Weimar Cinema, 1919–1933

Lilian Harvey

Willy Fritsch

„Emil un

Weimar Cinema, 1919–1933
Daydreams and Nightmares

Laurence Kardish

The Museum of Modern Art, New York

Photo Credits:

In reproducing the images contained in this publication, The Museum of Modern Art, New York, obtained the permission of the rights holders whenever possible. The Museum requests that information concerning the location and identity of any additional rights holders be forwarded, so that they may be contacted for future editions.

Unless noted below, all images in this book come from The Museum of Modern Art, New York.
Images on the following pages are courtesy Deutsche Kinemathek, Berlin: 2, 3, 4, 5, 8, 12, 13, 15, 18, 24, 25, 73, 74, 76 (top and bottom), 79, 81 (left), 83, 85, 89 (bottom), 91, 92, 95, 96, 103 (top and bottom), 104, 108, 110, 111, 113 (top and bottom), 114, 119, 120, 123 (top and bottom), 124, 127, 128 (bottom), 130, 131, 133, 134, 137 (top), 139 (top), 140, 143, 144, 150, 153 (top and bottom), 154 (bottom), 157, 161, 163 (top), 164, 167, 168 (top and bottom), 170, 171 (bottom), 173, 175, 179 (bottom), 181, 183 (bottom), 185, 186, 189 (bottom), 193, 194, 197, 199, 201 (top), 203, 205 (bottom), 206, 209, 211, 212, 216

Note:

In the essays that follow, English titles for German films are given in two styles: an official English-language release title is styled in italics, as in *Der letzte Mann* (*The Last Laugh*), whereas films without official English titles are given translations, in roman type with sentence-style capitalization, as in *Napoleons kleiner Bruder* (Napoleon's little brother).

Published in conjunction with the exhibition *Weimar Cinema, 1919–1933: Daydreams and Nightmares*, organized by Laurence Kardish, Senior Curator in the Department of Film, at The Museum of Modern Art, New York. November 17, 2010–March 7, 2011

Produced by the Department of Publications, The Museum of Modern Art, New York

Edited by Emily Hall
Designed by Amanda Washburn
Production by Christina Grillo
Printed and bound by Oceanic Graphic Printing, Inc., China
This book was typeset in Block Berthold and Futura.
The paper is 157 gsm Japanese White A Matt.

Published by
The Museum of Modern Art
11 West 53 Street
New York, New York 10019-5497
www.moma.org

© 2010 The Museum of Modern Art, New York

The catalogue of Weimar films (excluding review excerpts from English-language sources), Werner Sudendorf's essay, and the descriptions of Friedrich-Wilhelm-Murnau-Stiftung and Transit Film were translated from the German by Russell Stockman.

Library of Congress Control Number: 2010935437
ISBN: 978-0-87070-761-2

Distributed in the United States and Canada by D.A.P./Distributed Art Publishers, Inc., 155 Sixth Ave., 2nd floor, New York, New York 10013
www.artbook.com

Distributed outside the United States and Canada by Thames & Hudson Ltd., 181 High Holborn, London WC1V 7QX
www.thamesandhudson.com

Front cover: Kurt Gerron. *Ein toller Einfall* (*A Crazy Idea*). 1932; page 2: Wilhelm Thiele. *Die Drei von der Tankstelle* (*Three from the Filling Station*). 1930; page 3: Piel Jutzi. *Mutter Krausens Fahrt ins Glück* (*Mother Krause's Journey to Happiness*). 1929; page 4: Gerhard Lamprecht. *Emil und die Detektive* (*Emil and the Detectives*). 1931; page 8: G. W. Pabst. *Die Büchse der Pandora* (*Pandora's Box*). 1929; page 12: Robert Siodmak and Edgar G. Ulmer. *Menschen am Sonntag* (*People on Sunday*). 1930; page 24: Robert Wiene. *Das Cabinet des Dr. Caligari* (*The Cabinet of Dr. Caligari*). 1920; page 44: Anatole Litvak. *Das Lied einer Nacht* (*One Night's Song*). 1932; Kurt Bernhardt. *Die Frau, nach der man sich sehnt* (*Three Loves*). 1929; back cover: Fritz Lang. M. 1931

Printed in China

Foreword

Weimar Cinema, 1919–1933: Daydreams and Nightmares features eighty films made in Germany between the world wars, a period of cinema history that was extraordinarily fertile and influential in the development of the moving image. Since the mid-1930s, when the Nazis attempted to obliterate the cultural achievements of the Weimar Republic, The Museum of Modern Art has played a significant role in keeping alive the contributions of German filmmakers, first through national exhibition and eventually through preservation. Since the reunification of Germany in 1989, many Weimar-era films have been restored, and thanks to the special relationship the Museum's Department of Film has with film archives in Germany and elsewhere, we can present a comprehensive exhibition for the first time in the United States—a mix of classic films and motion pictures unseen since the 1930s—that will provide museumgoers with hours of enjoyment and students of cinema and the Weimar period with the opportunity to appreciate and reappraise the contributions of German filmmaking between the abdication of Kaiser Wilhelm II and the coming to power of the Nazis. It was during this period that film matured from a silent art, international in its visual expressiveness, into a more localized one, circumscribed by language.

The film program is augmented by an exhibition of posters and photographs of Weimar filmmaking in The Roy and Niuta Titus Theater 1 Lobby Gallery and by this illustrated book, with an extensive filmography supplemented by German criticism and essays by leading scholars of the period.

I want to thank Laurence Kardish, Senior Curator in the Department of Film, for initiating and organizing this project, and his collaborator, Eva Orbanz, Senior Curator for Special Projects at the Deutsche Kinemathek in Berlin and former President of FIAF, the International Federation of Film Archives, for her contributions to the film program. I am also grateful to Ron Magliozzi, Assistant Curator in the Department of Film, for co-organizing the gallery exhibition.

The participation of three organizations in Germany has proved essential to the realization of all aspects of this exhibition, and for their generous collaboration and cooperation MoMA is deeply appreciative of the Friedrich-Wilhelm-Murnau-Stiftung, Wiesbaden, holder of many of the original film materials of Weimar-era films, along with Transit Film, its distribution agency; the Stiftung Deutsche Kinemathek, Berlin, which in addition to films, loaned personnel, film posters, still photographs, and research materials; and the Bundesarchiv-Filmarchiv, Berlin, the national film archives of Germany, for providing access to its collections.

Glenn D. Lowry, Director
The Museum of Modern Art, New York

Acknowledgments

Weimar Cinema, 1919–1933: Daydreams and Nightmares is a major film program accompanied by an exhibition of Weimar-era film posters and still photographs and by this publication. In making possible this three-part initiative I want to thank first and foremost my collaborator, Eva Orbanz, Senior Curator for Special Projects, Deutsche Kinemathek, Berlin, and former President of the International Federation of Film Archives (FIAF), who organized the selection with me and acted as a liaison with archives in Germany and elsewhere. Her dedication and good humor graced this project from the start, and I could not have realized it without her. I am also grateful to Ron Magliozzi, Assistant Curator in the Department of Film, for his help in organizing the gallery exhibition.

I cannot thank enough the authors Thomas Elsaesser, Eric Rentschler, and Werner Sudendorf, who, despite their busy schedules, have written so illuminatingly, bringing new perspectives to the subject. My deep appreciation also goes to Ulrich Döge, who provided the book's invaluable filmography. His research is exemplary, and the materials he located are endlessly fascinating.

This exhibition owes everything to the support of Glenn Lowry, The Museum of Modern Art's Director, and Rajendra Roy, Chief Curator in the Department of Film. Their commitment and dedication to this project have been critical.

Without the participation of two excellent organizations in Germany, this exhibition would not have been possible: the Friedrich-Wilhelm-Murnau-Stiftung in Wiesbaden, which has been entrusted with the legacy of German film, and the Deutsche Kinemathek, Berlin. At the Murnau Foundation, my thanks go to Eberhard Junkersdorf, Chairman of the Board of Trustees; Helmut Possman, former Chairman of the Board; and Gudrun Weiss, who graciously made so many films available for us to view. At the Deutsche Kinemathek, I am grateful not only for the support of its director, Dr. Rainer Rother, who gave to this project in terms of loans and research materials, but also for the staff who have been so helpful, including Anke Hahn, Martin Koerber, Connie Betz, and Peter Latta.

Many other archives have been gracious in their loans, including the Bundesarchiv-Filmarchiv, Berlin (Karl Griep, Head, and Gisela Hofmann and Barbara Schuetz); the Filmmuseum München (Stefan Droessler, Director); Cineteca di Bologna (Gian Luca Farinelli, Director); Archives Françaises du Film, Bois-d'Arcy (Eric Le Roy, Head of Access and Collection Enrichment); British Film Institute National Archive, London (Nigel Algar, Senior Curator); the Motion Picture Department of the George Eastman House, Rochester, New York (Caroline Yeager, Assistant Curator); and Deutsches Filminstitut-DIF (Claudia Dillman, Director, and Michael Schurig, Curator). Thanks also go to two New York distributors of Weimar-era films: Kino International and Milestone Films.

The Goethe-Institut, New York, has also been exceedingly helpful, and particularly the valuable assistance of Gabriele Becker, Dr. Stephan Wackwitz, and Juliane Camfield. I would like to thank the historians, critics, writers, and students of the period who advised us: Vladimir Opela, Národní Filmový Archiv, Prague; Marleen Labijt, EYE Film Instituut Nederland, Amsterdam; Hans-Michael Bock in Hamburg; and, in Berlin, Rolf Aurich, Wolfgang Jacobsen, and Helmut Wietz. In the United States and Canada, I am grateful to Anton Kaes, Mark Langer, Kimberly O'Quinn, James Schamus, and Richard Traubner. I also want to acknowledge the support of Jane Klain, Juliane Lorenz, Oliver Mahrdt, and Marion Boulton Stroud.

For funding my research trips to Germany I want to thank MoMA's International Program (Jay Levenson, Director) and MoMA's International Council (Carol Coffin, Executive Director). My colleagues in the Department of Film have helped in myriad ways, and to my workmates either on West 53 Street or at the Celeste Bartos Preservation Center in Hamlin, Pennsylvania, I owe my thanks: Kitty Cleary, Sean Egan, Jenny He, Jytte Jensen, Mary Keene, Nancy Lukacinsky, Anne Morra, Josh Siegel, Charles Silver, Kate Trainor, Pierre Vaz, Arthur Wehrhahn, John Weidner, Peter Williamson, and especially Justin Rigby, who assisted me personally in the preparation of this exhibition. I also want to thank Kim Mitchell, Margaret Doyle, and D'Arcy Drollinger, of MoMA's excellent Department of Communications, for spreading the word of this exhibition. Thanks also go, in the Department of Exhibitions, to Jennifer Cohen and to David Hollely for the design of the gallery installation, and to Karlyn Benson, Registrar.

I was fortunate in having a very special group in MoMA's Department of Publications, headed by Christopher Hudson, and I am indebted to them, including David Frankel, Editorial Director; Emily Hall, who edited this book; Amanda Washburn, who designed it; Christina Grillo, Hannah Kim, Kara Kirk, and Marc Sapir, who all were involved in its production; Emily Nathan, for research; and Russell Stockman, for translation.

I am forever indebted to my wondrous and loyal companion in life, JWS, whose encouragement and criticism I hope never to take for granted.

Finally, I would be remiss in not acknowledging the extraordinary work of two pioneers of film study who believed early on that film was indeed an art and laid the foundation for this book: Iris Barry, MoMA's first film curator, who collected and exhibited films from Germany as the brilliance of that country's cinema was dimmed by the Third Reich, and Siegfried Kracauer, an important film critic and social historian, who, while in exile in New York during World War II and working at MoMA, wrote one of film culture's seminal texts, *From Caligari to Hitler: A Psychological History of the German Film*, on whose enormous legacy we hope, with this exhibition and book, to build.

Laurence Kardish
Senior Curator, Department of Film

Laurence Kardish

Transatlantic

Weimar and Hollywood

On May 28, 1931, New York mayor Jimmy Walker attended the reopening of a movie house in Yorkville, a Manhattan neighborhood with many German-speaking residents. The theater, formerly the Hippodrome, had been given a new name, the UFA Cosmopolitan Deutsche Sprechfilm Theatre, and for the next two years it screened only German-language films, sometimes with subtitles and sometimes not. The *New York Times* reported that the mayor, who in 1927 had visited Berlin (where he was warmly received and where he presumably raised his glass a few times, a pleasure denied him by Prohibition, whose dates are roughly coeval with the Weimar Republic), welcomed the competition good German films would give American films and hoped, he said, it would bring the two countries closer together.[1] The German consul general also gave a welcoming speech, in two languages, and the managing director of the great German movie studio Universum-Film AG, known as UFA, introduced the Cosmopolitan's inaugural offering, the recently completed *Der grosse Tenor* (The great tenor), directed by Hanns Schwarz and starring Renate Müller and Emil Jannings.

Jannings, a celebrated German actor who had come to America in 1926, would go on to win the first Academy Award given to an actor, in 1929, the year most Hollywood films became talkies, and would return to Germany that same year to continue his career unaccented, in his native tongue. A glance at the three films Jannings made before returning to Germany—two of which (*The Way of All Flesh* [1927], directed by Victor Fleming and now considered lost, and *The Last Command* [1928], directed by Josef von Sternberg) were cited by the Academy of Motion Picture Arts and Sciences as the reason for the award—shows us a fine example of the fecund relationship between the film industries of Germany and the United States in the 1920s. Jannings's third American film, *The Patriot* (1928), also considered lost, was made by a successful German filmmaker, Ernst Lubitsch, who had come to America in 1922, invited by Mary Pickford, and who ultimately directed and produced some of the most significant American films of the 1930s and '40s, and it was cowritten by another German émigré, Hanns Kräly. *The Last Command*, which is still shown in revival houses, was directed by an Austrian-born

American who went to Berlin in 1929 to make one of the key early sound films there, *Der blaue Engel* (*The Blue Angel*, *1930*), starring the ever-present Jannings and a (then) relatively unsung beauty, Marlene Dietrich, whom the director immediately brought back to America. The art director for both *The Patriot* and *The Last Command* was a German architect, Hans Dreier, who had come to Hollywood in the early 1920s.

Less than eight months after the UFA Cosmopolitan opened, the *New York Times* reported from Berlin on the premiere of a courageous antiwar film *Niemandsland* (*No Man's Land*, 1931); the article's writer thought that director Victor Trivas should be nominated for a Nobel Peace Prize in view of the film's pacifism at a time with "reactionaries . . . looming so threateningly in the background."[2] However, despite the praise of many contemporary critics, the film was not a commercial success, nor did it win approval from the perspicacious and progressive critic Siegfried Kracauer, who found the ending—in which World War I enemy combatants move almost hand in hand from the trenches of no-man's-land to a never-never land of fraternal respect—completely inauthentic.[3] In reviews and essays for the highly regarded newspaper *Frankfurter Zeitung*, Kracauer despaired of the German films that were successful both at home and abroad as the transition was made, in the late 1920s and early '30s, from silent motion pictures to sound films and as popular cinema ignored the encroaching threats to Germany's young and fragile democracy.[4] The films that did well in Germany and were exported to cinemas in America, like Erik Charell's *Der Kongress tanzt* (*Congress Dances*, 1931) and Paul Martin's *Ein blonder Traum* (*A Blonde Dream*, 1932), were mainly UFA films (frequently produced by one man, Erich Pommer) that the Berlin correspondent of the *New York Times* noted were of "chinchilla lightness . . . [with] swinging tunes . . . and good-natured sophistication," popular works that acted as social opiates.[5] In spite of the crisis of severe unemployment in Germany, sparked by Wall Street's collapse in late 1929, and the surprising success of the National Socialist (Nazi) party in the Reichstag elections of September 1930, these films, in imitation of the chronic happy endings of the Hollywood films then occupying about half the screens in Germany, either feigned obliviousness or made light of sinister realities.

Adolf Hitler was appointed chancellor of Germany on January 30, 1933, and in what probably was his first social appearance as head of state, on February 2, he went to the movies. Taking a place of honor in the first balcony of Berlin's palatial UFA-Palast am Zoo, he attended the premiere of Gustav Ucicky's *Morgenrot* (*Dawn*; fig. 1), a film that was not antiwar but prosacrifice, about members of a beleaguered World War I submarine crew who choose death so that other sailors might live. Hitler applauded the film, as did his new cabinet, including the chairman of UFA's board, the nationalist industrialist Alfred Hugenberg, formerly the leader of the German National People's Party, who in 1927 had rescued UFA from insolvency (brought on in part by the financial disaster that

Fig. 1. Rudolf Forster (center left) in Gustav Ucicky's *Morgenrot* (*Dawn*, 1933)

was Fritz Lang's *Metropolis* of the same year) and whom Hitler had just made minister of food and commerce of the new Germany.

Meanwhile, in early February of that year, while Berliners could see a film about dying nobly, New Yorkers had a choice of at least three frivolous films, the sort Kracauer thought debilitating daydreams that reinforced rather than subverted the rotten status quo: *Zapfenstreich am Rhein* (Tattoo on the Rhine, 1930), a musical drama directed by Jaap Speyer; *Eine Tür geht auf* (A door opens, 1933), a mystery directed by Alfred Zeisler; and *Ihre Majestät die Liebe* (*Her Majesty, Love*, 1931), a romantic comedy directed by Joe May.[6]

The summary of this historical moment is emblematic of three aspects of the transatlantic relationship between Weimar cinema and American movies: the rich interchange between Germany and the United States in artists both in front of and behind the camera; the esteem in which American film producers held German cinema from 1920 through 1933; and the significance of Kracauer's writings on German cinema, prewar in Berlin and postwar in New York, in shaping a critical perspective on Weimar cinema.

The interchange is indicated in part by the number of established German filmmakers who traveled to Hollywood, solicited by American studio heads (many of them also émigrés from German-speaking Central Europe or from Germany itself). German film artists tempted by offers from Hollywood or by the overall allure of America before the catastrophe of 1933 included the directors Lubitsch, Michael Curtiz, E. A. Dupont (who stayed briefly before going to London and then back to Germany), Paul Leni, Lothar Mendes, F. W. Murnau, Wilhelm Dieterle, Arthur Robison (who returned to Germany), Arnold Fanck (who stayed briefly), and G. W. Pabst (who returned to Austria); Pommer, the producer (who returned to Germany within a year); the actors Dietrich, Jannings, Pola Negri (who returned to Germany), and Conrad Veidt (who returned to Germany); the cameraman Karl Freund; the set designer Dreier; and the screenwriter Kräly.

Esteem may be measured by the number of citations garnered by German film-makers and films in the United States, at a time when the idea of such citations was still novel and quite limited. The *New York Times* published its first "10 Best" list in 1924 for films released in New York, and Lubitsch's American film *The Marriage Circle* was cited. His films were cited again in 1926, for *So This Is Paris*, and in 1928, for *The Patriot*. In 1927 the list included Murnau's first American film, *Sunrise: A Song of Two Humans*, which, with its fluid camera work, Expressionist-inflected sets, and Romantic tenor was a pure example of Weimar cinema. In 1932 two German-language films from 1931 made the list: Leontine Sagan's *Mädchen in Uniform* (*Girls in Uniform*), the first film by a woman to be included, and Géza von Bolváry's now virtually forgotten *Der Raub der Mona Lisa* (*The Theft of the Mona Lisa*). Curiously enough, the last Weimar film mentioned in the *Times* was *Morgenrot*, also acclaimed as one of the best foreign-language films of 1933 by the National Board of Review, an organization of film distributors and exhibitors, which in recognizing the achievements of imported cinema since 1929 accorded more "bests" to German films than to those of any other nation until the mid-1930s.

The American perception of Weimar cinema received an additional boost in 1933, a notable year for the public appreciation of cinema as an art, with the establishment of The Museum of Modern Art's Film Library. In 1929 the Museum's trustees had formed a committee to study the feasibility of establishing a curatorial department for film, and in 1932 the committee engaged Iris Barry, a British film critic and writer, to spearhead this study and eventually become the world's first film curator. Barry brought to MoMA an enthusiasm for certain postwar German films, which, with her subsequent support of Kracauer, helped elevate the status of Weimar cinema as German films were increasingly becoming creatures of a Nazi aesthetic. Some of the earliest films Barry collected for MoMA—to be exhibited, studied, and enjoyed in the same way as any of the other arts—were the films of Lubitsch, Lang, Murnau, and Pabst, four of the film-makers most commonly associated with Weimar cinema, and these were distributed to educational institutions around the country, accompanied by notes written by Barry, introducing some films and reintroducing others to a national audience.

In 1936 Barry wrote, "When German film first travelled abroad after the war, it was evident that a new school of cinematography, well worthy of study, perhaps of imitation was being evolved in Berlin. The first of the films to reach the United States was *Passion* in 1920, followed in 1921 by *The Cabinet of Dr. Caligari*. These represented two distinct varieties of German film."[7] The audience for *Passion*, whose original German title was *Madame Dubarry*, according to the trade journal *Variety*, "jammed New York's Capitol Theater" in December of 1920, where it "drew long and hearty applause" and was praised in an unsigned *New York Times* review as one of the most "pre-eminent motion pictures of the present cinematographic age . . . imported from

Europe, having originated in northern Germany . . . and directed by Ernst Lubitsch who is said to have a reputation of a cinematcian [*sic*] of the first rank abroad."[8] *Madame Dubarry*, a film about the French Revolution, was shot in Germany during a time of poverty, hunger, and social turbulence. At the time of its Berlin premiere in September 1919, street demonstrations were frequent and attempted seizures of power undermined the new democracy, but as Kracauer observed, it was not about politics but a romance that "reduced the revolution to a derivative of private passions."[9] Filmgoers in both Germany and the United States loved it, as did Barry, who, unlike Kracauer, was not bothered by the narrative's focus on emotions rather than political explication.

Robert Wiene's *Das Cabinet des Dr. Caligari* (*The Cabinet of Dr. Caligari,* 1920), with its theatrical style, architectonic sets, painted shadows, and loopy narrative, was quite another matter. *Dr. Caligari* represented a nightmare of sorts, taking place "in a world of intense relief and depth," according to the American poet and playwright George Scheffauer, who reported on its Berlin premiere in an article for *The Freeman* magazine, later quoted in the *Times,* adding that it was rare to find a motion picture in which "space has been given a voice . . . and becomes a presence."[10] When the film opened in New York in April 1921 another *Times* critic, echoing Scheffauer's sculptural reference, wrote, "The most conspicuous individual characteristic of the photoplay is that it is cubistic, or expressionistic. Its settings bear a somewhat closer resemblance to reality than say the famous 'Nude Descending a Staircase' . . . they are sufficiently unlike anything ever done on the screen before to belong to a separate scenic species."[11]

Having noted *Madame Dubarry* and *Dr. Caligari* were in the vanguard of the German film "invasion" (a prophetic word choice for 1936), Barry observed that German films "achieved their profound effects chiefly by lighting and by lively photographic devices. It was the German camerawork (in the fullest sense of the term) that most deeply impressed Hollywood. *Varieté* [*Variety*, Dupont, 1925] in particular was admired for its camera angles and *The Last Laugh* [*Der letzte Mann*, Murnau, 1924] for its unity of pictorial construction and the use it made of the travelling camera. . . . German talent engaged by American studios and the example of the German films combined to exercise a lasting influence."[12] As film historian Dave Kehr has written, the director John Ford, already famous for his railroad western *The Iron Horse* (1924), learned from Murnau, who had arrived at the Fox studio in 1926 to make *Sunrise*, "the use of forced perspectives and chiaroscuro lighting, techniques Ford would use to complement his own more direct, naturalistic style."[13]

These expressive visual strategies were not enough to convince Kracauer of the integrity of German cinema. He wrote from two perspectives which appear, at first glance, to be mutually exclusive: a Marxist inflection that insists that cinema act as a responsible and progressive social tool, and a more passive and descriptive psychological one, which posited cinema as something that manifests a community's unconscious

Fig. 2. Lya de Putti and Emil Jannings in E. A. Dupont's *Varieté* (*Variety,* 1925)

fears and desires, reflecting "those deep layers of collective mentality which extend more or less below the dimension of consciousness."[14] Although some German films, such as *Der letzte Mann* and *Varieté* (fig. 2), impressed both him and Hollywood with their plasticity as well as their ability to express introspection and a character's private life, he found many more of them a bane.[15] About three thousand feature films were made in Germany during the approximately 4,800 days of the Republic, and they were shown in the "countless new movie theaters" sprung up all over Germany during the 1920s, to which "all segments of the population stream . . . from the workers in suburban movie theaters to the haute bourgeoisie in movie palaces."[16] Many of them were nationalist and falsely nostalgic period melodramas and musicals set in Austro-Hungarian Vienna or Wilhelmine Potsdam and ubiquitous contemporary romantic comedies in which shop-girls married up and princes married down; Kracauer, faced with this slew of sugared versions of the past and cheery views of the present, opined that despite "some excellently crafted moments" in current German films, "lack of substance is the decisive trait of the totality of established film production."[17]

This assessment is harsh in light of the relief and, it is likely, pleasure many of these entertainments gave to contemporary audiences (and in recently restored versions still do), but Kracauer, perhaps sensing the end of a civil society, wanted the cinema to provide not an appeasement but a will to challenge the divisions within the Republic.[18] Some films, such as Phil Jutzi's *Mutter Krausens Fahrt ins Glück* (*Mother Krause's Journey to Happiness,* 1929) and *Berlin-Alexanderplatz* (1931) and Slatan Dudow's *Kuhle Wampe oder Wem gehört die Welt?* (*Whither Germany?,* 1932), cowritten by Bertolt Brecht, portrayed the difficulty of living decently under the constant pressure of unemployment, but for the most part motion pictures were, Kracauer observed, products fabricated by "capitalist entrepreneurs" who would hardly threaten their own world with possibilities that might destroy their wealth and comfort.

Kracauer knew what was at stake when Hitler came to power. With his wife, Lili, he fled Germany for Paris in 1933. In the summer of 1940, with German troops in Paris, the Kracauers and their Berlin friend and fellow critic Walter Benjamin made their way to Marseilles, hoping to cross the Pyrenees first into Spain and then to Portugal, where they expected to set sail from Lisbon to New York. Prevented from crossing into Spain, Benjamin committed suicide; the Kracauers persisted, and they arrived in New York on April 25, 1941. Within a week, and speaking little English, Kracauer reintroduced himself to Barry, whom he had met once before, in Paris in 1938. Barry quickly secured a Rockefeller Foundation grant for MoMA to engage Kracauer to prepare "a serious study of German wartime communication through film," several examples of which were already archived in the Film Library (along with the classic German films Barry had acquired from Berlin were a number of Nazi propaganda films bestowed—unsolicited— by the Reichsfilmarchiv).[19] Kracauer worked at the Museum, helping American wartime documentary filmmakers understand the effectiveness achieved by these propaganda films through the visceral power of calculated imagery rather than narration; he was also writing his first book in English, *From Caligari to Hitler: A Psychological History of the German Film*, which was published in 1947. He wrote primarily from memory of many films that were no longer available to him, but he was able to revisit some of the German masterworks Barry had begun collecting in 1936.

The text, a pioneering, classic, and indispensable—although limited—essay in film studies (and other disciplines), begins with an articulation of scope:

> This book is not concerned with German films merely for their own sake; rather, it aims at increasing our knowledge of pre-Hitler Germany in a specific way. It is my contention that through an analysis of the German films deep psychological dispositions predominant in Germany from 1919 to 1933 can be exposed—dispositions which influenced the course of events during that time and which will have to be reckoned with in the post-Hitler era.[20]

The book ignores for the most part those sophisticated comedies and charming musicals that played such a significant cultural role late in the brief life of the Republic; Kracauer was never their enthusiast, nor did they serve his thesis. As late as 1932, films such as Victor Janson's *Das Blaue vom Himmel* (*The Blue from the Sky*), Ludwig Berger's *Ich bei Tag und Du bei Nacht* (*Early to Bed*), and Kurt Gerron's *Ein toller Einfall* (*A Crazy Idea*) gave no clues to the darkening clouds, no hints of imminent savagery. But Kracauer thought that some other films did anticipate Germany's murderous future, especially those laden with ominous and dangerous characters; he theorized that the era's fetishistic obsession with the seductive allure of evil (embodied in monstrous beings, from Dr. Caligari to the child murderer of Lang's *M* [1931]) may have helped pave the way for totalitarianism.[21] He thus focused on the dark side of Weimar cinema, on the umbrageous and sinister, on those larger than life (and frequently undead) demagogues, hypnotists, madmen, and femmes fatales who seduced and destroyed willing victims over and over and over again, including but certainly not limited to Lang's Dr. Mabuse, a criminal master of disguises; Murnau's Nosferatu, an irresistible vampire; Pabst's Lulu, an insatiable man killer; and, of course, Dr. Caligari, whoever he may be.

Kracauer's perspective was confirmed by another German-Jewish film critic, Lotte H. Eisner, who fled to Paris and remained there during the Nazi occupation, barely surviving while working for the young archivist Henri Langlois, the founder of the Cinémathèque française. Her book, L'Écran démoniaque (The Haunted Screen), published in 1952, is another important firsthand account of Weimar cinema. Eisner, too, concentrates on the supernatural and the pagan, finding in these dystopic tendencies an expression of the people: "The weird pleasure the Germans take in evoking horror can perhaps be ascribed to the excessive and very Germanic desire to submit to discipline, together with a certain proneness to sadism."[22] Kracauer and Eisner were writing both from lively experience and in melancholy hindsight; there is understandably little sunlight or humor in their descriptions of this golden age of German cinema, but their converging assessments have provided, until recently, the critical template for the appreciation of Weimar filmmaking forged in reaction to the events of 1933.

Since German reunification in 1989, many forgotten Weimar-era films, including those Kracauer deemed meretricious in their "hymnic optimism" or just plain pitiful, have been restored and, for the first time in generations, been presented at festivals of classic films and shown at academic conclaves.[23] Concomitant with these revivals has come extended scholarship of the period suggesting broader approaches to the phenomenon of Weimar cinema. Writers and critics in Europe and America such as Hans-Michael Bock, Thomas Elsaesser, Sabine Hake, Anton Kaes, Bruce Murray, and Eric Rentschler, to name a few, have posited new ways and strategies of understanding German films between the wars including approaching this culture through the vectors of modernity, urbanism, and the lethal struggle among competing political parties.

In the last years of the Republic there were films such as Robert Siodmak's Menschen am Sonntag (People on Sunday, 1930) and Gerhard Lamprecht's Emil und die Detektive (Emil and the Detectives, 1931), which embraced the airy streets, light-dappled forests, and lakes surrounding Berlin. Billie Wilder, a brash young journalist and dance-hall enthusiast, worked on the scripts for both these films. While Kracauer and Eisner saw malevolence in the frequent trope of doubling (one being possessed by another and thus becoming two conflicting psychological presences), Wilder witnessed another form of doubling during the Weimar era: transvestitism, a staple of cabaret.[24] Men dressing as women (as do

Fig. 3. Jack Lemmon and Tony Curtis in Billy Wilder's *Some Like It Hot* (1959)

Reinhold Schünzel in *Der Himmel auf Erden* [Heaven on earth] and Curt Bois in *Der Fürst von Pappenheim* [*The Masked Mannequin*] [both 1927]) or women as men (as does Dolly Haas in *Liebeskommando* [Love's command, 1931]), in order to either escape detection or get closer to the object of their affection, is an inherently comic situation, especially when much to his or her surprise the cross-dresser begins to enjoy the disguise.

Billie left Germany before he directed a film of his own; as Billy he brought to Hollywood a vigorous appreciation of such absurdities of human behavior, along with the dry cynicism that distinguished Berlin humor and an enthusiasm for the syncopations of American jazz, a musical phenomenon welcomed in the German capital. Wilder, informed by his years in Berlin (to which he returned to make *A Foreign Affair* in 1948 and *One, Two, Three* in 1961), wrote and directed many dark and sophisticated American films, including *The Apartment* (1960) and *Some Like It Hot* (1959; fig. 3), a comedy, set during Prohibition, about gender confusion on a tonal par with Schünzel's *Viktor und Viktoria*, released in December 1933, eleven months into the Third Reich and the last musical to reflect the insouciance of the late Republic.

The transatlantic connection worked both ways. In 1922 D. W. Griffith, the great American filmmaker whose films tended to champion the underdog, heard about the suffering and the deprivations of the German people. Griffith began shooting *Isn't Life Wonderful* in the environs of Berlin in 1924, with a small American cast playing a refugee family in need and a large group of Germans as extras. The exterior scenes, immediate and modern, may be seen as a precursor of Neorealism; the interiors, shot partly in Griffith's studio in Mamaroneck, New York, belong to another era, more Victorian in sensibility. The film is deeply felt, and as MoMA curator Eileen Bowser wrote, it is "an intimate, sharply realistic study of . . . the debasement of people by the evils of war."[25] Griffith hoped the film would elicit the sympathy of Americans for civilians who through no fault of their own were barely coping with the ravages of inflation, unemployment, and a paucity of food. The film received favorable reviews in the United States but was a financial failure, and Griffith, who until now had produced his own films, lost his independence. *Isn't Life Wonderful* is a curious mix of sentiment and brutality, ending with a flourish of unexpected optimism. A young couple loses a wagonload of potatoes to a marauding group of the unemployed; he wakes up from having been beaten and, realizing what was lost, curses fate, while she looks up at the sky and sees the moon. Struck by the beauty of the fading night and impressed by their love for each other, she exclaims (in an intertitle, of course), "Isn't life wonderful!"

Griffith meant his title as an affirmation; history made it an irony, as it has for *Ins Blaue hinein* (*Into the Blue*), which disappeared for eighty years before it was restored by the Archives Françaises du Film, outside Paris. This, the only extant film directed by Eugen Schüfftan, *Menschen am Sonntag*'s master cinematographer, is an extraordinary thirty-six-minute film, made completely *en plein air*, with no studio artifice. The title is idiomatic, with connotations of the carefree and the spontaneous—a curious choice for a film about being unemployed. In a medium in which joblessness is usually portrayed as a grim state, *Ins Blaue hinein* celebrates being freed from an office as a liberation that may lead to good things. As the film opens, a firm closes, and the boss and his two workers plus a girlfriend go for a ride in the country, a jaunt that leaves them penniless, smiling, and hopeful. And indeed something serendipitous and positive does happen. It is a radical work not so much for its joyous sensibility that turns being out of work into happiness—a trope it shares with other late Weimar films, including Wilhelm Thiele's *Die Drei von der Tankstelle* (*Three from the Filling Station*, 1930)—but for its avant-garde camera work, which in its handheld wildness matches the film's unconstrained spirit. In its freewheeling photography, elliptical editing, and breathless pacing, *Ins Blaue hinein* anticipates the French New Wave by thirty years.

Schüfftan had worked in the special effects department of UFA, where he developed the Schüfftan process, a system for assimilating separate images that is still being used today, while working on Lang's *Die Nibelungen* (1924) and *Metropolis*. As a cinematographer in Germany he worked with a generation of filmmakers who later went into exile, many to the United States, where their training and experience enriched American cinema for decades to come. Schüfftan himself left Germany in 1933 for France, and when the Germans occupied Paris he came to America, where he became Eugene and in 1962 won an Academy Award for his cinematography on Robert Rossen's *The Hustler* (1961). In 1966 he once again captured the delirious spirit of *Ins Blaue hinein* in his camera work for *Chappequa*, Conrad Rooks's self-financed film about expanded consciousness. His life may be seen as a paradigm of the transatlantic connection between the cinema of two countries, an interchange extended by exile, in which the brilliance of American naïveté is made more interesting by the darkening shadows of German experience.

1. Mordaunt Hall, "The Screen," *New York Times*, May 29, 1931, p. 28.

2. C. Hooper Trask, "A Graphic War Film Stirs Berlin," *New York Times*, January 24, 1932, p. x5.

3. Siegfried Kracauer, *From Caligari to Hitler: A Psychological History of the German Film*, 1947, ed. Leonardo Quaresima, rev. ed. (Princeton, N.J.: Princeton University Press, 2004), p. 236.

4. Ibid., p. 208. Kracauer's *Frankfurter Zeitung* columns are collected in *The Mass Ornament: Weimar Essays*, trans. and ed. Thomas Y. Levin (Cambridge, Mass.: Harvard University Press).

5. Trask, "Berlin Turns to the Film Operetta," *New York Times*, November 13, 1932, p. X4.

6. *Her Majesty, Love*, an American film with the same English title, also set in Berlin, also from 1931, was adapted from the same German play by the dramatists Rudolph Bernauer and Rudolf Österrreicher, but this one was directed for the screen by Wilhelm Dieterle, a noted filmmaker, also a very recent émigré.

7. Iris Barry, program notes for *The German Influence*, a film series presented by The Museum of Modern Art, New York, April 7–8, 1936.

8. *Variety*, December 17, 1920; "The Screen," *New York Times*, December 13, 1920, p. 21.

9. Kracauer, *From Caligari to Hitler*, p. 49.

10. George Scheffauer, "The Vivifying of Space," *The Freeman*, November 24, 1920; quoted in "Cubism on the Screen," *New York Times*, November 28, 1920, p. 79.

11. "The Screen," *New York Times*, April 4, 1921, p. 22.

12. Barry, program notes, *The German Influence*.

13. Dave Kehr, "Long-Lost Silent Films Return to America," *New York Times*, June 6, 2010.

14. Kracauer, *From Caligari to Hitler*, p. 6.

15. Ibid., pp. 133, 206, 211.

16. Kracauer, "Film 1928," in *The Mass Ornament*, p. 308.

17. Ibid., pp. 316, 319.

18. This theme runs throughout *From Caligari to Hitler*, and Kracauer addresses popularity in "The Little Shopgirls Go to the Movies," *The Mass Ornament*, pp. 291–304.

19. See David Culbert, "The Rockefeller Foundation, The Museum of Modern Art Film Library, and Siegfried Kracauer, 1941," *Historical Journal of Film, Radio and Television* 13, no. 4 (1993): 495–511.

20. In the preface he wrote, "I am indebted to Miss Iris Barry, Curator of the Museum of Modern Art Film Library, to whom my book literally owes its existence; she not only suggested this study but assisted generously and in many ways towards its realization." Kracauer, *From Caligari to Hitler*, p. li.

21. Ibid., p. 77.

22. Lotte H. Eisner, *L'Écran démoniaque*, 1952, rev. ed. (Paris: Le Terrain Vague, 1965); published in English as *The Haunted Screen*, trans. Roger Greaves (Berkeley and Los Angeles: University of California Press, 1969), p. 95.

23. Kracauer, *From Caligari to Hitler*, pp. 211, 133.

24. On doubling, see ibid., pp. 29–31; and Eisner, *The Haunted Screen*, pp. 109–10. On Billy Wilder in Germany, see Glenn Hopp, *Billy Wilder: The Complete Films; The Cinema of Wit, 1906–2002* (Cologne: Taschen, 2003), pp. 10–13

25. Eileen Bowser, entry for *Isn't Life Wonderful*, in Bowser, ed., *Film Notes* (New York: The Museum of Modern Art, 1969), p. 55.

Thomas Elsaesser

Inside the Mind, a Soul of Dynamite?

Fantasy, Vision Machines, and Homeless Souls in Weimar Cinema

From the beginnings the German film contained dynamite. . . . Chaos spread in Germany from 1918 to about 1923, and as its consequence the panic-stricken German mind was released from all the conventions that usually limit life. Under such conditions, the unhappy, homeless soul not only drove straightway toward the fantastic region of horrors, but also moved like a stranger through the world of normal reality. . . . That free-wandering soul imagined the madmen, somnambulists, vampires and murderers who were haunting the expressionistic settings of the *Caligari* film and its like.

—Siegfried Kracauer[1]

Caligari and Company

Yes, it all began with *Das Cabinet des Dr. Caligari* (*The Cabinet of Dr. Caligari*), the 1920 film directed by Robert Wiene, produced by Erich Pommer, and starring Conrad Veidt, Lil Dagover, and Werner Krauss.[2] With it, some of the most spectacular and remarkable creations of cinematic horror ever produced suddenly appeared on German movie screens. The wave continued throughout the 1920s, more or less until the coming of sound in 1929–30.

Or so the story goes. Siegfried Kracauer, one of the most perceptive observers of Weimar culture and society at the time, was later convinced that the wave continued even beyond; for him the horrors of the screen foretold the terror of street violence, while the terror of political assassination grew, after 1933, into the horrors eventually perpetrated by a monstrous political regime. Writing immediately after Germany's defeat in 1945 and the revelations about the death camps, he called his book on the period of Weimar cinema *From Caligari to Hitler*; it was as if the movies had tried to exorcise the ghosts of World War I only to anticipate the even more unimaginable nightmares of World War II, which Kracauer in turn tried to exorcise with his own genealogy of evil.[3]

The bold comparison Kracauer drew between a fantasy figure from the cinema and a political figure from history has no doubt helped to give this moment and genre—whether we call the films Expressionist, fantasy, or horror—the ambiguous fascination

Fig. 1. Emil Jannings in F. W. Murnau's *Faust—Eine deutsche Volkssage* (*Faust*, 1926)

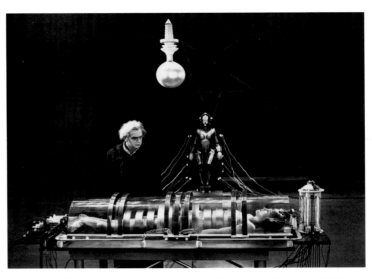

Fig. 2. Rudolf Klein-Rogge and Brigitte Helm in Fritz Lang's *Metropolis* (1927)

they have held ever since. But it may not explain the continuing appeal of *Dr. Caligari* and its progeny as cult films and cult figures for movie fans today. Creatures such as the Golem, Nosferatu, Dr. Mabuse, Orlac (from *Orlacs Hände* [*The Hands of Orlac*, 1924]), Jack the Ripper, Ivan the Terrible (from *Das Wachsfigurenkabinett* [*Waxworks*, 1924]), Mephisto (from *Faust—Eine deutsche Volkssage* [*Faust*, 1925; fig. 1]), and the scientist Rotwang and the robot Maria (from *Metropolis* [1927; fig. 2]) have become icons: their costumes, their makeup and body language, their fierce eyes and towering shadows have come back to haunt us in countless films, and the stories they animate have become archetypes, the basis for several movie mythologies. They have taken on a life outside of film as well, inspiring not only directors but designers and fashion trends to this day.

These figures, then, rather than embodying despotism in a time of political chaos or predicting incarnations of early-twentieth-century evil, have a power at once highly symbolic and highly cinematic. They are symbolic in that, like ogres and monsters in fairy tales, they evoke bodily sensations that feed the imagination, thus purging and cleansing the soul and allowing us to test our fears, moral judgments, and sense of real-ity against phantasms of pure evil. They are cinematic in that they confirm the medium's dual nature: realistic in its fantasies and fantastic in its realism. The philosopher Slavoj Žižek, for instance, has claimed that what he calls a "fantasy frame" (i.e., a subjective projection) is precisely what sustains our sense of reality, as well as of our sense of self.[4] Could it be that the fantasy figures populating Expressionist cinema, instead of exerting an ambiguous (political) fascination, retain our attention because they are mental images as well, thus speaking of an ambiguity that is epistemological as well as ontological?

Take, for instance *Das Cabinet des Dr. Caligari*, in which nothing is what it seems: the world of the film is inside out as well as upside down. After more than eighty years, there is still no agreement on what the narrative is actually about, or what genre it belongs to.[5] Is it a fantasy romance or a gothic tale of horror? Is it a detective story with a mystery twist or a medical case history? It could be the story of a sane person driven mad by an evil scientist, or it could be a demonstration of the powers and dangers of hypnosis at a time when psychoanalysis was just establishing itself as serious therapy; it could be a film about a war veteran simulating trauma and hiding in a clinic, or the deranged fantasy of a sick man imagining a scenario of persecution and murder set among his harmless fellow patients and casting his kindly and helpful doctor as the villain. Wiene's film, written by Hans Janowitz and Carl Mayer—two very different personalities—is a strange hybrid of all of these possibilities.[6]

In 1926 the art critic Rudolf Kurtz remembered the 1920 premiere of *Das Cabinet des Dr. Caligari* "like a fever dream," but he saw the film in light of contemporary political events, the unsuccessful Spartakus uprisings, giving it yet another meaning. For Kurtz the world of the asylum and the city fairground of the opening scenes was "surrounded by dark streets, across which echo commands shouted by republican paramilitary units; elsewhere, the piercing voices of street corner orators can be heard, and in the background, the center of town is plunged into total darkness, occupied by radical insurgents, machine-gun rattle, soldiers forming human chains, falling roof supports and hand grenades."[7] Kurtz's recollection of civil war and revolutionary unrest confirms Kracauer's analysis of the period as one of political turmoil, but he does not tell us why it was in Germany that the cinema so miraculously benefited from the turmoil, nor why it was assumed to be Expressionism, an artistic movement essentially of the prewar period, that became associated with the films' style and energy.

I said above that it all started with *Dr. Caligari*, but was that really the case? To get a sense of the possible origins of this genre and why it arose in Germany, we need a flashback to 1913 and to another period of unrest, this time in the world of the arts rather than in politics. Since 1909–11 German cinema had been trying to upgrade itself culturally and to be considered a serious art form, not least in order to combat the French influence and the economic hegemony of the film studios Pathé, Gaumont, and Éclair.[8] It needed the better-paying audiences of the rising middle classes, and it also wanted to attract the writers and actors from the theater, who had been looking down on the cinema as lacking status and respectability. As it still is for every new media technology, adoption by middle-class consumers was essential for economic survival. But the producers of the emerging film business also did not want to lose the mass audiences and therefore tried to retain them with lurid titles and sensationalist stories. During this period of debate about artistic value, the so-called *Autorenfilm-Debatte*, the studios tested several different genre formulas that combined high-culture status with popular appeal: the "social dramas" starring Asta Nielsen, for instance, who had been imported from Denmark with her husband, Urban Gad, or the melodramas and stage plays turned into films by Augustus Blom, Franz Hofer, and Max Mack.[9]

But the formulas the producers devised also included one initiated by the theater actor Paul Wegener, who had the idea of using story elements and visual motifs from nineteenth-century German Romanticism, especially fairy tales, folk legends, and gothic

Fig. 3. Paul Wegener (center right) in Henrik Galeen's *Der Student von Prag* (*The Student of Prague*, 1913)

or macabre literary tales. What Wegener was really interested in was film technique: he was fascinated by special effects, having seen some astonishing trick photography in a French film. Looking for someone in Berlin who could do similar work, he approached the cameraman and photographer's son Guido Seeber, and the two decided to look for suitable story material to display these special effects. They found it in the work of the well-known writer Hanns Heinz Ewers, who at their request wrote a remix of standard gothic motifs involving lost shadows, Faustian pacts, and doppelgängers—just what Wegener needed, since he wanted to astonish the world by playing opposite himself. Seeber later described how he overcame the difficulties of creating flawless cinematic doubles (after first experimenting with still photography), proudly noting that "the first large-scale application [of my new technique] was in *Der Student von Prag* [*The Student of Prague*], shot by me in 1913 with Paul Wegener in the lead and as his own double. The result caused a major sensation at the time. The illusion was so perfect that many experts simply would not believe me when I told them that I had exposed the relevant scenes twice in succession."[10]

In *Der Student von Prag* (fig. 3) we can identify the key thematic motifs of German Expressionist film as well as locate the thinking behind its origins. Wegener was attracted to the fantastic not only because it gave him a chance to explore different film techniques (such as trick photography, superimposition, special effects in the manner of Georges Méliès's *féeries*, Segundo de Chomón's stop-motion films, and Pathé's detective series); he also wanted to integrate these techniques into continuous-action narratives and to build dramatic stories with strong character-driven motivations around these separate moments of movie magic. In other words, he wanted to create longer narratives based on a supernatural or fantastic—which is to say, on a specifically cinematic-technical— causality rather than on real-world conflicts or melodramatic situations. In comedies, detective films, and *féeries*, human beings and the new machine of cinema were shown to complement each other, empowering its users; in Wegener's world, cinematic magic often deployed its darker forces as well, showing the seductive lure as well as the abuse of such power in the realm of appearances. Wegener's gothic fairy tales, such as *Der*

Rattenfänger von Hameln (*The Pied Piper of Hamelin*, 1917) or *Der verlorene Schatten* (Lost shadows, 1920), also overcame the hostility of the intelligentsia and the middle class by catering to the tastes of adults as well as children, thus exploiting cinema's unique popularity across generations and pioneering the idea of the "family audience."

The appearance and subsequent predominance of the fantastic in the German cinema of the 1920s may therefore be both simpler to explain and more devious than Kracauer's invocation of the lost world war, civil unrest, and the German soul. If we focus instead on Wegener, Seeber, and Ewers (Stellan Rye, the Dane nominally credited with directing *Der Student von Prag*, being still something of a mystery), then the revival of gothic motifs—from the writing of Alfred de Musset or E. T. A. Hoffmann and the Biedermeier settings inspired by the paintings of Caspar David Friedrich and Carl Spitzweg—makes more sense.[11] By imitating the Romantic *Kunstmärchen* (literary fairy tale) of Achim von Arnim and Clemens Brentano—rather than the tales of gothic horror from England by Joseph Sheridan Le Fanu, Ann Radcliffe, or Horace Walpole—Wegener and his colleagues not only made the cinema legitimate and respectable but also countered the dominance of films with French, Italian, or American locations by offering identifiably German subjects and settings, making them attractive also for export (especially to France), where German Romantic literature, philosophy, and visual art had been appreciated ever since Napoleon swept across the German principalities in the early 1800s.

Wegener's films thus set a pattern that repeated itself into the 1920s and even extended into the sound era: Romantic, nostalgic, and national themes joined with the experimental and avant-garde techniques favored by many filmmakers of the 1920s, who shared—much more than a single political outlook, whether of the communist left of the conservative right—a passion for advancing the medium's technical possibilities. Blending a middle-class concept of national literature with a pseudo-folk culture of popular entertainment for the masses, the Wegener formula made the fantastic film a mainstay of the German cinema for at least a decade (from 1913 until about 1923), before it left Romanticism behind and split into two versions of rococo: Ruritanian musical comedies and Prussian male melodrama.

Although this last development does not concern me here, it suggests that *Das Cabinet des Dr. Caligari* and the so-called Expressionist films came at the high point of the genre rather than, as is so often claimed, marking its beginning.[12] *Der Student von Prag*, the first compromise between high (artistic) culture and a low (technical) medium, is thus the place to seek the roots of the fantastic genre in German cinema. What breathed new life into the vogue for such films around 1920 was the extraordinary critical acclaim that *Dr. Caligari* received, first in France and subsequently in the United States.[13] It alerted German producers and directors to this new style and its promotional value, and led them to actively look for motifs that the export market would recognize as both German and artistic, that is, as Expressionist, a movement that had already established itself, after splitting off from French Fauvism, as a valuable quality label associated with Germany. This new cross-cultural context for the term helps to explain the temporal gap between German Expressionist art (1909–16) and German Expressionist cinema (1919–26).

Yet such characters as the mysterious Scapinelli in *Der Student von Prag* or the sinister doctor in *Dr. Caligari* are traditional figures of popular entertainment outside of Germany as well. Their Italian names refer back to the traveling showmen, the magicians, shadow players (*montreurs d'ombres*), and magic lanternists who with their phantasmagorias, visual spectacles, and optical toys had visited fairgrounds and toured cities all over Europe since the eighteenth century. Their manipulation of illusions finds, in many films, an elaborate and self-conscious parallel with cinema itself, suggesting the increasing social (and even political) power accruing to those who have control over the (moving) image, as in some key works of cinematic Expressionism from the early 1920s, such as *Das Wachsfigurenkabinett, Schatten* (*Warning Shadows*, 1923), and *Herr Tartüff* (*Tartuffe*, 1926). These fantastic films presented Mephisto figures as the tempters of young, petit bourgeois Fausts, with the key example being, of course, F. W. Murnau's *Faust—Eine deutsche Volkssage*, another traditional narrative serving as the vehicle for new cinematic techniques and amazing special effects. In theme and technique *Faust* recalled *Der Student von Prag*; in both cases a young man is first tempted and then seduced by an older man who promises power over the world of appearance and artifice. In the late nineteenth century Oscar Wilde's *The Picture of Dorian Grey* (1890) and Edgar Allan Poe's "The Oval Portrait" (1842) exploited similar Faustian themes, under the impact of photography and just before the invention of cinema. But while these literary works dramatize the gap between nature and art, the cinema highlights the new power relationship between culture and technology.

Der Student von Prag and *Das Cabinet des Dr. Caligari* do not share a common visual style; *Der Student von Prag* is naturalist and impressionist, with little resemblance to the angular sets and starkly stylized interiors of *Dr. Caligari*. What is more pertinent is the theme, in both films, of the double or dummy—Cesare in *Dr. Caligari*, the Faust character's doppelgänger in *Der Student von Prag*—as evidence of a kind of epistemological paranoia about both sense perception and the status of the self (already alluded to in connection with the "fantasy frame") and of a principle that is less stylistic than part of the period's cultural politics: story and style are driven by the exigencies of developing and testing state-of-the-art film technology. The films engaged with and intervened in a struggle over the realignment of cultural capital in Wilhelmine and Weimar Germany as the country became Europe's primary engineering nation, rather than (as Kracauer suggests) reflecting or representing the inner state of mind or the collective mentalities of the German soul, however much dynamite it might have contained.

Man and Machine, Nature and Technology

Expressionist films were not, however, cut off from current events or unresponsive to contemporary pressures. The prominent social and technological issues of the 1920s, usually summed up under the labels of "modernity" and "modernization," in the films of the fantastic found both expression and disguise, that is, an acceptably ambiguous representation-as-resolution. The revival of the gothic novel in the nineteenth century, like much of Romanticism's arsenal, was a Europe-wide phenomenon, usually attributed to a reaction against Enlightenment rationality, although in Britain it was also a more explicitly political response to the French Revolution, and in Germany to the Napoleonic Wars. The rapid industrialization in much of Europe that followed the defeat of Napoleon produced a major state of dislocation, which in literature and the arts was reflected in the theme of the contrast between city and country. Here the relation of man to nature was profoundly reconfigured, with nature often seeming familiar but uncanny, beautiful but haunted, a longed-for retreat but also a source of horror. The 1920s, after another devastating war, saw the introduction of major new technologies as well as another mass exodus from the country to the cities and another massive expansion of industry. It was as if these social conflicts from more than half a century earlier were restaged in a new medium for a new social class, the *Angestellten* (urban white-collar workers), as Kracauer rightly diagnosed in a pathbreaking sociological study.[14]

Especially popular in the mid-nineteenth century, for instance, were fantastic tales in which the natural world tried to avenge itself on those who despoiled it in search of mineral wealth or raped and ravaged the land by taking over rivers, lakes, and water-falls as sources of mechanical energy. Following the fairy tales of the Brothers Grimm but giving them a modern twist, the *Kunstmärchen* of the 1840s and 1850s invented figures such as Undine, Rumpelstiltskin, and the witch in the story of Hansel and Gretel. These tales allude to the split between the land, conceived as Mother Earth, and encroaching civilization, in the shape of mining industries and urbanization, bringing forth creatures that hover between man and woman, between evil spirit and supernatural being, and on whom the stories' young protagonists can project their fears as well as their fascination. Underlying these creatures' ambiguous representation is an urban bad conscience, if not outright guilt, about such encroachments and their consequences. This malaise leads to an inversion: natural habitats are portrayed as picturesque sites and idyllic spaces, but those who guard and protect them are dangerous monsters and malevolent apparitions. Such is the fate of Rübezahl the giant (celebrated in Wegener's *Rübezahls Hochzeit* [*Rübezahl's Wedding*, 1916]), haunting the woods and villages of the Erzgebirge (a mining region in Thuringia), and Alraune, an earth spirit with magical powers (in Henrik Galeen's *Alraune* [*Unholy Love*, 1927]). Even the figures of Mime, Alberich, and Etzel in Fritz Lang's *Die Nibelungen* (1924) have a mysterious communion with nature and at

Fig. 4. Fritz Lang's *Der müde Tod* (*Destiny*, 1921)

the same time pose a powerful threat to Siegfried and the Burgundian royal family, the film's more "civilized" protagonists.

    Stories in this tradition often revolve around contested forms of political authority or social control, with the elements of horror both disguising the historical conditions of socioeconomic struggles and foregrounding their destructive effects through super-natural forms of agency and legitimacy. Undine, for instance, is a creature of the sea, yearning to become human in order to marry a count, who is also being courted by another woman (who might be Undine's urban half sister and thus alter ego). Alternately threatened and protected by the spirits of the sea she left behind, Undine loses out to the other woman but resurfaces on a jet of water to interrupt her lover's wedding, reclaiming him for herself and the elements but thereby both killing him and frustrating her own desire to join the human race. Revived in the 1920s, such stories are either updated, as was *Alraune*, originally set in mythical times but now involving a scientist interested in heredity and eugenics, or they deal with contemporary issues, such as social justice or the consequences of financial speculation and conspicuous wealth, but projected back into another, more distant age. *Der Golem* (*The Golem*, 1915) is set in a medieval court; *Die Pest in Florenz* (*Plague in Florence*, 1917), *Lucrezia Borgia* (1922), episodes in *Der müde Tod* (*Destiny*, 1921; fig. 4), and *Faust* take place in Italy during the time of Renaissance principalities and city-states; and the struggles of the Reformation and Counter-Reformation provide the backdrop for the depiction of class relations, with protagonists acting out their antagonism toward the clergy and other father/authority figures, as in Wilhelm Dieterle's *Das Geheimnis des Abbé X* (*The Priest's Secret*, 1927).

Even elements in *Dr. Caligari*—Caligari's and Cesare's foreign origins and the mysterious medieval manuscript that the doctor tries to decipher—conform to this paradigm of displacement while still referring to topical issues such as psychoanalysis, hypnosis, and other contemporary treatments of mental illness or trauma.

In this sense the Expressionist films indeed signaled their own kind of politics—although instead of calling them protofascist, as Kracauer does, I would consider their message ecological: they express anxieties and fears about how modern men and women coexist with the natural environment under conditions of ever-advancing technologies, including the cinematograph, the telephone, and other machines of recording, surveillance, and control.

The Vision Machines, or the Powerless Power of the Look

Power relations in Expressionist films are most often articulated not through action or physical conflict but via the act of seeing and being seen: who controls the look, who looks at whom without being seen, who can immobilize by simply looking, and, finally, who controls what version of reality other people see. The most extreme example of this power structure activated through the eye is Lang's *Dr. Mabuse, der Spieler* (*Dr. Mabuse, the Gambler*, 1922). Throughout the film, Mabuse's hard stare resembles a totemic mask designed to terrify those who look at it; such an apparently empty look is not only an expression of power but can also be a dissimulation of it, used by Mabuse to control what version of himself he lets other people see. For instance, in the disguises that allow him to blend with the urban fabric, such as that of a Jewish peddler or a drunken working-class husband berating his wife, he slips into the diversionary gestures of metropolitan mimicry. At other times he is a kind of Mabuse-Medusa, as in the scenes in which he faces down the prosecutor, Dr. Wenk, at the gambling table and, as Dr. Weltmann, hypnotizes him. Vision thus assimilates or absorbs the look of others in the form of mimicry and camouflage, and wards it off in the form of the mask. In addition to foregrounding the act of looking, Lang's cinema also captures the power of the (male) gaze in a set of devices that lend human sight the illusion of new forms of mastery even as they mock its impotence.[15] Rather than demonstrating anticipatory parallels between Mabuse and Adolf Hitler, *Dr. Mabuse, der Spieler* is a cautionary tale, perhaps addressed to the director himself, about the filmmaker's ambiguous role as the master of the machinery of political power fantasies, predicting the political role the cinema would play in the totalitarian regimes of the 1930s and '40s.

Is Mabuse thus so memorable because through him the director can analyze the cinema as a locus of power—thus *through* the cinema warning *about* the cinema? It is an idea that joins the three Mabuse films, which, according to the critic Raymond Bellour, are "the most important reflection on the cinema ever produced by a director. The three films . . . deal with the central power of vision and diffusion, defined by the three major phases of the development of cinema: the cinema as such (silent cinema), sound cinema, and cinema confronting video and television."[16] Lang's Mabuse cycle is in this respect a veritable essay on the new social order of sound and image media, represented by modern technologies of surveillance as simulacra of society and community rather than as recording machines of reality. *Dr. Mabuse, der Spieler* makes its most explicit analogy between Mabuse as manipulator of vision and spectacle and Fritz Lang as cinematic metteur en scène in Mabuse's role as Dr. Weltmann, professional hypnotist and showman extraordinaire, who persuades his séance audience (and with them us, the film spectators) that they are seeing a desert caravan physically riding through the auditorium, a feat of conjuring magic which in turn is merely another layer of deception in the ongoing struggle between Mabuse and his adversary, Dr. Wenk. The properly political dimension of the analogy emerges more clearly in the triptych's second film, *Das Testament des Dr. Mabuse* (*The Testament of Dr. Mabuse*, 1933; fig. 5), made at the very beginning of the sound era, in which Lang singles out the human voice via loudspeaker and gramophone in order to demonstrate how readily it lends itself to the manipulation and production of "presence." A dummy Dr. Mabuse, wired to perform sinister deeds of simulated authority, issues commands and bellows instructions, intimidating his gang into believing him to be the more powerful for being heard but not seen. Finally, in *Die Tausend Augen des Dr. Mabuse* (*The Thousand Eyes of Dr. Mabuse*, 1960)—a sort of coda to, as well as retrospective reflection on, both the Weimar era and the Hitler years—it is the array of television screens, video monitors, and other, more diabolical surveillance devices installed at the Hotel Luxor, built by the Nazi secret service and used through the Cold War, with which Lang reinforces the notion of a looking glass world in which sight is not only the sense most easily deceived but also the one most easily seduced.

These technologies of vision, however, are "blind," that is, devoid of either affect or intent, of either love or hate, pleasure or fear—the usual attributes of human vision. With the empty look, the frozen stare, and the Medusa's gaze, Lang progressively descends into some very cold regions of post-human visuality, in which apparently no one is in control yet everyone struggles for control over others, suggesting that the look is no longer to be thought of as a metaphoric extension of power. In fact, power is what interrupts the exchange of looks by which human beings signal recognition of each other. For Lang the cinema, taken to its (techno)logical conclusion, is the ultimate metaphor not of social control effected through the power of the look but—more in line with Paul Virilio's thinking—proof of the end of this metaphor: the all-seeing eye of surveillance finally sees nothing at all.[17]

Fig. 5. Wera Liessem in Fritz Lang's *Das Testament des Dr. Mabuse*
(*The Testament of Dr. Mabuse*, 1933)

A similar obsession with seeing and being seen—although simpler because uncon-cerned with the philosophical implications of the new vision machines—is found in Karl Grune's *Die Strasse* (*The Street*, 1923), which employs the dialectic of guilty voyeurism and repressed exhibitionism. The protagonist, a middle-aged, henpecked husband, is lured to the city by the bright lights reflected on the ceiling of his stuffy room and ends up falling prey to a prostitute whose pimp frames him for murder. Eventually freed, he returns ruefully to his wife. Here, too, much of the drama of sudden temptation, moral fall, and therapeutic restitution plays out through metaphors of sight. A shot of the pros-titute blinking her eyes (rather like Cesare in *Dr. Caligari*) is followed by a huge pair of eyes, on a sign outside an optician's shop, suddenly lighting up, as if to mock the hero's curiosity. At a street corner a blind old man is led by his granddaughter, who makes a spectacle of herself in order to alert the police to the crime that has been committed. In one of the film's most phantasmagoric scenes, the soon-to-be-murdered victim, a man from the country, shows off his fat wallet to a prostitute who turns into a death's-head—a transformation that, since the hero looks straight into the camera, only the spectator is aware of—dividing the picture plane in two in a manner recalling the famous anamor-phic projection in Hans Holbein the Younger's *The Ambassadors* (1533), in which a skull falls like a blur across the frontal composition. In *Die Strasse* this division obliges the spectator to adopt two ocular points of view at once, one alluring, one horrific, as if the film were less concerned with punishing the hero's rebellion than with making a taboo of the spectator's visual pleasure, before giving it a demonic twist with its imagery of castration anxiety and violent murder.

Die Strasse here employs the indirect point of view and offscreen space in order to regulate but also suspend the characters' positions within the film. The protagonist finds himself included in a scene (but without any power over what he sees, as in the death's-head scene) and excluded from it (with no possibility of entering, as in a scene in which he longingly stares out the window at what we imagine is the street life below). Offscreen space in particular comes to represent a source of power—of suggestion, menace, anticipated dread—that forever escapes the protagonists' control; in both *Die Strasse* and the Dr. Mabuse trilogy there always seem to be more pairs of eyes than there are characters on the screen, a point that could be made about much of German Expressionist cinema. Perception—which, as I have pointed out, is the most fallible and deceptive of indices to truth—can be questioned by and subordinated to the power that resides in offscreen space. The question of the look's subject versus its object presents an additional problem: in these films a shot/reverse shot (also called "seeing/seen") has a different function from that in classical Hollywood, because the gaze in Expressionist cinema often does not have an object. Instead of the normal point of view structure, one finds no clear reverse-field relationship between the characters. Instead, the field of vision that a character has access to tends to lead to phobic or paranoid states, often connoted by the appearance of a double, which turns the subject into the other, divided and yet linked.

Sorcerers' Apprentices

Troubled perception and vicissitudes of looking both express epistemological ambiguity and signal its disavowal. As they were in the nineteenth-century literature of the fantastic, from Hoffmann via Poe to Fyodor Dostoyevsky and Henry James, such moments of uncertainty can be part of a strategy of defense, of psychic denial or traumatic forgetting. The uncanny element preserves the ambivalence of wanting to know and not wanting to know; it can be argued that the emphatic body language typical of Expressionism draws attention to the need to keep intact the body of the perceiver, to make himself master over his own lack of control of what is being perceived. This paradox between perception as knowing ("I see" meaning "I know") and perception as compensation for the dread of knowing (seeing as a protective cover from fully facing one's sense of impotence) may reveal the historical kernel of the films of the Weimar era. Such a notion of defense against too much knowledge might open up a new perspective on what Kracauer meant by the "psychic dispositions" of the contemporary audience: the films both address and give voice to the anxious sons of the Kaiser Wilhelm generation, robbed by the lost war and inflation not only of their savings and their jobs but of their dignity, their self-respect, and their manliness.[18] Driven by fear and resentment, unsure of social status and class identity—so Kracauer's theory goes—these sons saw the visions, dreams, and nightmares on the screen as speaking on behalf of their own inner selves. And, indeed, *Dr. Caligari*'s opening scenes involve class differences: Caligari, shortly after his arrival in Holstenwall, deferentially asks for a permit to put up his tent show, only to be insulted and humiliated by the town clerk and his subordinates. The scene deftly conveys the psychologically fraught experience of feeling at once outraged and powerless when faced with an arrogant, petty bureaucracy, and Caligari, in contrast with the impotent situation of contemporary spectators, is in a position to take revenge via his medium,

Cesare, murdering the clerk and thereby setting off the chain of events that make up the narrative. The spectators' feelings of resentment underwent a double inversion, with fear of humiliation first disguising itself as its inverse (ambition for social mobility and economic success) and then returning as horror with a sensation of uncanny recognition: the transgression is punished, the revolt of the sons against the fathers defeated. An additional, generic transformation makes the whole complex representable, with a very modern, metropolitan anxiety of a populace recently emerged from feudalism—how to survive in an upwardly mobile meritocratic-democratic society—becoming in *Dr. Caligari* a fantastic-gothic story from the distant past.

Even in this disguised form, the problem of social status is curiously disavowed. After its pointed beginning the narrative veers off in quite a different direction and never returns. Instead of Caligari's humiliation expressing itself in open revolt, his omnipotence, associated with his powers of hypnotism, ends up overcompensating for his social impotence in a manner that relates the story structurally to that of the sorcerer's apprentice: with Cesare, as with the Golem, Frankenstein, and other machine-men, a force is set free that escapes its creator's control and may even turn against him. One is never quite sure whether Cesare's nightly sorties are planned and ordered by his master or if they take on a momentum of their own. But Cesare is also Caligari's double: the medium is the embodiment of his master's rebellious, antiauthoritarian streak, itself an apparent contradiction of Caligari's own authoritarianism.

Another film of the same year, Ernst Lubitsch's *Die Puppe* (*The Doll*, 1919), seems to be a comedic response to *Dr. Caligari*'s questions of status anxiety and the master-slave dialectic. The plot is taken from a well-known Jewish marriage farce that had been adapted several times in the cinema since 1907. In Lubitsch's version a shy young man, forced to marry in order to inherit his uncle's fortune, takes refuge in a monastery to escape from an army of brides. The monks, eager to get their share of his wealth, suggest a ruse: why not marry a life-size windup doll? The doll maker's apprentice makes a fatal mistake, with farcical consequences that lead to a happy ending nonetheless. *Die Puppe* is also a parody of Hoffmann's "Der Sandmann" ("The Sandman," 1816), which Sigmund Freud famously used as his central literary example in his essay on The Uncanny. Lubitsch, however, makes fun of the male hero's anxiety about sex and sight, at the same time having a laugh either at the expense of (if we think of *Homunculus* [1916]) or anticipating (if we think of Maria from *Metropolis*) the tragic, melodramatic, and gothic-horror stories of doubles, homunculi, somnambulists, and automatons that German Expressionist cinema would tell through the 1920s.

The Frame Tale

The tales of sorcerers' apprentices also suggest anxiety about the social status of the Expressionist filmmaker himself, especially as compared with that of artists in other fields. Directors such as Wegener, Wiene, Lang, Paul Leni, Murnau, and Arthur Robison may have felt themselves misjudged and undervalued: their films can nonetheless be read as allegories of their professional dilemma and as manifestos of their cultural politics. Half seriously, half ironically, they portray themselves through their protagonists: the showmen, alchemists, hypnotists, and strange doctors are thus the masters and wizards of a new blend of science and the supernatural, and no one is quite sure whether this blend will turn out to be black or white magic. These sorcerers of a fabulous technology seem both reckless and wary of the forces they have summoned. In exercising control as artists but being afraid of losing control in the corporate bureaucracies of the giant film company UFA, they plundered, appropriated, and vampirized traditional high culture and the more established arts but also learned how to seduce the public. Thus they were both triumphant about their new manipulative prowess and concerned about its social consequences.[19]

This kind of cinematic self-reference might explain the unusual prominence given to the figure of the narrator, or more generally to the question of who or what is telling the tale. These uncanny (at once omnipotent and unreliable) master narrators in German Expressionist films include the mysterious figure of Scapinelli in *Der Student von Prag*, the itinerant showman of *Dr. Caligari*, and the equally itinerant *montreur d'ombres* in *Schatten*, who entertains the aristocratic company at the mansion with his truth-telling phantasmagoria. If one adds all the other string pullers of human puppets—Dr. Mabuse, Nosferatu, Tartuffe, and the figure of Death in *Der müde Tod*—then the list of master narrators is very long indeed, coinciding with, but by no means collapsible into, Kracauer's "procession of tyrants."[20] Some are external to the film's fiction, others are internally generated, as they are in *Dr. Caligari* and *Der Golem* but also in *Nosferatu. Eine Symphonie des Grauens* (*Nosferatu*, 1922) and *Die Nibelungen*. In *Nosferatu*, in particular, there are so many sources of narrative authority that the meaning of the tale is crucially altered, because they all compete with each other. But instead of feeling threatened by the narrators' tyrannical power (as Kracauer maintains), the spectator is more likely threatened by a lack of control, acutely aware of the absence of a reliable voice of truth. Despite the many narrators, it is clear that these figures are not to be trusted and thus add yet another layer of uncertainty.

The device that most readily introduces these further uncertainties is probably also the most distinctive feature of narration in Weimar films: the frame tale. The very term "frame" suggests a stabilizing function, a way of containing textual excess, but instead its deployment seems more often designed to complicate matters. The best-known example of such complication is, of course, the framing device of *Dr. Caligari*, whose origin and function has given rise to so much discussion and surmise that it has become a crux of film history in itself.[21] In *Dr. Caligari* the narrative is framed by another tale that acts as a motivation, a commentary, and thus an interpretation of the events immanent to the text. But since the frame tale, too, is overturned at the end, the *mise en abyme* denies or subverts the truth value of what one has just seen in a more radical fashion, with doubt about the reliability of the narrators as well as about their very sanity. Even the final frontal shot of the good doctor hardly reassures about his state of mind, never mind his intentions.

The frame not only complicates the story for viewers but also suspends the reality of the world in which the characters move, so that it is possible to argue that it acts as a lure or trap for the protagonists, an inducement either to give themselves away or give away a secret, as in *Schloss Vogelöd* (*The Haunted Castle*, 1921) and *Herr Tartüff*. Yet framing a story can also be used, as it is in *Schatten*, in a more ambiguous, open-ended way, as a protocinematic performance—arranged in a complicated form of doubling as a Balinese shadow play—that serves as a screen for projection and becomes the film we are actually watching. Used by the magician for ultimately benevolent, therapeutic ends, the frame ostensibly allows the characters to confront themselves, to attain a degree of self-knowledge about their fears, obsessions, jealousies, and murderous rages.

Other Minds, Other Worlds

A rich legacy of German Expressionist cinema from the 1920s passed to American cinema of the 1930s, with the critical success of Wiene's film likely paving the way for public acceptance of both the Universal Studios' horror films in the 1930s (directed by the likes of James Whale and Edgar G. Ulmer) and the film noir that began to appear in the mid-1940s (directed by Otto Preminger, Lang, Billy Wilder, Robert Siodmak, and Kurt Bernhardt). In the films of these genres, often seen as stylistic offspring of cinematic Expressionism or made by German directors, some of whom had found refuge from the Nazis in America, we see the return of the monsters from the 1910s and 1920s in different guises (Frankenstein, Dracula, mad scientists, homunculi), as well as many films with an amnesiac protagonist, a regular motif of the film noir directed by Siodmak and Bernhardt and thus referring back to Francis, the hero/victim of *Dr. Caligari*.[22] More than lighting or Expressionist stylization, it is the techniques of deferred narration—of flashbacks, multiple voices, and frames—that constitutes the legacy that *Dr. Caligari* and Weimar cinema took into exile, as well as the use of offscreen space to give the spectator that sense of dread or doom that so often overcomes film noir's weak, drifting male protagonists.[23]

German Expressionist cinema has become topical again in past decades not only because of the continuing popularity of film noir, nor because so many of the films are about the terror of being watched and observed and not being able to trust one's own eyes. *Dr. Caligari* is an epistemological and psychoanalytical puzzle, and it is in part this philosophical feature of the film (and its cousins) that we appreciate today: the endless reversibility of its truth claims, put in place by the frame tale and sustained by the narrative *mise en abyme*. However many times we tell ourselves the story of Francis and Jane, of Caligari and Cesare, we never know whom to believe and therefore never quite resolve what part of the story is real and what is imagined: if we believe Francis, the doctor is a dangerous madman; if we believe the doctor, Francis is a poor deranged soul. It may seem a trivial point, but it touches on the philosophical problem of other minds: what would it mean to know what goes on in someone else's mind, and what proof do I have that other minds exist? *Das Cabinet des Dr. Caligari* could also thus be seen as an example of the paradox of self-reference—all Cretans are liars, says a Cretan. But *Dr. Caligari* is also a fable about the lack of ontological ground; although it does not quite pose the problem in such terms, it raises the related ontological problem of other worlds: if the world I live in is merely someone else's fiction, where is the outside, the point from which I might see that I am trapped inside—if not inside someone else's inside? Perhaps anyone who poses these sorts of questions should be called paranoid. Yet today it seems that popular cinema has finally caught up with *Das Cabinet des Dr. Caligari* in this respect, and spectators of films like *The Matrix* (1999) or *eXistenZ* (1999) should have no difficulty sympathizing with Francis's dilemma; in those films, too, the protagonists want to know the identity of the Other who organizes all. And we might consider, on the same theme, television series such as *Twin Peaks* (1990–91), *The X-Files* (1993–2002), and *Lost* (2004–10); movies hyped via the Internet as "documentaries," such as *The Blair Witch Project* (1999); and films such as *The Truman Show* (1998), *Being John Malkovich* (1999), *Memento* (2000), or *Minority Report* (2002). Moviegoers today seem attracted to the fantastic, to science fiction, to horror and film noir as if it were a version of reality rather than its opposite, perhaps precisely because this oscillation among competing versions of reality now seems more truthful to our intuitions, to the quasi-metaphysical doubts and insecurities we have about political power, our abilities to control our lives, and being in the world.

These parallels between today's films and those of Germany in the 1920s suggest that Expressionist films and Weimar cinema do have a philosophical message, or at least pose a philosophical problem, namely that there is no firm ground for our thinking: that we can neither have epistemological certainty (that is, attain truth in what we know and how we know it), nor can we have ontological security (that is, a self-present ground of our existence). It is therefore not altogether far-fetched to argue that an alternative title for Kracauer's book might have been *From Caligari to Heidegger*—after the philosopher who published *Being and Time*, a masterpiece of ontological uncertainty, in 1927, seven years after *Dr. Caligari*.

What are we to make of these various parallels and retroactive anticipations? Do the anxieties and ontological doubts reflected by today's cinema mean, as Kracauer would almost certainly suggest, that we are heading toward a new authoritarianism, with the films casting "warning shadows" about what is to come? Or, as I have argued, do they act out these doubts so we may better anticipate its consequences by learning to live with both doubt and risk? I would say that these cinematic grandchildren of *Dr. Caligari* prove that we have become mature enough to live with such radical skepticism, that we enjoy ambiguity and reversibility rather than being driven insane by it. This would indicate that popular culture, in this case cinema, has achieved what the German cinema of the fantastic may not have set out to do but accomplished all the same: it has played a role in modernizing our philosophical thinking in addition to our lifestyles and design aesthetics. What used to be shocking and cause drear anticipation is now an intellectual pleasure, a game with possibilities, a frisson of disorientation. This is not as frivolous as it may sound, and films like *Dr. Caligari*—once considered scandalous works of twisted imaginations—deserve to be recognized for becoming part of our common, shared culture, part of a family of modern classics, still serving as a film to think with and not just fearfully recalled at anniversaries of political upheavals or fondly shown at retrospectives.

1. Siegfried Kracauer, "Notes on the Planned History of the German Film," 1944; quoted in Volker Breidecker, ed., *Siegfried Kracauer/Erwin Panofsky: Ein Briefwechsel* (Berlin: Akademie Verlag, 1996), p. 17.

2. Several of this essay's arguments appear in more amplified form in the chapter "Caligari's Family: Expressionism, Frame Tales and Master Narratives," in Thomas Elsaesser, *Weimar Cinema and After* (London: Routledge, 2000), pp. 61–104.

3. Kracauer, *From Caligari to Hitler: A Psychological History of German Film* (Princeton, N.J.: Princeton University Press, 1947).

4. On the fantasy frame, see Slavoj Žižek, *The Sublime Object of Ideology* (London: Verso, 1997), pp. 105–19.

5. For an overview of different interpretations of *Das Cabinet des Dr. Caligari*, see Mike Budd, ed., *The Cabinet of Dr. Caligari: Texts, Contexts, Histories* (New Brunswick, N.J.: Rutgers University Press, 1990); and David Robinson, *Das Cabinet des Dr. Caligari* (London: BFI Film Classics, 1997).

6. For a characterization of Carl Mayer, see Bernhard Frankfurter, ed., *Carl Mayer: Im Spiegelkabinett des Dr. Caligari: Der Kampf zwischen Licht und Dunkel* (Vienna: Promedia, 1997).

7. Rudolf Kurtz, *Expressionismus und Kunst* (Berlin: Lichtbildbühne, 1926), p. 46. Translation by the author.

8. On Franco-German film relations prior to 1918, see Elsaesser, "The Presence of Pathé in Germany," in Michel Marie and Laurent Forestier, eds., *La Firme Pathé Frères, 1896–1914* (Paris: Association Française de Recherche sur l'Histoire du Cinéma, 2004), pp. 393–406.

9. On the *Autorenfilm-Debatte*, see Anton Kaes, "Literary Intellectuals and the Cinema: The Kino-Debatte," *New German Critique* 40 (Winter 1987): 7–34.

10. Guido Seeber, "Doppelgängerbilder im Film," *Die Kinotechnik*, no. 1 (1919): 17. See also Seeber, *Der Trickfilm* (Berlin, 1929); reviewed by Sergei Eisenstein in *Close-Up*, May 1929.

11. Caspar Tyberg, "The Faces of Stellan Rye," in Elsaesser, ed., *A Second Life: German Cinema's First Decade* (Amsterdam: Amsterdam University Press, 1996), pp. 151–59.

12. Taking their cue from Kracauer's title, most overviews of German cinema begin with a discussion of *Das Cabinet des Dr. Caligari*.

13. On *Dr. Caligari*'s reception in France and the United States, see Kristin Thompson, "Dr. Caligari at the Folies Bergère," in Budd, ed., *The Cabinet of Dr. Caligari*, pp. 121–69.

14. Kracauer, *Die Angestellten: Aus dem neuesten Deutschland* (Frankfurt: Sozietäts-Druckerei, 1930); published in English as *The Salaried Masses: Duty and Distraction in Weimar Germany* (London: Verso, 1998).

15. On Fritz Lang as the director of the look and the stare, see the essays assembled in Steve Jenkins, ed., *Fritz Lang: The Image and the Look* (London: British Film Institute, 1981). On the illusion of mastery, see Elsaesser, "Fritz Lang: The Illusion of Mastery," *Sight & Sound*, January 2000, http://www.bfi.org.uk/sightandsound/feature/43.

16. Raymond Bellour, "La Machine à hypnose," *CinémAction* 47 (1988): 71. Translation by the author.

17. See Paul Virilio, *The Aesthetics of Disappearance*, trans. Philippe Beitchman (New York: Semiotext(e), 1991).

18. The ideas of "psychic dispositions" and "psychological patterns of a people at a particular time" are developed by Kracauer in the introduction to *From Caligari to Hitler*, especially pp. 8–9.

19. In the interviews he gave throughout his career, Lang was always conscious of the cultural prejudices he encountered as a film director, and he staunchly defended filmmaking on the cinema's own terms. See "Kitsch, Sensation, Kultur und Film," in Fred Gehler and Ullrich Kasten, eds., *Fritz Lang: Die Stimme von Metropolis* (Berlin: Henschel, 1990), pp. 202–6.

20. "Procession of Tyrants" is a chapter in Kracauer, *From Caligari to Hitler*, pp. *77–87*.

21. In addition to discussions by Hans Janowitz, Hermann Warm, and Erich Pommer in Helga Belach and H. M. Bock, eds., *Das Cabinet des Dr. Caligari* (Munich: edition text + kritik, 1997), see also Kracauer, *From Caligari to Hitler*, pp. *61–72*; Walter Kaul, ed., *Caligari und der Caligarismus* (Berlin: Stiftung Deutsche Kinemathek, 1970); and Robinson, *Das Cabinet des Dr. Caligari*. Another account of the story's origins is given in Leonardo Quaresima, "Wer war Alland? Die Texte des Caligari," in Frankfurter, ed., *Carl Mayer*, pp. *99–118*.

22. The prototype is discussed in Kracauer, *From Caligari to Hitler*, p. *212*.

23. In addition to the films of Robert Siodmak and Kurt Bernhardt, one could call Jacques Tourneur's female melodrama *Experiment Perilous* (1944) and his film noir *Out of the Past* (1947) outstanding examples of the Weimar style transposed to Hollywood. Film noir from the 1940s and melodramas from the 1950s are generally considered the genres most likely to extend the limits of classical narrative. In both genres, seeing/seen is frequently enfolded in the drama of imaginary or deficient sight, indicating their affinity (or pedigree) with Weimar cinema narration.

Das Lied einer Nac

Eric Rentschler

The Situation Is Hopeless but Not Desperate

UFA's Early Sound-Film Musicals

Beyond the Haunted Screen

"The Weimar cinema has never been a particularly popular cinema," writes Thomas Elsaesser. "It has always been something of a filmmakers' or a film scholars' cinema."[1] In his assessment, the films made in the Weimar Republic stand out above all by dint of the formal accomplishment and intellectual appeal of "individually authored art films."[2] Those who share this opinion applaud the masterpieces of Ernst Lubitsch, Fritz Lang, F. W. Murnau, and G. W. Pabst and focus on the mean streets, dread spaces, and eccentric narratives of what Lotte Eisner called "the haunted screen," from *Das Cabinet des Dr. Caligari* (*The Cabinet of Dr. Caligari*, 1920), *Nosferatu. Eine Symphonie des Grauens* (*Nosferatu*, 1922), and *Dr. Mabuse, der Spieler* (*Dr. Mabuse, the Gambler*, 1921) to *Metropolis* (1927) and *Die Büchse der Pandora* (*Pandora's Box*, 1929), along with other films of the fantastic, street films, chamber-room melodramas, and big-city symphonies.[3] The hallmarks of the silent era, critics like Elsaesser submit, have without a doubt played a much more estimable role in the history of German cinema than the productions made after the coming of sound and the Nazi takeover. Despite its truth, this argument has also fostered a partial and occluded view.[4] A more inclusive approach enables us to consider, along with the period's canonized productions, its less well-known genre films.

At first blush, most German sound features from the late 1920s and early 1930s seem to be decidedly out of synch with the harsh and harried zeitgeist, a time of mass unemployment, economic instability, political unrest, and existential disquiet.[5] Indeed, the vast majority of genre films from the Weimar Republic's last years, especially the many musical comedies, would seem best characterized as *ungleichzeitig*, or out of keeping with the times.[6] Here we behold performers who move with grace and ease, language that is perky and insouciant, lavish set designs that bear few traces of grim realities. There is an intrepid vitality and an abundance of good cheer, even in the midst of crisis; despite imposing odds, the denizens of these fantasy worlds remain chipper and unflappable. Produced in a country that was dancing on a volcano, these films provide light fare for hard times. The situation may be hopeless, they suggest, but it is not desperate.[7]

In Weimar film musicals, which are largely operettas, bodies and spaces are constantly in motion; these symphonies of silliness celebrate mobility and transport. At the start of *Die Drei von der Tankstelle* (*Three from the Filling Station*, 1930), a car hurtles down a country lane; the top is down, and its male occupants are in the finest of fettles. Trees zoom by, and the camera alternates between a whirring front wheel and a rear view from a side mirror. The entire scene unreels to the accompaniment of a spirited song ("Sunny day, lovely day/Heart aflutter and the motor running!/Agreeable goal, agreeable start/And a most pleasant journey") and a spunky score.[8] *Quick* (1932) begins in an exclusive spa with state-of-the-art fitness machinery devised to make muscles taut and faces firm. The resort's finicky guests, fixated on the state of their health, devote their abundant leisure time to the pursuit of diversion. Echoing the dramatic prologues from Arnold Fanck's mountain films, *Die verliebte Firma* (*The Company's in Love*, 1932) commences with some dissolves over breathtaking panoramas—but as the light musical treatment intimates, the first impression is illusory: after measuring the sublime immensity of the Alpine landscape, the camera narrows in on a singing romantic couple. This film about the making of a film quickly takes leave of the authentic location and moves to a big-city studio setting.

These sound fantasies are time machines as well. *Das Flötenkonzert von Sanssouci* (*Flute Concert at Sanssouci*, 1930) spirits us to Dresden in 1756, sampling conversations among a gathering of emissaries from countries conspiring against Prussia. The opening tracking shot lasts a full four minutes, granting us ample occasion to school our gaze in the play of signs and signals. Everything is coded here, we learn, even the musical accompaniment, so that seemingly innocuous phrases ("Isn't politics also a matter of not talking about politics?") assume political meanings. In *Der Kongress tanzt* (*Congress Dances*, 1931), cannons mark the start of a new day in 1814 at the Congress of Vienna. A voyeuristic camera sidles through a room full of people eagerly awaiting the latest developments. The most recent arrivals to the conference confirm that all of Europe is represented at the event; meanwhile, cannons continue to sound as nervous officials sneeze with equal loudness. From this antechamber we move to Count von Metternich's bedside where, in a touch reminiscent of Lubitsch, world history takes place behind closed doors.[9] Over breakfast, the statesman monitors the vast proceedings via an elaborate network of minions and machines.

With great emphasis, these features implement the means of audiovisual reproduction, putting gramophones, radios, and projectors on conspicuous display. *Das Lied einer Nacht* (*One Night's Song*, 1932) opens with the sound of a voice and the shadow of a microphone, which yield to the shadow of an announcer and then the shadow of a performer. A dissolve to a long tilt up radio towers is followed by another dissolve to an antenna on a building top and a pan across a window and into a living space. The mediated voice has, we see, found an audience, a dog sitting in front of a radio and listening to a loud male singer. The camera cuts seamlessly to a man with his mouth wide open—not a performer but a patient at the dentist's office. There is an inordinate energy and irreverence in the subsequent cuts between places, faces, and spaces, as the film catapults from Vienna to Budapest to Bucharest and as we track the path of a telegram and the transmission of a text over the wires while a train travels through the night.

Einbrecher (Burglars, 1930) takes us behind the scenes and offers a hands-on view of a technology that creates artificial worlds. The first shot provides a close-up of a singing torero, an animated figure straight out of a tale by E. T. A. Hoffmann, and opens up to a gathering of costumed cyborgs, stand-ins for the make-believe beings who people the film we are about to see. A Walt Disneyesque *metteur en scène* directs the proceedings in a laboratory for mechanical puppets. Later in the film, a song reiterates the imaginary trappings of the world before us:

> The dog looks alive,
> The child speaks,
> A world of simulations.
> Everything moves in turns.
> Inside her is only clockwork,
> Not a heart.

The Cultivation of Distraction

One might say, as Weimar contemporaries often did, that most early German sound endeavors were vapid and formulaic, indeed clockwork constructions without a heart.[10] Film studios certainly realized that this thought was on many critics' minds—and did not hesitate to acknowledge it. Toward the end of *Die Koffer des Herrn O. F.* (*The Trunks of Mr. O. F.*, 1931), for instance, two executives from OTAG (Ostend Feature Film, Inc.) reflect on how their studio's new features might best respond to the strained economic climate. Their recipe for success is standardized light fare with only the most modest variations. The studio head gestures proudly to posters of coming attractions, images of romantic pairs who will appear in future operettas: *Ich liebe, Du liebst, Er liebt, Wir lieben, Ihr liebt*—and, finally, to fill out this grand ensemble of six films, *Alle lieben*. And that is not all—there are also plans for similar productions with a martial aspect, as we see in a further profusion of posters: *Kasernenduft: Eine Tonfilm-Operette* (The aroma of the barracks: a sound-film operetta), *Kasernenzauber* (The magic of the barracks), *Es ist lustig zu marschieren* (It's fun to go marching), and *Kasernenluft* (The air of the barracks). In this economy, revue films coexist cozily with military reviews.[11] "A film with deeper

"You want to humiliate me...that's why you came!"

Fig. 1. Jeanette MacDonald and Maurice Chevalier in Ernst Lubitsch's *The Love Parade* (1929)

meaning," maintains the studio boss, facing the camera in a close-up, "is of interest to no one. A film without deeper meaning is what a big city needs."

German features of the early sound era, outside of a few notable exceptions, have indeed been seen as lacking deeper meaning. Weimar cinema, by and large, is equated with the silent era before 1929; it has gone down in film history as a site of modernist endeavor that contributed substantially to international understanding of the medium's expressive potential and exercised an indelible influence on the very notion of what constitutes a film. Its chief significance for the scholars who established its critical reputation abides in its status as a "motor of modernity," as an entity that in crucial ways fueled Germany's belated and conflicted attempts to become a modern nation.[12] Features of the era at once enact and embody the tug and pull within this national body between the old and the new, between modern and antimodern initiatives. German films of the early 1930s, apart from unquestioned masterpieces like Lang's *M* (1931) and *Das Testament des Dr. Mabuse* (*The Testament of Dr. Mabuse*, 1933), seemed, in comparison, devoid of substance and seriousness. If there is anything modern about early German sound films, it would seem to be their industrialized uniformity.

Even though comedies constituted a full one-third of the features produced during the Weimar era, they invariably take a backseat to German films of the fantastic and surely suffer when placed aside contemporary generic counterparts made in France and the United States. No German director of the 1920s, beyond the young Lubitsch and, on occasion, Reinhold Schünzel and Ludwig Berger, receives particular recognition; discussions about German film comedies more often than not focus on performers.[13] Early German musical comedies do not hold up well when compared to works by René Clair, Lubitsch, or Rouben Mamoulian: *Die Drei von der Tankstelle* pales next to *Sous les toits de Paris* (*Under the Roofs of Paris*, 1930) and *Der Kongress tanzt* is surely no *Love Parade* (1929; fig. 2). And the only German filmmaker who could rival Busby

Berkeley's masses in motion would be Leni Riefenstahl. The popular early musical comedies, especially those produced by Erich Pommer of Universum Film AG (UFA), were frequently chided as being escapist and negligible.[14] There were, to be sure, several realist films that addressed social circumstances and confronted unresolved political problems; *Kameradschaft* (Comradeship, 1931) and *Westfront 1918* (1930) by Pabst, and Slatan Dudow's *Kuhle Wampe* (*Whither Germany?*, 1932) are often-noted exceptions to the rule. Josef von Sternberg's *Der blaue Engel* (*The Blue Angel*, 1930) had musical numbers, but no one would mistake it for a comedy. The much larger ensemble of films, it was—and often still is—said, sought to transform the gravity of reality into a kinder and gentler unreality. Lightweight fare (which did not necessarily have a light touch) was a preferred approach: operettas and revues, social comedies, romances, and farces with a folksy flair. "Again and again," Rudolf Arnheim wrote about German film releases of 1931, "we note with dismay that we must flee into a void when we want to amuse ourselves."[15]

Three concerns have strongly inflected discussions of early German sound comedies. First, contemporary commentators met the coming of sound in general with suspicion, claiming, as did Arnheim, that it would mean the death of cinema as an art because its higher level of realism threatened to undermine "all the exceptional qualities of silent film that we had loved."[16] In a retrospective assessment, Siegfried Kracauer elaborated on how the presence of sound divested the image of its suggestive and evocative power. Verbal statements, he submitted, tend to articulate intentions whereas camera shots apprehend the unintentional and the unspoken. Silent films probed "levels below the dimension of consciousness, and since the spoken word had not yet assumed control, unconventional or even subversive images were allowed to slip in. But when dialogue took over, unfathomable imagery withered and intentional meanings prevailed."[17] He went on to note that both talkies and silent films contain ideological inscriptions, "although analysis of these attitudes is hampered rather than facilitated by the addition of spoken words."[18] Béla Balázs was hopeful that sound films might "teach us to analyse even chaotic noise with our ear and read the score of life's symphony"—in short, that they might train the human ear, just as silent films had trained the human eye.[19] Unfortunately, he later admitted, these great hopes would rarely find fulfillment in the sound era.[20]

A second complaint was that the sound comedies intensified film's powers of distraction. The UFA musicals of the early sound era were seen, in Arnheim's words, as film confections.[21] They appeal to "what is bad and stupid in man" and ensure "that dissatisfaction shall not burst into revolutionary action but shall fade away in dreams of a better world." These industrial commodities legitimate the status quo and stultify the possibility of collective resistance;[22] they fortify belief in the church and the power of capital; they also propagate the sanctity of marriage and the home.[23] According to Ernst

Bloch, writing in 1929, distraction fuels emotion without creating momentum and "dams life back to nothing but youth, to inflated beginnings, so that the question concerning the Where to never arises."[24] Distraction is evasion, a deception "which is supposed to conceal the place and ground on which it occurs"; life becomes fully determined by the interests that govern the status quo: tedium by day, escape by night.[25] People come to regard their material limits and experiential lacks through the eyes of the powerful and big business. "In the evening, when lit, the dust of the day looks really colourful and alluring. This entices, but does not fulfil, does not create the desire for more genuine things, but for things that are always new."[26]

A third objection was even more emphatically political. The most prominent escapist sound comedies issued from UFA, which was owned by the media mogul Alfred Hugenberg and dominated, since his takeover in 1927, by his right-wing agenda. These productions colluded with nationalist and reactionary designs, increasingly so after Hugenberg, as chairman of the supervisory board, allowed political dictates to determine the studio's direction. In 1930 the critic Hans Sahl spoke out against Hugenberg's upbeat panegyrics for the German military, his *Zapfenstreiche*, saying that they agitated against reflection, transforming the sound film into "a German tragedy." Hugenberg, Sahl elaborated, "is fortunate in his control of a contingent of cinemas which permit him to add these films to the repertoire without drawing any attention."[27] The films that stirred the masses and provided emotional sustenance during the last years of Weimar, Klaus Kreimeier has observed, were not leftist productions by Pabst or Brecht or Willi Münzenberg but rather UFA's melodramas, comedies, Prussia films, waltz fantasies, and barracks comedies. The progressives simply failed to understand collective dispositions and thus remained unable to address the masses' inner cravings.[28]

While still sensitive to the objections of critics such as Arnheim, Balázs, and Kracauer, recent commentators have suggested that we might approach the early sound films in less dismissive ways and regard them as integral parts of the Weimar legacy.[29] In reconsidering the significant exemplars of UFA sound operettas made before the Nazi ascent to power, we gain a sense of critical awareness and a decided self-consciousness; the films are very much self-aware products of their times and not just regressive, symptomatic texts. If we put these works into dialogue with films of other genres, we encounter different answers to similar dilemmas, diverse strategies for dealing with times of crisis and the crises of the times. Seen together with other contemporary productions, these exercises enable us to comprehend the diversity of ways in which the Weimar Republic was both experienced and cinematically represented.[30] The seeming antagonisms of apparently nonsynchronous film artifacts, as Karsten Witte once observed, "can in fact produce historical insights."[31]

Fig. 3. Lilian Harvey and Willy Fritsch in Wilhelm Thiele's *Die Drei von der Tankstelle* (*Three from the Filling Station*, 1930)

Communities of Circumstance

In 1930 the German Reich was 1.7 billion reichsmarks in debt, and 4 million people were unemployed. An article in the trade paper *Film-Kurier* in July 1931 related a question very much on the minds of UFA studio executives: "What then would be more needed now than an offering of films that might lead audiences out of this spiritual vacuum and offer something that is both uplifting and distracting?"[32] *Die Drei von der Tankstelle* (fig. 3), produced by Pommer, put this upbeat resolve into practice and became the most successful film of the 1930–31 season.[33] Three friends (Willy Fritsch, Heinz Rühmann, and Oskar Karlweis) return from a long vacation to find their servants gone and their belongings impounded. "Something very unpleasant happened during your absence," says their lawyer. An earthquake? they wonder. Or maybe a change of government in Lippe-Detmold? This was after all a time of unpleasant surprises, particularly in Lippe-Detmold, where two years earlier the Nazis had won their first regional election. And in the state elections on September 14, a day before the film's premiere, the Nazis had scored a decisive breakthrough. Asked if his wife perhaps might have had a blond child, the lawyer (played by a German Jew, Kurt Gerron) replies, "Even worse than that: you're bankrupt."

The production registers the state of economic emergency and political turmoil, all the better to make light of it. Nonetheless, the rise of the Nazis along with a tweak of Jewish anxiety do not go unacknowledged. The bankrupt trio remains unmoved by the challenge to their financial status; they bounce about in unison, cheerfully contemplating all the things they will have to do without, singing, "Great God, we're bankrupt." Werner R. Heymann's five songs bring an undeniable vigor to the film, as does Franz Planer's intimate lighting, for instance, in the romantic duet, "Liebling, mein Herz lässt Dich grüssen" [Darling, my heart sends its love to you], fine touches that make up for Wilhelm Thiele's often clunky mise-en-scène (particularly his maladroit blocking and circus-ring staging) and the sometimes less-than-fluid editing. Hoping to recoup their losses, the three comrades sell their car and buy a filling station on a heavily trafficked road in the boonies. Sharing the chores of attendant, all three become enamored by Lilian (Lilian Harvey), a sprightly blonde in a shiny convertible, though only one of them (as casting policy dictated, her real-life romantic partner, Fritsch) will gain her favor.

Through it all, what the film speaks of as "the three meshugga musketeers" never break a sweat; by no fault of their own, the sunny boys become executives in the Gas Station Corporation, owned by Lilian's father. Even if reality intrudes in a brief documentary glimpse of the working day in a factory, this drab prospect is tempered by its protagonists' free and easy perspective: "We've seen work from the distance/And even from the distance it was not a pretty sight." As in many contemporary UFA features, the pleasures of the male bond seem more compelling than the obligatory romantic union.[34] In the final moments, Willy (Fritsch) shakes hands with his friends and carries Lilian away from the scene. They pass through a curtain and suddenly stand before a spotlight. Looking into the camera, Lilian is astonished. There are people out there, she says, an audience! "Yes, indeed. A bunch of total strangers!" What are they doing there? What are they waiting for? Lilian quickly comes up with an answer: an operetta has not reached its end until after the finale; to that end, the film offers a closing extravaganza in a protracted take that unites the entire cast of players.

An altogether different "bunch of total strangers" occupies a shabby rooming house in Robert Siodmak's *Abschied* (*Farewell*), of the same year; here the impact of hard times becomes far more palpable and poignant. In this anti–Grand Hotel people live in close quarters; intrusions by strangers into private spheres and personal affairs are common occurrences. Everyone is at loose ends and hopeful that things will get better. The film's key romantic couple sustains a candid conversation about their prospective monthly income, minutely calculating how, if all goes well, their savings will accrue over time and what that accumulated amount will mean for their future well-being. Siodmak's drama, which grants nary a glimpse of exterior spaces, presents a community of circumstance, an ensemble that negotiates dire straits. In the end, we see Brigitte Horney, left high and dry by her lover, sitting alone in a darkness of emotional devastation. This finale is anything but a celebration: "Everything in life is also like a song/Fading and vanishing, a farewell."[35]

Fig. 4. Willy Fritsch and Lilian Harvey in Erik Charell's *Der Kongress tanzt* (*Congress Dances*, 1931)

Too Lovely to Be True

The haunting theme song of *Abschied* evokes the ephemeral and precarious nature of human endeavor: "How quickly we forget, what once was/Nothing remains of everything that once was."[36] The signature tune of *Der Kongress tanzt* (fig. 4) does something similar, albeit in a far more reassuring fashion: "Today all fairy tales become true/Today one thing is clear to me/That only happened once/That never happens again/That's too lovely to be true."[37] The catch phrase "Das gab's nur einmal" (That only happened once) has now come to incarnate the nostalgic embrace of precious moments and past delights, a yearning for yesteryear's hit tunes or cinematic evergreens.[38] The past on view in this "superoperetta" (which cost a hefty 4 million reichsmarks), directed by the master showman Erik Charell, is a simulacrum of Vienna, a site of court intrigue, balls and waltzes, of sentimental schmaltz over *Heuriger* in Grinzing, and of *Wiener Mädln* and snappy marching cavaliers.[39] A love affair between the shopgirl Christel (Harvey) and Czar Alexander (Fritsch) unfolds while the congress convenes. Hoping to distract Alexander from decisive deliberations, Metternich hires a seductive agent to waylay him; the czar in turn engages the dim-witted Uralsky (also played by Fritsch) as a body double.[40] Christel and Alexander thus have time for assignations while the gathered nations plot Europe's future. Upon learning that Napoleon has returned to France, however, Alexander puts an end to the whirlwind affair and bids Christel farewell.

Although the film was the uncontested box office hit of the season, it met with the extreme displeasure of influential critics. Kracauer deemed it "a senseless gathering of decorations"; in the name of amusement, the historical revue diverted attention from the true state of crisis and awakened "illusions and desires which can only serve the forces of reaction, and whip up a dust storm that totally blinds the audience."[41] Arnheim's assessment was every bit as harsh. It was a pity, he remarked, that members of the audience lacked the czar's power to deputize doubles: "I can think of people who would have liked to have sent stupid Uralsky to the film" in their place.[42] And yet, if *Der Kongress tanzt* is an illusory concoction, it is one that makes no bones about its creation of illusions. Doubles stand in for characters in this fiction just as the film actors play their roles. The first view of Christel shows her responding to a foreigner's question: "Do you speak English?" No, she replies, which of course belies the contemporary spectator's better knowledge that the film star Harvey grew up in London. Metternich is a master surveillor, akin to Dr. Mabuse or the Frederick the Great of *Das Flötenkonzert von Sanssouci*, who at once monitors comings and goings as well as puts things in motion. In that way his interventions enable the spectator's own sensory ubiquity; as a guiding hand, he also figures as an on-screen surrogate for the director. His panoptic point of view is primarily aural; from his bedside control center he asks to hear what is going on in a room, and we then see what he hears—and in this way both share and exceed his access to the flow of information.

The film's famous theme song exalts a lovely moment that has passed and will not return. This might be read as a celebration of nostalgia, but if one considers the lines more carefully, it would seem to be a nostalgia for something that perhaps never really happened, for an experience that was "too lovely to be true"—much like the film we are watching, which glorifies cinema's powers of illusion and makes them transparent. Sights and sounds unreel in an unceasing flow of motion that seems real but is of course imaginary. Precisely at the moment when Harvey sings of things being "too lovely to be true," memorializing what Witte called the "glorious promise of the *status quo ante*," costumed cable carriers enter the image.[43] The song describes this profusion of light and movement as "ein goldner Schein," which in German has a double meaning. This "golden gleam" renders things bright and brilliant, so much so that it sometimes blinds us. In the film's rousing set piece, the song itself exerts a contagious appeal in its performance in and passage through a number of social spaces, from the city to the countryside, with a cast of various social classes singing the catchy lyrics and confirming the tune's irrepressible popularity. In the process, the film shows us the mediation of a self-conscious mass culture as well as revealing its illusory and false constitution, a dream machinery that openly acknowledges the spurious quality of its productions—"zu schön, um wahr zu sein."

The Limits of Make-Believe

As a fictional artifact that reveals its own sense of possibility and discloses its production of meaning, *Der Kongress tanzt* was anything but unique. A number of UFA operettas lay bare the cinematic apparatus and, in so doing, made it apparent just how self-consciously the studio's talented and sophisticated creators had crafted their productions. Berger's *Ich bei Tag und Du bei Nacht* (*Early to Bed*, 1932), in fact, could be said to ironize UFA operettas. In this regard it was hardly an anomaly, for features that poked fun at film conventions, as Jörg Schweinitz has argued, abounded during the Weimar era.[44] Nonetheless, for all his critical awareness, director Berger was surely no Brecht, espousing anti-illusionism in the name of political enlightenment. Indeed, Berger first gained notoriety as a filmmaker enamored of fairy tales, as his whimsical Cinderella adaptation, *Der verlorene Schuh* (*Cinderella*, 1923) attests. He crafted escapist scenarios endowed with *Stimmung*, hoping to shed light on the "golden gleam" of UFA's fantasy worlds and to provide a kind of enchantment in which spectators might find refuge without being blinded.

After his return to Germany from a disappointing three-year sojourn in Hollywood, Berger declined UFA's offer to direct *Der Kongress tanzt*. *Ich bei Tag und Du bei Nacht*, shot also in English and French, would become his masterpiece. Two denizens of Berlin share a bed in the same rooming house, but in shifts. Grete (Käthe von Nagy) works as a manicurist by day; Hans (Fritsch) waits on tables in an upscale nightclub. (If the disposition were reversed, quipped critic Willy Haas, "this would not be an operetta, but rather a moral tragedy.")[45] Grete and Hans meet by chance on the street, each mistaking the other for someone of a higher-class station. The narrative's obvious destiny, of course, is the moment when the confusion of identities is resolved so that the two can sleep next to—rather than after—each other.

The narrative of *Ich bei Tag und Du bei Nacht* contrasts escapist fantasies with everyday pursuits and shows how they interact. Each morning on his return to his part-time lodgings, Hans walks past a cinema and talks to the projectionist Helmut. The film's opening sequence shows the start of *Dies alles ist Dein* (All of this is yours), a Bombastik-Film production that outdoes any UFA extravaganza (even *Der Kongress tanzt*) in its excessive escapism and opulent over-the-topness. Helmut is enthusiastic about the new release, quoting an approving critic on how this "real-life fairy tale" makes clear that "the golden moment" will one day come to all of us. Grete, likewise, repeatedly compares her everyday life to what she sees at the cinema and seems happiest when the two overlap so that things "are just like the movies." Hans is not smitten by screen fantasies and, suspicious of being taken in by anything or anyone, considers films to be lies (*Schwindel*). Negotiating between these poles of naive acceptance and cynical reason, Berger's feature presents a modern world in which the media is an integral part.

We hear popular songs emanate from projectors and phonographs as well as radios, so incessantly that we readily understand a landlady's complaint that "hit tunes are spreading like the plague." Characters carry the movies with them in their real-life encounters. During an outing to Sanssouci, Hans and Grete manage to get locked in the music room of Frederick II. When they hear a flute being played, it is as if the ghost of the Great King were present, albeit in the form of a reprise from UFA's Prussia film of several seasons back, *Das Flötenkonzert von Sanssouci*, starring Otto Gebühr. While in the castle, the couple also sees Expressionist shadow plays straight out of Murnau or Lang. The reality of their world (and this film) reminds them (and us) of other films.

The reality that *Ich bei Tag und Du bei Nacht* represents, however, is also that of contemporary Berlin. Although the film was shot almost without exception in a Babelsberg studio, it provides a primer on the navigation of modern times and urban spaces. Characters dwell in part-time quarters that are anything but cozy or commodious. We see a glimpse of Hans's wallet, which is all but empty. Again and again we view price tags and hear characters talk about how much things cost and how one cannot afford them.[46] We encounter a swank bar from the perspective of a waiter who works there rather than that of its well-heeled patrons. Berger depicts the uneasy facts of everyday life that give rise to fantasies; he also shows various ways in which the producers of mass culture respond to and capitalize on collective dreams of a better world. The film legitimates the necessity for imaginary spaces that take people away from their vicissitudes and dissatisfactions.

Many Weimar films, both sound and silent, insistently and persistently interrogated the medium of cinema and disclosed the constructive capacities and abusive powers of a nascent mass culture. In the final shot of *Das Cabinet des Dr. Caligari*, we quite literally see double and cannot determine whether the figure of authority is a benevolent doctor or a homicidal lunatic. *Die Strasse* (*The Street*, 1923) revels in the enticements of urban life in the form of a cinematic experience and at the same time demonstrates the perils of such seductive spectacles. Ironic epilogues leave us with all-too-happy endings in *Der letzte Mann* (*The Last Laugh*, 1924) and *Geheimnisse einer Seele* (*Secrets of a Soul*, 1926). Lang's *M* exhibits how urban subjects apprehend increasingly abstract living spaces through visual and verbal mediations—which, as the film itself makes apparent, are usually inconclusive and, as such, quite often unreliable. UFA's early sound musicals, to varying degrees, represent self-conscious exercises in wishful thinking where a yearning for distraction coexists, not always amicably, with the reality principle.

Ich bei Tag und Du bei Nacht ends where it starts: at the movies. During the pyrotechnic finale of *Dies alles ist Dein*, the camera tracks down rows of delighted viewers and fixes on a smiling Hans and Grete; they go in for a kiss as the lights come up and the audience rises to leave. We cut back to the screen and, while the curtains close, see

Ende before the image darkens. If you are looking for succor, this UFA comedy suggests, you can find it in cinema's illusions, but only for a moment; for lasting happiness, look elsewhere. In these late-Weimar productions, fantasies of a better life gained fulfillment in the form of conciliatory reveries that were, however, clearly marked as fictions and therefore not meant to be taken seriously. For all its regressive properties, observed Kracauer, distraction possesses a truth potential: it has the power to expose the world's true state of disarray and fragmentation rather than masking it.[47] These early sound comedies surely do not go quite that far in their pursuit of distraction; they do, however, mark the limits of make-believe and caution the spectator about the downside of confusing cinematic illusions with social solutions.

1. Thomas Elsaesser, "Film History and Visual Pleasure," in Patricia Mellencamp and Philip Rosen, eds., *Cinema Histories, Cinema Practices* (Frederick, Md.: University Publications of America, 1984), p. 81.

2. Ibid., p. 71.

3. See Lotte H. Eisner, *L'Écran démoniaque*, 1952, rev. ed. (Paris: Le Terrain Vague, 1965); published in English as *The Haunted Screen: Expressionism in the German Cinema and the Influence of Max Reinhardt*, trans. Roger Greaves (Berkeley and Los Angeles: University of California Press, 1973).

4. To this day, many observers persist in equating Weimar cinema with Expressionist film—a mighty feat of abbreviation, both reductive and inaccurate, given that of the more than 3,500 German features that premiered during that era only a handful of them bear the earmarks of the period style. For a detailed and differentiated account of German Expressionist film, see Jürgen Kasten,

Der expressionistische Film: Abgefilmtes Theater oder avantgardistisches Erzählkino? Eine stil-, produktions-, und rezeptionsgeschichtliche Untersuchung (Münster: MAkS, 1990).

5. The philosopher Karl Jaspers, in his important 1931 diagnosis of the precarious final years of the Weimar Republic, wrote that people have "been uprooted. . . . It is as if the foundations of being had been shattered. . . . The foundations of life quake beneath our feet." Jaspers, *Die geistige Situation der Zeit* (Berlin: de Gruyter, 1931); published in English as *Man in the Modern Age*, trans. Eden and Cedar Paul (New York: Anchor, 1957), p. 2.

6. *Ungleichzeitigkeit* is the key concept of Ernst Bloch's seminal analysis *Erbschaft dieser Zeit* (Zurich: Oprecht & Helbling, 1935); published in English as *Heritage of Our Times*, trans. Neville and Stephen Plaice (Berkeley and Los Angeles: University of California Press, 1991).

7. The phrase is a variation of Karl Kraus's often-quoted phrase, "Die Lage ist hoffnungslos, aber nicht ernst." Kraus, *"Erlaubt ist, was missfällt": Karl Kraus zum Vergnügen*, ed. Günter Baumann (Ditzingen: Reclam, 2007).

8. "Sonniger Tag! Wonniger Tag!/ Klopfendes Herz und der Motor ein Schlag!/Lachendes Ziel! Lachender Start/und eine herrliche Fahrt!"

9. The comparison to Ernst Lubitsch comes from Karsten Witte, "Too Beautiful to Be True: Lilian Harvey," trans. Eric Rentschler, *New German Critique* 74 (Spring–Summer 1998): 38.

10. See Rudolf Arnheim, "Escape into the Scenery (1932)," in *Film Essays and Criticism*, trans. Brenda Benthien (Madison: University of Wisconsin Press, 1997), p. 190. Speaking of recent German features, he wrote, "There is little of note as regards the development of sound film—as is the case everywhere in contemporary film production."

11. See Witte's seminal essay on German revue films, "Visual Pleasure Inhibited: Aspects of the German Revue Film," trans. J. D. Steakley and Gabriele Hoover, *New German Critique* 24–25 (Fall–Winter 1981–82): 238.

12. Anton Kaes, "Film in der Weimarer Republik: Motor der Moderne," in Wolfgang Jacobsen et al., eds., *Geschichte des deutschen Films*, 2nd rev. ed. (Stuttgart: Metzler, 1993), pp. 39–98.

13. See Georg Seesslen, "Das Unterhaltungskino II: Das Spiel mit der Liebe—Aspekte der deutschen Stummfilmkomödie," in Harro Segeberg, ed., *Die Perfektionierung des Scheins: Das Kino der Weimarer Republik im Kontext der Künste* (Munich: Fink, 2000), pp. 95–96.

14. UFA's early sound musicals include *Melodie des Herzens* (Hanns Schwarz, 1929), *Liebeswalzer* (Wilhelm Thiele, 1930), *Die Drei von der Tankstelle, Einbrecher, Ihre Hoheit befiehlt* (Schwarz, 1931), *Nie wieder Liebe* (Anatol Litvak, 1931), *Bomben auf Monte Carlo* (Schwarz, 1931), *Der Kongress tanzt, Zwei Herzen und ein Schlag* (Thiele, 1932), *Das Lied einer Nacht, Quick* (Robert Siodmak, 1932), *Ein blonder Traum, Ich bei Tag und Du bei Nacht, Ich und die Kaiserin* (Friedrich Hollaender, 1933), *Ein Lied für Dich* (Joe May, 1933), *Walzerkrieg* (Ludwig Berger, 1933), *Saison in Kairo* (Reinhold Schünzel, 1933), and *Viktor und Viktoria* (Schünzel, 1933).

15. Arnheim, "Hans Albers (1931)," in *Film Essays and Criticism*, p. 220.

16. Arnheim, "Sound Film Gone Astray (1932)," in ibid., p. 42.

17. Siegfried Kracauer, *From Caligari to Hitler: A Psychological History of the German Film* (Princeton, N.J.: Princeton University Press, 1947), p. 205.

18. Ibid.

19. Béla Balázs, *Theory of the Film*, 1945, trans. Edith Bone (New York: Dover, 1970), p. 204.

20. Ibid., p. 194.

21. In his scathing review of *Der Kongress tanzt*, Arnheim calls it "a gumdrop" and mockingly cites approving words about the film that appeared in the *Lichtbildbühne*: "What's been concocted is a confection that will tickle the palates of the unknown millions to whom this film is dedicated, like manna from heaven." Arnheim, "Partly Expensive, Partly Good (1931)," in *Film Essays and Criticism*, p. 175.

22. Arnheim, *Film*, trans. L. M. Sieveking and Ian F. D. Morrow (London: Faber & Faber, 1933), p. 171. In 1931 two influential analyses of the commercial film apparatus's regressive workings appeared in German translation: Ilja Ehrenburg's *Die Traumfabrik: Chronik des Films/The Dream Factory* (Berlin: Malik, 1931) and René Fülöp-Miller's *Die Phantasiemaschine/The Fantasy Machine* (Berlin: Zsolnay, 1931).

23. Arnheim, *Film*, p. 176.

24. Bloch, *Heritage of Our Times*, p. 25.

25. Ibid., p. 26.

26. Ibid., p. 36.

27. Hans Sahl, "Zapfenstreiche bei der Ufa," in *"Und doch. . .": Essays und Kritiken aus zwei Kontinenten*, ed. Klaus Blanc (Frankfurt am Main: Luchterhand, 1991), p. 99. Translation by the author.

28. Klaus Kreimeier, *Die Ufa-Story: Geschichte eines Filmkonzerns* (Munich: Hanser, 1992), p. 208.

29. Notable endeavors in this vein include contributions on UFA operettas by Thomas Koebner, Jörg Schweinitz, and Corinna Müller in Koebner, ed., *Diesseits der 'Dämonischen Leinwand': Neue Perspektiven auf das späte Weimarer Kino* (Munich: edition text + kritik, 2003), pp. 341–408; Michael Wedel's well-researched and comprehensive monograph, *Der deutsche Musikfilm: Archäologie eines Genres, 1914–1945* (Munich: edition text + kritik, 2007); and Müller's *Vom Stummfilm zum Tonfilm* (Munich: Fink, 2003). In English, see Elsaesser, "It's the End of the Song: Walter Reisch, Operetta and the Double Negative," in *Weimar Cinema and After: Germany's Historical Imaginary* (London: Routledge, 2000), pp. 330–58.

30. The bicycle race between the two window washers in *Ein blonder Traum* recalls the opening sequence of *Kuhle Wampe*, but with a decided tonal difference: the friends are having fun, which cannot be said of Bertolt Brecht's desperate job seeker. Villa Blitz, the country squatter's hut in *Ein blonder Traum*, likewise, brings to mind the homeless community called Kuhle Wampe. The life of the disfranchised

in the UFA feature was decidedly at odds with the situation presented in Slatan Dudow's short documentary, *Zeitprobleme. Wie der Arbeiter wohnt* (*Contemporary Problems: How the Worker Lives*, 1930).

31. Witte, "Wie Filmgeschichte schreiben?" *epd Kirche und Film* 34, no. 12 (December 1981): 12: Translation by the author.

32. Described in Kracauer, "Not und Zerstreuung: Zur Ufa-Produktion 1931/32," *Frankfurter Zeitung*, July 15, 1931: Translation by the author.

33. The titles of several films from 1932 were even more unabashed in their attempt at uplift: *Man braucht kein Geld* (*You Don't Need Money*) and *Es wird schon wieder besser* (*Things Will Get Better*).

34. Lilian Harvey and Willy Fritsch, the German dream couple, appeared together in a dozen films between 1926 and 1939. As stars, however, their popularity did not extend beyond Germany. And, without question, the chemistry between them was not exactly explosive. When they come together at the end of films, their union is invariably sealed with a kiss, but the viewer remains hard-pressed to imagine that it might lead to further intimate activity. More than anything they are comrades, very much along the lines of Ben Barr Lindsey's *The Companionate Marriage* (1927), an American guide to domestic designs that was quite popular at the time in Germany.

35. "Alles im Leben ist auch wie ein Lied/Verklingt und entflieht, ein Abschied."

36. "Wie schnell vergisst man, was einmal war/Nichts bleibt züruck, alles war einmal."

37. "Heut' werden alle Märchen wahr,/heut' wird mir eines klar:/Das gibt's nur einmal,/Das kommt nicht wieder,/das ist zu schön, um wahr zu sein."

38. Film critic Curt Riess's voluminous panegyric about the stars and productions of classical German cinema echoes the song's title. See Riess, *Das gab's nur einmal: Das Buch der schönsten Filme unseres Lebens*, 2nd rev. ed. (Hamburg: Verlag der Sternbücher, 1957).

39. Kracauer, *From Caligari to Hitler*, p. 208.

40. Fritsch would also play double roles in UFA's *Walzerkrieg* (*Battle of the Waltzes*, 1933) and *Amphitryon* (1935).

41. Kracauer, "Kunst und Dekoration," *Frankfurter Zeitung*, October 13, 1931: Translation by the author.

42. Arnheim, "Partly Expensive, Partly Good (1931)," p. 176.

43. Witte, "Too Beautiful to Be True," p. 38.

44. Schweinitz, "'Wie im Kino!': Die autothematische Welle im frühen Tonfilm," in *Diesseits der 'Dämonischen Leinwand*,' pp. 373–92.

45. Willy Haas, "Ich bei Tag und Du bei Nacht," *Film-Kurier*, November 29, 1932: Translation by the author.

46. In *Ein Blonder Traum* there is a long scene in which the protagonists calculate the cost of a better life in minute detail.

47. Kracauer, "Cult of Distraction: On Berlin's Picture Palaces," in *The Mass Ornament: Weimar Essays*, trans. and ed. Thomas Y. Levin (Cambridge, Mass.: Harvard University Press, 1995), p. 328.

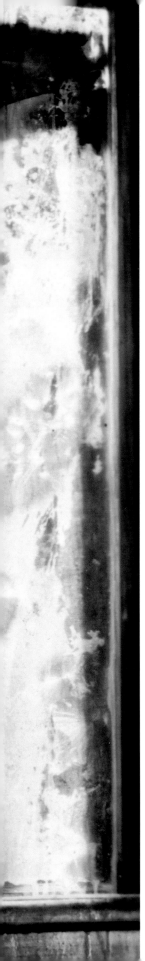

Werner Sudendorf

Neither Lulu nor Lola

Marlene Dietrich before The Blue Angel

If only Marlene Dietrich had told us about her early years. Her youth under Kaiser Wilhelm II, the films she saw, what life was like during the Weimar Republic, the many artists with whom she acted and made films. Did the winds of modernism sweep through her life like a hurricane, or did she scarcely feel a breeze? She surely remembered all this, but she didn't permit such questions. Her early years in Germany, her stage and film appearances didn't count. Those were only "tiny, unimportant walk-ons,"[1] films of no significance, and in fact before *Der blaue Engel* (*The Blue Angel*, 1930) she was "completely unknown, a complete Nobody."[2] Her film career began with Josef von Sternberg and *Morocco* (1930). Period. Finished. End of discussion. She once assured an interviewer in all seriousness that her name appeared only at the very bottom in the credits for *Der blaue Engel* and that it wasn't included at all on the movie poster.[3] That when Sternberg discovered her she was still studying under Max Reinhardt. In truth, by that point she had already appeared in roughly sixteen films and almost twice as many stage productions.

Despite her refusal to talk about her years up to *Der blaue Engel*, it is possible to reconstruct something of them. Marlene (born Marie Magdalene) Dietrich came from an extremely conservative family. Her mother was the daughter of a wealthy jeweler, and her father was a police officer, a philanderer more interested in ladies than in his job. Her uncle Hermann Dietrich was a member of Alfred Hugenberg's German National People's Party and a dignitary, the vice president of the National Assembly as well as a member of the Prussian parliament. The family drove about in carriages, and regularly consorted with their wealthy relatives.

Dietrich loved the cinema, especially Henny Porten and her maidservant dramas. But no hint of modern social developments or Expressionist art or literature was admitted into the household. Obedience and breeding were what mattered most. It was not for nothing that Dietrich referred to her mother as "a good general."[4] Even at eighteen she was slapped for coming home too late after waiting to get an autograph from an adored actor. During the revolutionary days of 1919 she wrote in her diary, "Why do I have to experience this dreadful time; I wanted to have a golden, blissful youth. And now it has come to this."[5] Dietrich was anything but a revolutionary or rebellious champion of modern ideas.

That we still do not know all the German films she appeared in is not her fault alone: they are not part of the canon with which film historians define Weimar cinema. Dietrich acted almost exclusively in productions without major artistic pretensions, in dreary melodramas, cheap burlesques, or genre pictures, films targeted at an audience that went to the cinema either to laugh or cry at other people. Many of these productions are either considered lost or else survive only in fragments. One writer insisted that she was an extra in Ernst Lubitsch's *Das Weib des Pharao* (*Loves of Pharaoh*, 1922), and it is true that Lubitsch always filled the front rows of his crowd scenes with students of the Reinhardt school.[6] But it is impossible to check this, for there are hundreds of costumed extras in *Das Weib des Pharao*. The fact that her husband, Rudolf Sieber, worked as a production assistant on Lothar Mendes's *Der Mönch von Santarem* (The monk of Santarem, 1924) leads us to believe that she was in that film as well, and the actor Willy Fritsch remembers her from Alexander Korda's film *Der Tänzer meiner Frau* (My wife's dancer, 1925), but both films are assumed lost.[7] It has been claimed that she can be seen with John Loder in a dance scene in the Korda film *Madame wünscht keine Kinder* (*Madame Wants No Children*, 1926), but no one has actually managed to identify her.[8] There was a persistent rumor that in G. W. Pabst's *Die freudlose Gasse* (*The Joyless Street*, 1925) she stood next to Greta Garbo in a row of starving women, but that was untrue. It is possible that she was one of the many prostitutes in *Die Liebe der Jeanne Ney* (*The Loves of Jeanne Ney*, 1927), but this, too, is uncertain. One can therefore concur with Dietrich that these were "unimportant walk-ons"—if they happened at all—that gave no hint of the young actress's potential. But was there potential? And where could she display it?

Her first known appearance in a film was in Georg Jacoby's *Napoleons kleiner Bruder* (Napoleon's little brother, 1922), which was also distributed under the titles *Der kleine Napoleon* (The little Napoleon) or *So sind die Männer* (That's how men are). Even though the film is not completely preserved (the last reel has disappeared), from what survives it is clear that neither director Jacoby nor scriptwriter Robert Liebmann nor cameraman Max Schneider made any effort to provide it with wit or refinement. Dietrich was in a role of no importance to the plot, and contemporaries relate that Schneider didn't like her and often placed her in such a way that she was obscured by others.[9] But in one scene she appears completely alone, as a maid standing in a doorway, looking somewhat confused.

It was also in 1922, when Dietrich was twenty, that she met the production manager Rudolf Sieber, and they were married on May 17, 1923. Sieber was scouting for an actress to play a demimondaine in Joe May's *Tragödie der Liebe* (Tragedy of love, 1923). May was a well-known, experienced, and often excellent director, and *Tragödie*

Fig. 1. Marlene Dietrich and Fritz Kortner in Kurt Bernhardt's *Die Frau, nach der man sich sehnt* (*Three Loves,* 1929)

der Liebe, a fast-moving, exciting blend of melodrama, crime film, and social study, had a splendid cast. Emil Jannings, its star, would later play Professor Rath in *Der blaue Engel,* but it is likely that he never noticed the young Dietrich.

Dietrich plays the girlfriend of a public prosecutor. She speaks to him on the telephone, and in one brief scene in the courtroom, with a monocle clamped in one eye, she plays him off against his young assistant with hand gestures and glances. The film was originally produced in four parts, and it is sad that all that survives of it is a shorter version from 1929. The actor Wladimir Gajdarow remembered a scene that the shorter version does not contain:

> [It] began with the woman of easy virtue played by Marlene Dietrich taking a bath. The telephone rings and the maid picks up the receiver. In the background you can see Dietrich up to her neck in the bath water. The maid tells her that the prosecutor would like to speak to madame about something important, and Dietrich stands up. As she begins to move, a close-up shows only the little telephone table with its velvet tablecloth. Then a naked arm extends into the picture and picks up the receiver, then we see a naked shoulder and back, then Dietrich's face, then a naked leg, and finally the other arm clutching the velvet cloth to her waist like a robe as Dietrich begins her conversation. This introductory sequence was made expressly in order to get the most luscious parts of Marlene Dietrich's body into the picture, especially her legs.[10]

Dietrich's body was virtually dissected, reduced to the sex appeal of its parts. She was thus presented as another example of a typical Weimar Republic girl (although we might imagine the Weimar girl to be less curvy), with hair like a mop rather than in a pixie cut.[11] The ideal of beauty was still dominated by Wilhelmine tastes, with that era's fondness for voluptuousness. In the pinups and promotional photographs Dietrich later posed for, the focus is exclusively on her legs. Even in the film *Die Frau, nach der man sich sehnt* (*Three Loves,* 1929; fig. 1), Fritz Kortner stares lasciviously at her legs, which suddenly appear in close-up. In 1924 the theater critic Alfred Kerr still remembered the name of her character in a play only "because of her flesh."[12] In 1927 she lamented that, thanks to her role in *Tragödie der Liebe,* "I was unfortunately typed as the demimondaine and adventuress, although I would naturally have far preferred to play something else."[13] The woman of easy virtue would continue to be her trademark role in Hollywood as well, although, to be sure, on a distinctly higher level.

In 1926 Dietrich played a scheming lady of the court in Arthur Robison's lavish costume film *Manon Lescaut.* The same year, in Korda's *Eine Dubarry von heute* (*A Modern*

Dubarry) she is not even given a name but is simply listed as "a coquette." In theater productions, too, she often played a modern girl untroubled by notions of morality—sometimes with a monocle, sometimes without.

In the nineteenth century monocles were worn mainly by aristocrats. They were clearly a status symbol and came to be thought of as a stereotypical attribute of the Prussian officer. The *neue Frau* (new woman) of the Weimar Republic adopted this symbol as a means of thumbing her nose at the values of the Wilhelmine era. In her public appearances, although not as clearly as in her film roles, Dietrich seemed to be the quintessential emancipated *neue Frau*. She was mobile and independent, drove a car, and, in *Das Schiff der verlorenen Menschen* (*Ship of Lost Men*, 1929), directed by Maurice Tourneur, she became an airplane pilot—a profession considered by only the most daring and modern of women. In 1927 she allowed herself to be photographed as Thomas Gainsborough's *Blue Boy*, took boxing lessons, played in revues, and sang naughty songs.

And then there were those legs! That women had legs at all was a well-kept secret during the Wilhelmine era, and by the beginning of the Weimar Republic, skirt lengths had risen only as far as the ankle. But a woman with things to do needed to have her legs free, and it was impossible to dance the newest dances in long, tight skirts. Freedom, leisure time, and amusement were all desired by the *neue Frau* (although it was never mentioned that the concomitant erotic freedom had many losers and few winners). The same year that Dietrich went to Hollywood, Dada artist Hannah Höch celebrated the liberation of women's legs in *Marlene* (1930), a collage in which male eyes gaze upward at two naked legs atop an antique pedestal, with Dietrich's smiling mouth at the top edge. Are the legs a fetish? Are they an offering? Is Dietrich smiling at the men or because of them?

Dietrich experienced all the glamour of the cinema and the stage but still felt unfulfilled. In October 1926 she noted in her diary, "I play in theaters and films and make a lot of money. But as for myself I experience nothing. Nothing as a woman, nothing as a person."[14] By this time she had experimented in comedy in *Der Juxbaron* (The imaginary baron, 1926), directed by Willi Wolff, and the sensational film *Der grosse Bluff* (The big bluff, 1927), directed by Harry Piel. Her role in *Der grosse Bluff*, which she probably owed to her husband, at the time a producer with Piel, was a sidekick, a bit more than an interchangeable piece of stage decoration. *Der Juxbaron* was aimed at lower-middle-class masses overwhelmed by the new realities, celebrating their backwardness in the form of the burlesque, and its humor is all dirty jokes and male locker-room banter. In a few scenes Dietrich once again wears a monocle, this time as a sign of capriciousness in spite of all her good breeding.

After these relatively unimpressive engagements Dietrich decided, in 1927, to leave Berlin and make a new start in Vienna. But there the situation was no different from the one she had left. At Vienna's Kammerspiele and Theater in der Josefstadt, she played one girl among many and one student among others in the plays *Broadway* and *Die Schule von Uznach* (The school at Uznach). And while fulfilling these obligations on stage, she worked on the film *Café Electric*, under the young director Gustav Ucicky (who would later go to Berlin and manage to continue his career before, during, and after Hitler's seizure of power), a picture meant to warn young women about the enticements of the demimonde. In Germany the film was given the racy title *Wenn ein Weib den Weg verliert* (When a woman loses her way).

In *Café Electric* a prostitute (played by Vera Salvotti) wants to return to middle-class life; Dietrich plays her counterpart, a well-bred young woman who takes up with petty hoodlums and pimps but is finally rescued. It was hardly a novel plot, and one critic suspected that *Café Electric* was not a new film at all but one that had been distributed earlier as *Die Prostitution* (Prostitution, 1919). Although her stay in Vienna did not further her career, it brought some unexpected benefits: the actor Igo Sym, who played a young, charming lover in *Café Electric*, happened to know how to play the musical saw, a quirky musical instrument often featured in stage revues, and he taught Dietrich how to play it and later presented her with one as a memento. She took it with her to the United States, and during World War II she used it in her USO performances for American soldiers.

By March 1928 Dietrich was back in Berlin, where she took up her old life. With her theater engagements, film roles, and advertising photos, she was earning more money than her husband. She enjoyed balls and receptions, and she was always fresh, sexy, and refined. She had appeared on stage with all the greats of the Berlin theater, but public appreciation for her acting talent was no match for its interest in her physical charms. One critic observed that in Heinz Hilpert's staging of George Bernard Shaw's *Misalliance* (1909–10), with Otto Wallburg and Heinz Rühmann, Dietrich had "a way of sitting that one cannot really call very decent. Even if she showed less, it would still be enough."[15]

But why not show those gorgeous legs? They were an asset that Dietrich deliberately marketed. She appeared in ads for women's stockings, allowed herself to be photographed in skimpy clothing for magazines, and posed with a Champagne glass in her hand and her legs outstretched for a New Year's Eve greeting, the rest of her covered by a black wall, as though the photographer had anticipated the elements of Höch's collage. Photographs of her from that time fell into two distinct types: the frivolous girl lifting her skirt (or not needing to, since she had already taken it off) and official theater and film images that showed her as a serious, buttoned-up, and somewhat unsophisticated actress. Sternberg would see to it that a single, very different figure was created out of Dietrich's two incarnations in her US career; in this sense *Der blaue Engel* was the last appearance of the woman of easy virtue that Dietrich had tried to project in Germany.

Dietrich was living well and enjoyed the erotic provocation of acting. In 1928 she issued her first recording, with songs from the revue *Es liegt in der Luft*, in which she had appeared with the chanteuse Margo Lion singing "Wenn die beste Freundin" (When a best girlfriend). The two women appeared onstage in identical costumes, each wearing a bunch of violets—a lesbian symbol—at her shoulder, although in her memoirs Dietrich downplayed her obvious and exemplary competence in all erotic arenas, insisting, "I did not know then the meaning that had been attached to violets ever since the play by Edouard Bourdet, 'The Prisoner' [*La Prisonnière*, 1926], had seen the light of German stages. I liked violets, that was all."[16] Not as well known is the duet she sang with Hans Carl Müller, "Cleptomaniacs," whose lyrics proclaim, "Wir tun's aus sexueller Not" (We do it out of sexual frustration). "*That* I understood and did not need to ask for clarification," Dietrich confirmed in the manuscript of her autobiography, although in the end she did not allow this sentence to published.[17]

At the beginning of 1929 the Berlin film world was debating whether there was any future for the sound films coming from the United States. Would the new technique prevail, or was it just a temporary craze? There was no question that it was the dernier cri, and it certainly increased box-office receipts. Dietrich, with the graying heartthrob Harry Liedtke, was making the film *Ich küsse Ihre Hand, Madame* (*I Kiss Your Hand, Madame*; fig. 2), an easygoing comedy set in high society with an excellent cast and staged with a light hand by Robert Land. Dietrich plays the Madame whose hand is kissed, but her importance is somewhat limited to the title; the film mostly deals with Liedtke's harem fantasy, with differences in class and rank that are made to vanish with a few dramatic twists, and with a fat little man (Karl Huszar-Puffy) who makes the lovers look all the more appealing. The setting is Paris—where else? It was the first time Dietrich sneaked her talisman into a film, an African doll that later showed up in both *Der blaue Engel* and *Morocco*. But at least she was now playing a major role, acting in expensive costumes, and being idolized. With Paris and high fashion she became more a lady than a girl, and her admirers were mature men rather than boys. She was not a sensation, not even a discovery, but, as the critic Hanns G. Lustig called her, "A lovely guarantee of the future."[18]

The film's real sensation was a short sound sequence in which Richard Tauber lip-synched the title song, a recording of which played during each screening to simulate a sound film, much like the technique employed in Germany in the 1910s (and no match for the new sound films from the United States, which were longer, technically superior, and much more entertaining). *Ich küsse Ihre Hand, Madame* had all the charm of a boulevard play; it was perfectly crafted, and did not pretend to be anything more than good entertainment.

Dietrich had now demonstrated that she was competent to play major parts. The young Kurt Bernhardt was the first director to choose her for a truly demanding, multifaceted role. He was considered a rising talent; since 1924 he had made seven films,

Fig. 2. Marlene Dietrich and Harry Liedtke in Robert Land's *Ich küsse Ihre Hand, Madame* (*I Kiss Your Hand, Madame,*1929)

and he was now engaged by Terra-Film to direct *Die Frau, nach der man sich sehnt* (*Three Loves*, 1929), from the 1927 novel by Max Brod. It was Bernhardt who fought for Dietrich and discovered her true affinity for the camera. "What fascinated me about Marlene," Bernhardt recalled,

> was her personal charisma as an especially beautiful and exciting woman. There was an erotic aura about her that I could not see in any other actress from these years. She played the role with commitment and lots of hesitations. . . . When I suggested her to the Terra-Film directors for the leading role, I encountered the most powerful resistance, for she was wholly unknown in film circles. Fritz Kortner, on the other hand, was a known stage actor who played leading roles at the Staatstheater, and was immediately accepted. After an extended discussion they gave in to me and engaged Fräulein Dietrich for the main role.[19]

Both the director and Curt Courant, the cameraman, were only thirty years old and, with their fondness for stylized imagery, were very different from the old pros Dietrich had previously worked for. The film's central themes were the younger generation's lack of perspective, its imprisonment in the mindset of its parents, and its attempts to escape. Bernhardt presents Dietrich as erotically alluring, with an aura of glamour and mystery. When Henri (Uno Henning) first sees her, he gazes up at her as if she were some kind of apparition. Steam rises from the railway platform, a blind is raised in a train compartment, and there is Dietrich's face, framed by frost patterns. Then the blind is closed again by her companion, Dr. Karoff (Kortner). To Henri, who has just gotten married and is on his way to his honeymoon, this fleeting vision combines forbidden desire and freedom. Dietrich plays her role with greater reserve and concentration than she did in her earlier films; she was already directing herself, searching out shadows from which to step into the light and speaking more with her eyes and body than with

Fig. 3. Marlene Dietrich and Gary Cooper
in Josef von Sternberg's *Morocco* (1930)

words. Bernhardt recognized a very simple reason for her acting technique: "Marlene was afraid that her nose gave her an unattractive profile and never stepped out of the light, so that she often spoke to her partners only with her eyes and never turned toward them the way a person normally would."[20] Hesitation was another technique employed by Sternberg and Dietrich to build, in her American films, the kind of excitement that made her so interesting and mysterious. But the contemporary critics in Germany disliked the new Dietrich, declaring her acting stiff and cold.

Her next film, announced as a major production, was an artistic and commercial flop. *Das Schiff der verlorenen Menschen*, with Kortner as her costar once again, bobbed along on a sea of tedium and, as early as the day after the premiere, met with loud whistling from the audience. Dietrich and Kortner had planned on taking a bow but didn't even step onto the stage. With Fred Sauer's *Gefahren der Brautzeit* (*Dangers of the Engagement Period*, 1929), her last silent film, she returned to the prewar reactionary figure of the vulnerable girl. Perhaps Willi Forst, who played the male lead, helped her ignore the bad script and the miserable production.

Dietrich's roles in her German films before *Der blaue Engel*, with the exception of some parts of *Die Frau, nach der man sich sehnt*, are projections of a kind of femininity with roots extending well back into the Wilhelmine era, a male fantasy that represents the fears of the petit bourgeois fathers of modern women. She is usually a daughter, naughty rather than insolent, unchaperoned and therefore in danger; in the end she is saved, ends tragically, or becomes grotesque in her determination to make her own decisions. Most often she is hounded by insistent warnings not to abandon the path of virtue, and she lives in fear of eternal damnation. Although Weimar cinema is often admired for its progressive, modern, and avant-garde style, the majority of films made during the era were just this kind of middle-of-the-road tale; by chance, rather than by intention, Dietrich ended up representing the economically and sexually independent—and thus dangerous—woman of the Weimar Republic. It was Sternberg, in *Der blaue Engel*, who provided Marlene Dietrich with a new morality uniquely her own, allowing her to abandon the path of virtue. Thus her star began to rise, and she took her chance with both hands. Her first film in America, *Morocco* (fig. 3), would be made from a book of her choice.[21]

1. Marlene Dietrich, "You Svengali–Me Trilby" (chapter in her autobiography, copy of the original manuscript), p. 1. Stiftung Deutsche Kinemathek–Marlene Dietrich Collection Berlin (SDK–MDCB). All quotations cited in this essay are from this English manuscript, which was translated into German by Max Colpet (aka Kolpe) and published as *Nehmt nur mein Leben: Reflexionen* (Munich: Bertelsmann, 1979). It was translated back into English by Salvatore Attanasio for the US edition, *Marlene* (New York: Grove Press, 1989).

2. Dietrich, in *Marlene*, directed by Maximilian Schell (BR Deutschland/Frankreich/Tschechoslowakei, 1983–84).

3. Dietrich, interview with Bengt Feldreich for Sveriges Television, recorded July 31, 1971, Copenhagen, broadcast August 8, 1971.

4. Dietrich, "Childhood I" (chapter in autobiography manuscript), p. 19. SDK–MDCB.

5. Dietrich, November 9, 1918, entry, unpublished diary. SDK–MDCB.

6. Anonymous, "Marlene—Gestern und Heute," *Filmwelt* (Berlin), September 10, 1932, n.p.

7. Willy Fritsch, in undated notes by Jimmy Jungermann from a meeting about the publication of Fritsch's autobiography. Stiftung Deutsche Kinemathek, Berlin.

8. Homer Dickens, *The Films of Marlene Dietrich* (New York: Cadillac Publications, 1968), pp. 58–59. The film is included in most Dietrich filmographies.

9. Marika Rökk, *Herz mit Paprika* (Munich: Universitas, 1988), pp. 124–25. Rökk refers to the unpublished memoirs of her husband, the director Georg Jacoby, which are now part of the Marika Rökk Collection at SDK.

10. Wladimir Gajdarow, *W teatre i w kino* (Moscow: Iskusstvo, 1966), pp. 134–35.

11. Verena Dollenmeier, ed., *Glamour! Das Girl wird feine Dame: Frauendarstellungen in der späten Weimarer Republik* (Berlin: Seemann Verlag, 2008), p. 135.

12. Alfred Kerr, review of *A Summer Night's Dream* at the Theater in der Königgrätzer Strasse, *Berliner Tageblatt*, February 10, 1924.

13. Dietrich, "Man darf nie 'nein' sagen," *Mein Film* (Vienna), no. 100 (1927): 19.

14. Dietrich, October 18, 1926, entry, unpublished diary. SDK–MDCB.

15. Ludwig Sternaux, quoted in Renate Seydel, ed., *Marlene Dietrich: Eine Chronik in Bildern* (Berlin: Henschel Verlag, 1984), p. 64.

16. Dietrich, "Youth" (chapter in autobiography manuscript), p. 59c. SDK–MDCB.

17. Ibid.

18. Hanns G. Lustig, "Filmlärm und das stumme Gesicht einer Frau" *Tempo*, January 18, 1930; quoted in Gero Gandert, ed., *Der Film der Weimarer Republik, 1929* (Berlin: Walter de Gruyter, 1993), p. 306.

19. Kurt Bernhardt, interview with Christian Blackwood, Norddeutscher Rundfunk, Hamburg, 1978.

20. Ibid.

21. Josef von Sternberg, cable to Dietrich on board the SS *Bremen*, April 2, 1930, 12:15 pm: "Congratulations to us both stop new film will be called Morocco based on story Amy Jolly from book you slipped into my luggage stop you will be at least fabulous. Jo." Maria Riva, *Marlene Dietrich* (New York: Knopf, 1993), p. 80.

Catalogue of Weimar Films

Compiled by Ulrich Döge

(entries on *Niemandsland, Der Mann, der seinen Mörder sucht,*
and *Razzia in St. Pauli* compiled by Eva Orbanz)

The documentation that follows is dedicated primarily to German films produced in the era of Germany's Weimar Republic (1919–33) and is based mainly on several printed and virtual sources of data: censorship cards; advertising material provided by the film's distributor; production news items and reviews published in trade papers such as *Lichtbild-Bühne* and *Film-Kurier;* and monographs, among them biographical reference works and filmographies of movie directors, such as Hans-Michael Bock, ed., *CineGraph: Lexikon zum deutschsprachigen Film* (Munich: edition text+kritik, 1984–); and Ulrich J. Klaus, *Deutsche Tonfilme: Filmlexikon der abendfüllenden deutschen und deutschsprachigen Tonfilme nach ihren deutschen Uraufführungen*, 15 vols. (Berlin-Berchtesgaden: Klaus, 1988–2006). Details about various release dates and screenings were obtained from contemporary reviews in the *New York Times* and *Variety.*

While there is plenty of literature concerning a small group of prominent German and Austrian directors of this era—as the number of publications dedicated to F. W. Murnau, Fritz Lang, and Ernst Lubitsch demonstrates—for the great majority of their lesser-known and unknown colleagues, basic biographical information is scarce or missing. Thus some biographies include more detail than others.

Titles: English titles are generally those of a film's first English release. When this title differs from the circulating title used by The Museum of Modern Art, the original title is given with the film's US or British premiere date.

Year: The year refers to a film's first release in its country of origin.

Cast, film credits, and music: The cast and crew lists identify major participants, but they are not exhaustive.

The credits for silent-film music are limited to composers of original scores and those conductors and arrangers of the music performed at premieres who would presumably have been known in the United States. Although this appears to dismiss the musicians who performed the music, it is in fact because we don't know who they were. However, most major silent productions were released with an accompanying score, sometimes—if a production company had a big budget at its disposal—an original score by a famous composer. At the first-run cinemas in larger cities, these would be performed by orchestras, at least at the film's premiere. More frequently, scores arranged by the performer and/or conductor from music by other composers were performed. Even in the smallest towns, cinema owners hired local pianists to accompany screenings with musical passages meant to make the mood of a scene audible.

Exile: Exile forms an important part of a director's biography, unless he (or occasionally she) died before 1933, the year the National Socialist party assumed absolute power. Some directors left Germany well before 1933 to continue their work abroad, but eventually simply living abroad became exile.

Austria became the provisional country of exile, primarily for German-Jewish directors but for some non-Jewish directors as well, from 1933 to the Anschluss, in March 1938, when Austria was annexed to Nazi Germany. So not every German director who worked in Austria in this period was automatically in exile. Starting in 1934 much of the private Austrian film industry freely fulfilled the Nazi politicians' demands not to employ Jewish cast and crew on films for the commercially critical German market. Only a small number of independent production companies in Austria deliberately engaged German-Jewish exiles, and the German authorities forbade the import of the resulting films.

Reviews: Excerpts from reviews are taken almost exclusively from German periodicals contemporary with the films themselves, preferably, but not limited to, trade papers. Both prominent and unknown authors are included in order to demonstrate the rich culture of film criticism in Weimar-era Germany.

Statements by directors and other crew members come either from the same sources as well as from monographs published decades later. German periodicals cited were published in Berlin unless otherwise indicated.

Censorship: During the Weimar Republic, two boards were responsible for film censorship: the Filmprüfstellen in Berlin and Munich and the Filmoberprüfstelle in Berlin, a superior board for appeals, both under the Reichsinnenministerium (Federal Ministry of the Interior). Once the Nazis came to power, the criteria and organization of film censorship changed fundamentally, becoming a ministry, under Joseph Goebbels, of Volksaufklärung und Propaganda (Public Enlightenment and Propaganda). A number of films produced in the Weimar era were retroactively censored by the National Socialists, especially those with perceived pacifist, leftist themes (such as *Cyankali*, *Kuhle Wampe*, and *Niemandsland*) made during the transition from democracy, even in an already authoritarian form, to dictatorship. Conflicts with the various agencies, leading to the mutilation of circulating copies of films or to the banning of public screenings, are noted in the Film Notes section. —U.D.

Anders als die Andern 1919
Different from the Others

Germany
Director: Richard Oswald
Screenplay: Richard Oswald,
  Dr. Magnus Hirschfeld
Cinematography: Max Fassbender
Art direction: Emil Linke
Science advisor: Dr. Magnus
  Hirschfeld
Production company: Richard Oswald-
  Film, Berlin
Producer: Richard Oswald

Cast
Conrad Veidt: Paul Körner, virtuoso
  violinist
Leo Connard: his father
Ilse von Tasso-Lind: his mother
Alexandra Willegh: his sister
Ernst Pittschau: her husband
Fritz Schulz: Kurt Sievers, friend of Paul
Wilhelm Diegelmann: his father
Clementine Plessner: his mother
Anita Berber: Else, his sister
Reinhold Schünzel: Franz Bollek,
  blackmailer
Karl Giese: Paul as a schoolboy
Helga Molander: Frau Heilborn
Magnus Hirschfeld: doctor and sex
  researcher

Premiere: May 28, 1919, Berlin

Richard Oswald (born Richard Ornstein)
Born November 5, 1880, Vienna;
died September 11, 1963, Düsseldorf.
Exile: 1933: fled from Germany to
Vienna; 1934: went into brief exile in
France, the Netherlands, and England;
1935–36: moved back and forth
between Vienna and Berlin; 1939:
moved with family to the US by way of
Italy, Vienna, London, and France

Selected Weimar films: *Die Prostitution*
(1919), *Lucrezia Borgia* (1922), *Feme*
(1927), *Der Hund von Baskerville*
(1929), *1914. Die letzten Tage vor
dem Weltbrand* (1931)

Paul has felt drawn to his own sex since childhood, and his parents' attempts to marry him off to a woman have come to nothing. At a concert, he meets Kurt, and they fall in love. Kurt's parents forbid him to have any contact with Paul. Paul is blackmailed by his former acquaintance Franz Bollek for violating Paragraph 175 of the criminal code, which forbade sex between men. Paul eventually reports him to the police, and Franz is sentenced to jail time, although Paul, too, has to spend a week in jail for violating Paragraph 175. Before he begins his sentence, his acquaintances avoid him; desperate, he kills himself. A doctor is able to convince Kurt, now tired of life, not to kill himself but to fight against social and state discrimination against homosexuals.

"This work towers above the flood of seamy pornography unleashed by the first enlightened films in its praiseworthy intent, its sci-entific seriousness, and altogether tasteful treatment of the awkward subject matter. In it Oswald is uniformly content with subtle suggestions that never overstep the boundaries of decency and good taste and moreover presents a film drama of highly dramatic forcefulness."

  Dr. J. B. [Jürgen Bartsch], "Ist der Film *Anders als die Andern* unsittlich?" *Film-Kurier*, no. 39 (July 19, 1919).

Film Notes:
Banned by the censors on August 18, 1920, with closed screenings permitted for professionals in schools and research centers. The original version had long been assumed lost, but a copy with Ukrainian intertitles, discovered in the USSR in the 1970s, was identified as the shortened version, *Gesetze der Liebe*, which had been reedited by Magnus Hirschfeld in 1927. The Filmmuseum München has restored both films and issued them on a DVD that also includes the English-language version.

Die Austernprinzessin 1919

The Oyster Princess

Germany
Director: Ernst Lubitsch
Screenplay: Ernst Lubitsch, Hanns Kräly
Cinematography: Theodor Sparkuhl
Art direction: Kurt Richter
Production company: Projektions-AG Union (PAGU), Berlin
Producer: Paul Davidson

Cast

Victor Janson: Mister Quaker, America's oyster king
Ossi Oswalda: Ossi Quaker, his daughter
Harry Liedtke: Prince Nucki
Julius Falkenstein: Josef, servant, Nucki's friend
Max Kronert: Seligsohn, marriage broker
Curt Bois: orchestra director
Gerhard Ritterband: kitchen boy
Also featuring: Albert Paulig, Hans Junkermann

Premiere: June 20, 1919, Berlin

Ernst Lubitsch

Born January 29, 1892, Berlin; died November 30, 1947, Los Angeles. Exile: 1922 onward: directed films for various studios in the US

Selected Weimar films: *Die Puppe* (1919), *Rausch* (1919), *Sumurun* (1920), *Anna Boleyn* (1920), *Die Flamme* (1922)

Ossi Quaker, the spoiled daughter of the wealthy American oyster king, wants to marry a prince as soon as possible. The marriage broker Seligsohn recommends the so-called Prince Nucki. Nucki, in fact penniless, sends his servant and friend Josef to Ossi to impersonate him and find out if the Quakers are really millionaires. Ossi forces the false Prince Nucki to marry her immediately. During the lavish wedding the real Prince Nucki shows up and, after all the confusion is resolved, finds the love of his life in the oyster princess.

"Whether the idea is strong or weak makes no difference in a Lubitsch comedy. Here it is a matter of 'how,' not 'what.' He realizes an idea in such a way that it becomes good. The entire comedy . . . is elegant, and executed in a style never before seen in a German comedy. It is an elegant style on the whole, one that has verve. . . . No other German director can match his cutting technique, his close-ups, and his song titles actually derived from the situation. . . . The comedy is witty, amusing, perhaps hilarious. Is it zany? Is it comical? One laughs, but one does not laugh spontaneously and heartily. Just when you think you can really laugh, suddenly there's another scene where you say: fabulous! What an idea! Amazing set! But then you don't laugh, you simply—marvel. . . . '250,000 marks! Amazing set! Three hundred servants.' Why? Only because America thrives on superlatives? . . . Have you read of the film cities in America, of the seventy thousand actors in the film *Intolerance* [D. W. Griffith, 1916]? Judging by numbers is subjective. We will never be able to match that. Our strengths lie elsewhere."
Bobby E. Lüthge, *Film-Kurier*, no. 15 (June 22, 1919).

Madame Dubarry 1919

Passion

Germany
Director: Ernst Lubitsch
Screenplay: Fred Orbing (aka Norbert Falk), Hanns Kräly
Cinematography: Theodor Sparkuhl
Second camera: Fritz Arno Wagner
Technical supervision: Kurt Waschneck
Art direction: Kurt Richter, Karl Machus
Costume design: Ali Hubert
Composer and conductor at premiere: Frank Schirrmacher
Production company: Projektions-AG Union (PAGU), Berlin, on behalf of Universum Film AG (UFA), Berlin
Producer: Paul Davidson

Cast
Pola Negri: Jeanne Vaubernier, later Madame Dubarry
Emil Jannings: Louis XV
Reinhold Schünzel: Duc de Choiseul, minister of state
Elsa Berna: Comtesse de Gramont, his sister
Harry Liedtke: Armand de Foix, medical student
Eduard von Winterstein: Count Jean Dubarry
Karl Platen: Guillaume Dubarry
Gustav Czimeg: Duc d'Aiguillo
Paul Biensfeldt: Lebelle, king's chamberlain
Magnus Stifter: Don Diego, Spanish ambassador
Willy Kaiser-Heyl: commander of the guard
Fred Immler: Duc de Richelieu

Premiere: September 18, 1919, Berlin
US premiere: December 12, 1920, Capitol Theatre, New York

Ernst Lubitsch
See page 73

Thanks to a string of influential aristocratic lovers, Jeanne Vaubernier, an employee in a Paris dress shop, becomes the mistress of King Louis XV, called Madame Dubarry. Even her strongest antagonist, Choiseul, a minister of state, cannot stop her. She energetically promotes her former fiancé, Armand de Foix, seeing to it that the king pardons him for shooting her first lover, the Spanish ambassador Don Diego, in a duel. Later, as the most powerful woman in France, she arranges to have the beloved Armand promoted from soldier to officer. But her unlimited and unofficial reign is of short duration. When the king dies of smallpox, Choiseul uses the opportunity to ban Jeanne from the court. In the revolution of 1789, the enraged populace brings down the monarchy, and the king's former mistress, too, is targeted by the new rulers of the Terror. Her trial ends with a death sentence. Armand, who is the chairman of the revolutionary tribunal, has to announce the verdict. His attempt to save Jeanne fails, and he is arrested and killed. Jeanne dies at the guillotine, surrounded by a crowd of eager spectators.

"Shooting in [the PAGU studio in the Berlin district] Tempelhof. In the huge hall, which is filled with the most varied sets, stands the Paris Opera around 1789. . . . King Louis's bedroom in Versailles. Genuine gleaming parquetry, gold, velvet, tapestries. Imposing design. Jannings lies in a lace shirt on a wide bed. The king. He has large, dark sores on his face and chest. The king is ill. He does not want to die, he refuses! His weak figure lies motionless in the pillows, his sharp profile with the Bourbon nose prominently presented. His hands play nervously above the coverlet. The doctors determine that His Majesty has the pox. Extreme revulsion of the chamberlains and others. The cardinal of Paris and three priests come with incense, a cross, and the Host. ¶'Get away! What do you want? I don't want to die.' He throws the Bible at their heads, sinks back, and dies. . . . ¶'Pola Negri!' Now 'she' comes, delicate, sensitive, her nostrils quivering, looking radiantly about and smiling. Diva through and through. They greet each other. . . . Comtesse Dubarry with a tall, white wig and wearing a heavy silk rococo frock like a picture by Watteau. ¶'You approach the bed and see at once that the king is dead.' Lubitsch gives instructions and shows what he wants. ¶'Music!' ¶A run-through, and then it begins. She stands still for a moment and shuts her eyes. Her body begins to tremble, as if a stream of electricity were coursing through her; then she lunges forward, stares at the pockmarked, waxen face of the dead Louis. ¶A scream . . . then she flings herself across the bed and the corpse, her hands clawing at the silk. A pearl necklace breaks. She sobs and quivers. . . . Now she straightens, her breast heaving. And when she staggers close to the camera, big tears, genuine tears, stream down across her sobbing face. . . . ¶'Thank you, Polachen, thank you!' ¶Lubitsch takes her arm and leads her to her chair."
B. E. L. [Bobby E. Lüthge], "Paris in Berlin," *Film-Kurier*, no. 15 (June 22, 1919).

Algol. Tragödie der Macht   1920
Algol

Germany
Director: Hans Werckmeister
Screenplay: Hans Brennert, Friedel Köhne
Cinematography: Axel Graatkjær (aka Axel Sørensen)
Art direction: Walter Reimann
Production company: Deutsche Lichtbildgesellschaft (Deulig), Berlin

Cast
Emil Jannings: Robert Herne, miner
John Gottowt: Algol, devil
Hanna Ralph: Maria Obal
Gertrud Welcker: Leonore Nissen
Hans Adalbert Schlettow: Peter Hell and his son, Peter
Ernst Hofmann: Reginald Herne
Erna Morena: Yella Ward
Käte Haack: Magda Herne
Sebastian Droste: dancer

Premiere: September 3, 1920, Berlin

Hans Werckmeister
Born 1879, Berlin; died July 3, 1929, Berlin

Selected Weimar films: *Margots Freier* (1919), *Die Kleine vom Film* (1922), *Die Brigantin von New York* (1924), *Weil Du es bist* (1925), *Der Kampf um den Mann* (1927)

Robert Herne, a miner, accepts a tempting offer from the devil Algol: complete control over the unlimited energy provided by the mysterious star of the same name. Rays emitted by this star are concentrated in a power plant. Only Robert knows the secret of the energy production, and he alone determines who receives it in exchange for food, thus allowing him to rule nearly all mankind. Only a single, largely rural country preserves its independence, and Maria Obal, Robert's former girlfriend, has moved there. Peter, Maria's son, asks Robert to use the power plant for the good of mankind, but in vain. When the last free population finally submits, the tyrant believes he has realized his dream of absolute power. But his brief triumph turns into misery and decline: his wife, the former entrepreneur Leonore Nissen, suffers a fatal accident when she touches a cable through which the Algol current flows, and their son, Reginald, basking in luxury, is in thrall to Yella Ward, a seductive, unscrupulous American who urges him to take over the world in place of his father. Recognizing that he has given in to excessive lust for power, Robert destroys the fateful Algol machine and dies before Reginald can take it from him by force.

"The fantasy film set a precedent, and keeps producing more and more offshoots, more or less beautifully constructed, but always interesting. *Algol* falls into this category. Following the trend of the time, it hopes to show that even dominating the world and its natural forces does not make one happy, that happiness rather lies in sticking to one's own turf, in peaceful work, in the bosom of one's family. . . . The film is an odd amalgam of realism and fantasy. Scenes of workers' revolts, country life, ministerial conferences, and such alternate with fantastic visions, bizarre texts, and pictures of the power plant and Robert Herne's home rendered in a kind of Expressionist style. . . . In the interior scenes the abundance of ornamental decoration is almost suffocating, and the actors are difficult to see against a background saturated with lines and colors. One might have wished for greater unity in the film as a whole, but one has to admit that it leaves behind a powerful impression. ¶Emil Jannings plays Robert Herne, all will and strength, rampant in his delirium of power yet controlled in every movement, a restrained force of nature superior to all the rest not only physically but also intellectually."

> *Der Kinematograph* (Düsseldorf), no. 713 (September 12, 1920).

Film Notes:
Biographical information about Werckmeister is scarce. He began his career as an actor in the German theater at the end of the nineteenth century and toured Italy, Greece, Turkey, and Egypt. From 1911 to 1916 he directed the municipal theater in Cologne, and from 1917 to 1920 he was the managing director of Deulig-Film. The first film he directed was *Der Friedensreiter* (1917), with Werner Krauss in the lead role.

Das Cabinet des Dr. Caligari 1920
The Cabinet of Dr. Caligari

Germany
Director: Robert Wiene
Screenplay: Carl Mayer, Hans
    Janowitz
Cinematography: Willy Hameister
Art direction: Hermann Warm, Walter
    Reimann, Walter Röhrig
Costume design and intertitles: Walter
    Reimann
**Conductor and musical arrangement
    for Berlin premiere:** Leo Zelinsky
Musical arrangement for US premiere:
    Samuel Lionel "Roxy" Rothafel,
    Ernö Rapée
Production company: Decla-Film-
    Gesellschaft, Berlin
Producer: Erich Pommer

Cast
Werner Krauss: Dr. Caligari
Conrad Veidt: Cesare
Friedrich Féher: Francis
Lil Dagover: Jane
Hans Heinrich von Twardowski: Alan
Rudolf Lettinger: Dr. Olfen, medical
    officer and Jane's father
Rudolf Klein-Rogge: criminal

Premiere: February 26, 1920, Berlin
First US screening: April 3, 1921,
    Capitol Theatre, New York

Robert Wiene
Born April 27, 1873, probably in
Breslau, German Empire (now
Wrocław, Poland); died July 15, 1938,
Paris. Exile: 1935: went into exile
in London; 1936: moved to Paris

Selected Weimar films: *Die verführte
Heilige* (1919), *Genuine* (1920),
I.N.R.I. (1923), *Panik in Chicago*
(1931), *Taifun* (1933 [banned 1933;
altered and rereleased as *Polizeiakte
909*, 1933])

In a garden, Francis sees his wife, Jane, walking in front of him as though in her sleep. The sight triggers a memory, and Francis begins to tell a strange story to a companion. Shortly after the opening of the annual fair in a small Northern German town, the local newspaper reports that a high official was murdered the night before; one of the carnival entertainers, Dr. Caligari, had been humiliated by the victim when applying for a permit for his show. Francis attends Caligari's performance at the fairgrounds with his friend Alan. Caligari wakes his medium, Cesare, out of a deep sleep, and in a trancelike state the young man predicts the future. When Alan asks how long he will live, Cesare answers: until the crack of dawn. His prophecy comes true when Alan is murdered during the night. Francis suspects Caligari, but the police apprehend another man. With the help of Jane's father, Dr. Olfen, Francis shadows Caligari. At the fair Jane meets Caligari, who shows her Cesare; his appearance shocks her, and she runs away. On orders from his master, Cesare breaks into Jane's bedroom that night, but he is overcome by her beauty and chooses not to kill her. He abducts her and flees through alleys and across rooftops, pursued by Dr. Olfen's servants. As they come closer and closer, Cesare is forced to leave his victim behind, still alive, and he finally collapses, hounded to death. Francis is stunned by the incident. Following Jane's report, the police and Francis compel Caligari to open Cesare's casket, where, in his place, they find a mannequin. Caligari escapes into an institution for the insane, and Francis

follows him there. With the help of clinic documents, Francis explains the mad serial killer's double identity and motive. Caligari is restrained in a straightjacket and placed in a cell. As Francis ends his story, the garden in which he and his companion find themselves is revealed to be part of the institution. We recognize the other patients: Jane, who thinks she is a queen, and Cesare, not dead, engrossed in looking at a flower. When Caligari appears, Francis becomes aggressive and is forcibly led away. Caligari, visiting Francis in his cell, feels that he is curable and explains to him that he knows both the cause of his psychic affliction and the appropriate kind of therapy.

"Naturalism and Impressionism had had a generation all to themselves, then suddenly in 1909–10 there was a countermovement everywhere that turned against what was left of historicism, in short, against all realistic art. This countermovement is called Expressionism. . . . Through Expressionism we now have a profound sense of how irrelevant reality is and how powerful the unreal: what has never been, what is only felt, the projection of a mental state onto one's surroundings. . . . The technique of film automatically lends itself to the depiction of the unreal, specifically its depiction in the manner of Expressionism. In it the requirement that the picture be flat is fulfilled, in it the colors function wholly as atmospheric values. For film is by no means an art of black and white, as everyone thinks; it has a great deal to do with colors. Why else would artists design decorations and cos-

tumes in the most appealing colors? The colors take on importance . . . in the film as light values. . . . ¶Then there are the forms in which the artist, turning his back to nature and looking outward from within, represents his experience. . . . The film dramatist will have the fairy-tale forest and the magical palace and all the settings in which the imagination of an E. T. A. Hoffmann is at home constructed by the Expressionist, so that they mysteriously whisper of an artistic sense of things that are not of this world, and of which our book learning does not allow itself to dream—unless it were to suddenly stop knowing and begin to dream unscientifically. But the dreamer would not relate what he thinks in ordered speech: he would speak simply in cries, in screams, just as the Expressionist writer would prefer to. These cries and screams are the 'titles' that even the Expressionist film drama cannot do without."

Robert Wiene, "Expressionismus im Film," *Berliner Börsen-Courier*, July 30, 1922.

Der Golem, wie er in die Welt kam 1920

The Golem: How He Came into the World

Germany
Directors: Paul Wegener, Carl Boese
Screenplay: Paul Wegener
Cinematography: Karl Freund
Art direction: Heinz Poelzig (drafts),
Kurt Richter (construction)
Costume design: Rochus Gliese
Composer: Hans Landsberger
Conductor at premiere: Bruno Schulz
Production company: Projektions-AG
Union (PAGU), Berlin
Producer: Paul Davidson

Cast
Paul Wegener: Golem
Albert Steinrück: Rabbi Loew
Lyda Salmonova: Mirjam, his daughter
Ernst Deutsch: Rabbi Famulus
Otto Gebühr: Kaiser Rudolf II
Lothar Müthel: Count Florian
Hanns Sturm: Rabbi Jehuda,
congregation elder
Max Kronert: temple attendant
Greta Schröder: little girl with a rose
Loni Nest: little girl with an apple

Premiere: October 29, 1920, Berlin
First US screening: June 1921,
Criterion, New York

Paul Wegener
Born December 11, 1874,
Arnoldsdorf, German Empire (now
Jarantowice, Poland); died September
13, 1948, Berlin. No exile

Wegener directed only one other film
in Weimar-era Germany, *Lebende
Buddhas* (1920); he primarily worked
as an actor in, for example, *Sumurun*
(Ernst Lubitsch, 1920), *Monna Vanna*
(Richard Eichberg, 1922), *Die
Weber* (Friedrich Zelnik, 1927), and
Unheimliche Geschichten (Richard
Oswald, 1932).

From his study of the position of the stars, Rabbi Loew suspects that the Jews in the ghetto are about to suffer a catastrophe. As it happens, the kaiser commands that they leave his dominion. To protect his congregation from the forced expulsion, Loew, with his assistant, Famulus, creates the Golem out of a piece of clay, following an ancient ritual. The kaiser summons Loew to a celebration at court in order to entertain the public with magic. Loew presents the Golem and reminds the kaiser and his noble entourage of the wandering of the Jews in the wilderness. Because one of the participants in the celebration ignores his admonition to be silent during talk of the Exodus, the imperial palace nearly collapses. Loew has the Golem support the roof. In gratitude, the kaiser rescinds his edict against the Jews. The Golem has thus fulfilled his function; Loew changes him back to a shapeless clump of clay. But Famulus secretly brings the creature to life again in order to kill the hated nobleman Florian, who enjoys the affections of Loew's lovely daughter Mirjam and who has already spent a night with her. Florian flees from the powerful monster into a tower, falls to the ground, and dies. Suddenly the Golem takes on a life of its own and sets fire to the ghetto. In the end a little girl is able to subdue the monster and save the Jews.

"This second Golem film [following *Der Golem* in 1915] is a milestone in the history of the cinema. Namely because it creates a new relationship to modern art. Not the way *Das Cabinet des Dr. Caligari* and *Genuine* [both Robert Wiene, 1920] relate to Expressionist painting, but to an imaginary architecture of a symbol-filled sculpture. . . . ¶The Golem is Paul Wegener. Of gigantic proportions, clumsy, naive, fierce, beastly, and then, when he smells the scent of a rose or takes a child up into his arms, with an inner goodness that spreads across the broad, angular face with its Mongoloid eyes, until he collapses in death. He is monumentally impressive as he gropes his way through the alleys with the stride of a wound-up automaton, chops wood with angular, precisely measured movements, or silently and eloquently lets his heavy head sink down onto his chest."

Eugen Tannenbaum, *BZ am Mittag*,
October 30, 1920.

Film Notes:

In 1914 Wegener and Henrik (born Heinrich) Galeen wrote a screenplay with a similar plot that became Galeen's *Der Golem* (1915). The film had nothing to do with Gustav Meyrink's novel of the same name (1915).

Carl Boese

Born August 26, 1887, Berlin; died
July 6, 1958, Berlin. No exile

Selected Weimar films: *Die Tänzerin
Barberina* (1920), *Die schwarze
Schmach* (1921 [banned 1921]),
Die Frau im Feuer (1924), *Ossi hat
die Hosen an* (1928), *Drei von der
Kavallerie* (1932)

Von morgens bis mitternachts 1920
From Morn to Midnight

Germany
Director: Karlheinz Martin
Screenplay: Karlheinz Martin, Herbert Juttke, from the play by Georg Kaiser (1916)
Cinematography: Carl Hoffmann
Art direction, costume design, and figurines: Robert Neppach
Production company: Ilag-Film, Berlin
Producer: Herbert Juttke

Cast
Ernst Deutsch: the teller
Erna Morena: the lady
Hans Heinrich von Twardowski: the young man
Eberhard Wrede: the bank director
Edgar Licho: the fat man
Hugo Döblin: the junk dealer
Frieda Richard: the grandmother
Lotte Stein: the wife
Roma Bahn: the daughter/the beggar girl/the coquette/the mask/the girl from the Salvation Army
Lo Heyn: the lady at the ball
Also featuring: Mary Zimmermann Ballet Company

First German screening: autumn 1920, probably in the Ruhr region
First Japanese screening: December 1922, Tokyo

Karlheinz (also: Karl Heinz) Martin
Born May 6, 1886, Freiburg im Breisgau, German Empire; died January 13, 1948, Berlin. No exile

Weimar films: *Die Verwandlung* (1920), *Das Haus zum Mond* (1921), *Die Perle des Orients* (1921); as dialogue director: *Berlin-Alexanderplatz* (Phil Jutzi, 1931)

An embittered, married bank teller despises his bourgeois life. He steals money from the bank and quietly leaves his family. He dives into a metropolitan adventure, attending a sports tournament, a nightclub, and a meeting of the Salvation Army. A young female missionary betrays him to the police, and he commits suicide.

"Karl Heinz Martin approached his first film with radical intentions. . . . The script . . . was closely based on the play. Only the female figures were blended into a single figure. Martin wished to get away from specifics—he was more interested in the timeless and universal. His figures are 'a teller,' 'a girl,' and 'a mother'—no private individuals. . . . ¶The figures are reduced to a few, prominent features. The rhythm of their existence is shifted to their gestures. . . . The set designer worked in black and white: figurines, landscapes, interior decorations—everything was meant to create a graphic effect, the movement of surfaces and lines, light and dark. The road into the night, a winter tree; a white serpent flattened into dark planes; and in front a massive tree, the play of spreading branches. The cameraman Hoffmann has adapted to the designer's intentions: everything comes out gray on gray. The figures have shed their organic forms, are merely formal elements within the decorative scheme, contribute to the picture space, are dismembered by spots and stripes of light painted on them. This movement of people who merely function as shapes prevents the viewer from being drawn into the film. What he sees are grimaces and distortions, coldness, stiffness—he is filled with alienation."

Rudolf Kurtz, *Expressionismus und Film*, 1926, eds. Christian Kiening and Ulrich Johannes Beil (Zurich: Chronos, 2007), pp. 66–69.

"The altogether successful images in which the fleeing teller strides through a snowy landscape and the six-day racers speed past have an astonishing spatial effect. Here it is a matter of a new form of representation, one that deliberately diverges from reality, and yet every viewer will recognize and interpret it as flawless."

Unsigned review, *Rheinisch-Westfälische Zeitung*, undated and quoted in an Ilag-Film advertisement; reprinted in *Der Film*, no. 42 (October 16, 1920): 89.

Film Notes:

As a theater director, Martin directed the play *Von morgens bis mitternachts* at Hamburg's Thalia Theater in 1918.

The film was shot in the first half of 1920 and approved for public viewing by the censors on August 15, 1921. Even though a press preview took place in Munich in early February 1922, the film, for unknown reasons, never had a normal release in Germany. It was considered lost for many years, but on January 21, 1963, a copy of the restored version, provided by the National Film Center/ National Museum of Modern Art, Tokyo, was shown in East Berlin. In 1985 the same Tokyo institution provided a copy to the Filmmuseum München; the film, reconstructed in a different way, premiered on March 10, 1993, at the Musée d'Art Moderne de la Ville de Paris as part of the exhibition *Figures du moderne: L'Expressionisme en Allemagne*. The first German screening of this newly restored version followed on June 25, 1993, at the Filmmuseum München.

Hintertreppe 1921

Backstairs

Germany
Directors: Leopold Jessner, Paul Leni
Screenplay: Carl Mayer, from the play
   Juana (1918) by Georg Kaiser
Cinematography: Karl Hasselmann,
   Willy Hameister
Art direction: Paul Leni (drafts), Karl
   Görge (construction)
Composer: Hans Landsberger
Production company: Henny Porten-
   Film, Berlin, on behalf of Gloria-
   Film, Berlin
Producers: Hanns Lippmann, Henny
   Porten

Cast
Henny Porten: housemaid
Wilhelm Dieterle: craftsman
Fritz Kortner: letter carrier

Premiere: December 11, 1921, Berlin

Leopold Jessner
Born March 3, 1878, Königsberg,
German Empire (now Kaliningrad,
Russia); died December 13, 1945,
Los Angeles. Exile:1933: left Berlin
with his ensemble on a tour through
Belgium, Holland, and England;
1936: while ensemble was performing
in Tel Aviv, went into exile in the US

Weimar films: *Erdgeist* (1923); as
artistic supervisor: *Täter gesucht*
(Carl Heinz Wolff, 1931)

Paul Leni
Born July 8, 1885, Stuttgart; died
September 2, 1929, Hollywood.
Exile: 1926: with his wife, left
Germany for the US to work with the
producer Carl Laemmle at Universal
Picture Corporation, and directed four
films there

(continued)

After a monotonous day's work for a wealthy family, a housemaid meets her fiancé, a craftsman, in a square in front of the house. The happy lovers are observed by a shy, crippled letter carrier from his cellar window. He is consumed with jealousy; he, too, desires the young housemaid. One day her fiancé fails to show up for their usual rendezvous and does not get in touch with her for a few days. Has something happened to him? Has he found another? The housemaid's agonizing uncertainty drives her to despair. Finally the letter carrier hands her a comforting letter from her fiancé. In a happy mood she visits the letter carrier at home to thank him for the good news but is surprised to find him writing another letter to her, as false as the first. Her horror and disappointment give way to increasing sympathy, as she recognizes that his false comfort arose out of pity. What she does not know is that for many days her fiancé has been unconscious in the hospital following an accident at work. One evening, as the letter carrier and the housemaid settle down to a fine supper together in his room, the craftsman unexpectedly returns, completely recovered. He is killed by the letter carrier. The housemaid commits suicide out of despair.

"In this ambiguous manuscript the directing and acting are oddly congenial. ¶In the first part, when it is necessary to show the work of a housemaid, the endless sequence of identical chores day after day, Jessner presents a series of identically animated scenes that are unusual in that nothing unusual happens in them. They are simply extracts, both in space and in time; one almost never sees a whole room, only the corner where Henny happens to be working. She makes beds, she polishes boots, she clears the table, she washes the glasses. . . . And Henny Porten does all this as a matter of course, as though she had never been a film diva but spent her whole life as a housemaid. It is very difficult to show a person at work, to bring him to life through his work. Mayer, Jessner, and Henny Porten have accomplished it by means of film."

Hans Siemsen, "Die lehrreiche
Hintertreppe," *Die Weltbühne*, no. 3
(1922): 72.

Leni worked most frequently as a set
designer or art director in, for example,
Tragödie der Liebe (Joe May, four
parts, 1923); as director: *Prinz Kuckuck*
(1919), *Patience. Die Karten des
Todes* (1920), *Die Verschwörung zu
Genua* (1921)

Dr. Mabuse, der Spieler 1922

Dr. Mabuse, the Gambler

Germany
Director: Fritz Lang
Screenplay: Thea von Harbou, from the novel by Norbert Jacques (1921–22)
Cinematography: Carl Hoffmann
Art direction: Otto Hunte, Carl Stahl-Urach, Erich Kettelhut, Karl Vollbrecht
Costume design: Vally Reinecke
Production company: Uco-Film, Berlin, on behalf of Decla-Bioscop, Berlin

Cast
Rudolf Klein-Rogge: Dr. Mabuse
Bernhard Goetzke: District Attorney von Wenk
Alfred Abel: Count Told
Gertrude Welcker: Countess Dusy Told
Aud Egede Nissen: Cara Carozza, dancer
Anita Berber: dancer
Paul Richter: Edgar Hull, millionaire
Hans Adalbert Schlettow: Georg, chauffeur
Georg John: Pesch, servant
Grete Berger: Fine, servant
Julius Falkenstein: Karsten, Wenk's friend
Robert Foerster-Larrinaga: Spoerri, secretary
Lydia Potechina: Russian woman
Julius E. Herrmann: Schramm, proprietor
Karl Huszar-Puffy: Hawasch, counterfeiter
Karl Platen: Told's servant

Premiere, part 1: April 27, 1922, Berlin
Premiere, part 2: May 26, 1922, Berlin
First US screening: August 6, 1927, Fifth Avenue Playhouse, New York

Part 1: *The Gambler*
"Dr. Mabuse is the archetype, the very image of the ingenious criminal. With his phenomenal intellectual powers he is able to subjugate everyone around him. He knows all of mankind's faults and weaknesses, and he knows how to exploit them for his own purposes. . . . He does not merely wish to rob one or more people, he wishes to be the master—master of the city he lives in, master of the country he lives in, master of mankind. . . . Mabuse pops up now here, now there, now in a casino as a passionate gambler, now in gin mills as a drunken sailor, now on the stock exchange as a financier, now in the lecture room as a professor, now with sick people as a doctor or psychoanalyst. . . . ¶His assistants—Georg, the chauffeur; Hawasch, the director of the mint; the weakling Spoerri, a drunk and cocaine addict; and Pesch—all merely tools with no will of their own, trembling at his approach. Two women are devoted to Mabuse: Cara Carozza, the dancer from the music hall, and Fine, a woman of the streets. They idolize him and unquestioningly carry out all his commands."

> Program notes for the Berlin premiere, UFA-Palast am Zoo, 1922.

"It is not the plot that accounts for the success of this work, which explodes the closed form of the drama with its electrifying savagery, but rather the episode, not the action in its totality but symbolic single events most vividly expressive of the times. . . . Conglomeration of dance and crime, gambling and cocaine addiction, jazz band and raid. . . . In this fresh delirium of dehumanized mankind there is no sense, no logic—only play. But while the others indulge him at the bar, Dr. Mabuse plays with men and human fates. . . . A brilliant criminal in countless masks and metamorphoses."

> Eugen Tannenbaum, *BZ am Mittag*, April 28, 1922.

"In fifty or a hundred years the film *Dr. Mabuse, der Spieler* will show people a time that they could perhaps scarcely comprehend without such period pieces. . . . The extravagance of the newly rich, the rabid gambling on the stock exchange, the clubs, the addiction to pleasure, the speculation, the vast amount of smuggling, counterfeiting, the reawakened superstition, mankind's penchant for the extrasensory, the faith in spiritualism, the spread of hypnosis for criminal purposes, and not least the effect of the agitation of fanatic 'saviors' on the misled masses."

> *Berliner Illustrierte Zeitung*, April 30, 1922.

Part 2: *King of Crime*
Mabuse loses his omnipotence. His adversary, the public prosecutor Wenk, devises a plan to catch Mabuse, using Countess Told and the already arrested dancer Carozza, but at first it fails. Mabuse wants to exploit the countess himself. He abducts her and drives her husband, Count Told, to suicide. But Mabuse does not manage to get rid of Wenk, who stays on his tail. Police surround and storm the house in which Mabuse has barricaded himself with his accomplices. They successfully defend

(continued)

Fritz (born Friedrich Christian Anton) Lang

Born December 5, 1890, Vienna; died August 2, 1976, Beverly Hills. Exile: 1933: in July went into exile in France, directing *Liliom* in Paris on behalf of Fox-Europe for producer Erich Pommer; 1934: moved to the US; 1935: became US citizen; 1956–60 shot two films in the Federal Republic of Germany

Selected Weimar films: *Harakiri* (1919), *Der müde Tod* (1921), *Die Nibelungen* (two parts [*Siegfried* and *Kriemhilds Rache*], 1924), *Spione* (1928), *Das Testament des Dr. Mabuse* (1933 [banned from domestic distribution 1933])

themselves in a savage shoot-out, but then the army arrives. At the last moment Mabuse manages to escape into his counterfeiting workshop. The police finally arrest him, but he has lost his mind.

"The way he [Dr. Mabuse] is surrounded and hunted, the way he loses one card after another, the way horrible masks of people who have been under his spell close in on him, the way dead objects come alive and threaten to throttle him with their tentacles, it is all once again constructed with consummate virtuosity and technique. . . . Very good when the suggestive words of Dr. Mabuse, flashing like lightning, illuminate the road on which public prosecutor Wenk is supposed to drive his car into the abyss. . . . Wonderful the way two racing automobiles turn out of the bright glare into a dark side street."

BZ am Mittag, May 27, 1922.

"The photography of Carl Hoffmann is a true delight and a surprise. He has finally made available to film the convincing, astounding nighttime shot. Without dyeing or tinting even a single picture, he has photographed purely for atmosphere and nonetheless achieved the subtlest shadings. Some ideas are extremely exciting, for example, the eyes of Dr. Mabuse shooting forward toward the viewer, the animated intertitles suggestively growing bigger and bigger, the view through the opera glasses, which changes from a cloudy blur to clarity as the focus is adjusted."

Vorwärts, April 30, 1922.

Film Notes:

The novel by Norbert Jacques was originally published as a series in a Berlin magazine. The first English edition was *Dr. Mabuse, Master of Mystery* (London: Allen & Unwin, 1923).

The first American screening was a shortened version (just sixty-three minutes, with 150 English intertitles) titled *Dr. Mabuse*. The first version released in the US combined the film's two parts, which were shown separately in Germany.

Nosferatu. Eine Symphonie des Grauens 1922
Nosferatu

Germany
Director: F. W. Murnau
Screenplay: Henrik Galeen, from the novel *Dracula* (1897) by Bram Stoker
Cinematography: Fritz Arno Wagner
Assistant camera: Günther Krampf
Art direction: Albin Grau
Costume design: Albin Grau
Composer and conductor at premiere: Hans Erdmann
Production company: Prana-Film, Berlin
Producers: Albin Grau, Enrico Dieckmann

Cast
Max Schreck: Count Orlok/Nosferatu
Alexander Granach: Knock, real estate agent
Gustav von Wangenheim: Hutter, Knock's secretary
Greta Schröder-Matray: Ellen Hutter, his wife
Georg Heinrich Schnell: Harding, ship-owner, Hutter's friend
Ruth Landshoff: Ruth, his sister
John Gottowt: Professor Bulwer, follower of Paracelsus
Gustav Botz: Professor Sievers, town physician
Max Nemetz: captain of the *Empusa*
Wolfgang Heinz, Albert Venohr: sailors

Premiere: March 4, 1922, Berlin
First German screening: March 15, 1922, Berlin
First US screening: June 3, 1929, Film Guild Cinema, New York

F. W. Murnau (born Friedrich Wilhelm Plumpe)
Born December 28, 1888, Bielefeld, German Empire; died March 11, 1931, Santa Monica, California. Exile: 1926: signed a four-year contract with William Fox and left Germany for
(continued)

Count Orlok seeks a residence in Wisborg. Knock, a real estate agent, dispatches Hutter, his secretary, to Orlok's remote castle in the Carpathian Mountains to offer him a property. As Orlok's guest, Hutter discovers his host sleeping in a coffin and flees, horrified. Meanwhile Ellen, his young wife at home, is plagued by terrifying dreams, so she is greatly relieved to see her beloved husband return unharmed. A ship arrives in Wisborg carrying a coffin, which contains Orlok—the vampire. The captain and the other sailors are dead. Suddenly rats overrun the port city and plague spreads everywhere, killing countless residents. Orlok moves into a house across from Hutter. Ellen figures out how to destroy the light-shy monster. She lures Orlok into her room and allows him to bite her, causing him to forget the time. When the first rays of the sun strike the vampire, he disintegrates into dust.

"The sets for the film are far more the work of the painter than the architect. . . . Art is inspiration, not reproduction (Herwarth Walden [aka Georg Lewin, gallery owner, publisher, musician, patron of the avant-garde]). Applied to film, set architecture should not try to be anything more than an atmospheric frame . . . nothing more than the major key to which the plot is attuned: the 'acting space' harmonizes with the action of the scene. ¶It is obvious that light is what is most important for the art decoration. . . . Light is not there to illuminate the set but to bring the picture to life—scenery and action—in terms of form. . . . In the decoration we have to create shadowed areas, that is, places that absorb the light to a greater or lesser degree. This is possible by using color, with its varied light sensitivity. Thus color comes to play an important role in our black-and-white art."
Albin Grau, "Licht-Regie im Film," *BZ am Mittag*, March 5, 1922.

"We are assured that a number of ladies who . . . attended the *Nosferatu* premiere had a bad night. And this seems perfectly credible, for in the field of literature only Hoffmann, Poe, and [writer, cabaret artist, and filmmaker Hanns Heinz] Ewers have succeeded in injecting horror into art with such perfection. . . . The *Nosferatu* film is a sensation, for it radically departs from the well-worn path of the hundreds of newly resurrected love stories and the mechanical adventure. . . . The story of the spooky vampire Nosferatu, who spreads death, plague, and terror, has been presented in film with spellbinding forcefulness. Atmospheric elements are included wherever the camera could find them: bleak high-mountain ravines, crashing waves, wind-whipped clouds, eerie ruins. A textbook example of how film has exploited the moods of landscape for its own purposes."
H. W. [Hans Wollenberg], *Lichtbild-Bühne*, no. 11 (March 11, 1922).

Film Notes:
A version restored by the Filmmuseum München, premiered February 20, 1984, at the International Film Festival in Berlin.

1389/8   Die zwölfte Stunde

the US, where he made *Sunrise: A Song of Two Humans* (1927), *Four Devils* (1928), and *Our Daily Bread/ City Girl* (1930)

Selected Weimar films: *Der Knabe in Blau/Der Todessmaragd* (1919), *Der Bucklige und die Tänzerin* (1920), *Schloss Vogelöd* (1921), *Tartüff* (1925), *Faust—Eine deutsche Volkssage* (1926)

Das alte Gesetz 1923
The Old Law

Germany
Director: E. A. Dupont
Screenplay: Paul Reno, from
    Erinnerungen, 1810–1840 (1909)
    by Heinrich Laube
Cinematography: Theodor Sparkuhl
Art direction: Alfred Junge, Kurt Kahle
Costume design: Ali Hubert
Art advisor: Avrom Morewski
Production company: Comedia-Film,
    Berlin

Cast

THE GHETTO FIGURES
Avrom Morewski: Rabbi Mayer
Ernst Deutsch: Baruch, his son
Grete Berger: his mother
Robert Garrison: Ruben Pick
Werner Krauss: Nathan, professor
Margarete Schlegel: Esther, his
    daughter

THE THEATER FIGURES
Jakob Tiedtke: theater director
Olga Limburg: his wife
Alice Hechy: their daughter
Julius M. Brandt: old comedian

THE VIENNESE FIGURES
Henny Porten: Archduchess Elisabeth
    Theresia
Ruth Weyher: lady-in-waiting
Hermann Vallentin: Heinrich Laube,
    director of the Burgtheater
Wolfgang Zilzer: page
Also featuring: Philipp Manning

Premiere: October 29, 1923, Berlin

E. A. (Ewald André) Dupont
Born December 25, 1891, Zeitz,
German Empire; died December 12,
1956, Los Angeles. Exile: 1933:
moved to the US

Selected Weimar films: *Das Geheimnis
des Amerika-Docks* (1919), *Die
Geierwally* (1921), *Zwei Welten*
(1930), *Peter Voss, der Millionendieb*
(1932), *Der Läufer von Marathon* (1933)

It is the middle of the nineteenth century. In an Eastern European ghetto Rabbi Mayer is celebrating the traditional feast of Purim. To him the Old Law, according to which a religious Jew may not perform in the theater, is sacred. His son, Baruch, however, feels drawn to the stage. He leaves the ghetto and joins a troupe of actors touring the Habsburg empire. The Archduchess Elisabeth Theresia, who is in the audience of a performance in Vienna, falls in love with the good-looking young actor and recommends him to Heinrich Laube, the director of the famous Burgtheater. Despite initial misgivings, Laube is impressed by Baruch's talent and engages him. As Rabbi Mayer once again celebrates Purim, Baruch captivates the Viennese public in a production of Hamlet. At the urging of the cadger Ruben Pick, Baruch visits his father to reconcile with him, but he is rebuffed by the pigheaded old man for his blasphemous way of life. While in the ghetto Baruch encounters Esther, his early love, who follows him to Vienna, where the two marry. Pick convinces the rabbi to join him at one of Baruch's premieres. Thrilled by his son's magnificent acting, the father accepts his transgression of the Old Law.

"*Das alte Gesetz* is unusual in one particular aspect . . . that demonstrates how well the director Dupont commands the specific genre of film. This is when Laube has the actor audition, a scene basically foreign to film. Here the entire effect was to come from Laube's contrary responses as he listens. To this end it was necessary to give him some visible activity: Laube is eating breakfast. The way Hermann Vallentin heedlessly drinks his coffee, chews, stops for a second, becomes attentive, returns to his breakfast, and finally stops altogether—is even better than his police interrogation in *Tragödie der Liebe* [Joe May, 1923]."

Herbert Ihering, *Berliner Börsen-Courier*,
November 1, 1923.

Schatten 1923
Warning Shadows

Germany
Director: Arthur Robison
Screenplay: Rudolf Schneider, Arthur Robison, from an idea by Albin Grau
Cinematography: Fritz Arno Wagner
Art direction: Albin Grau
Costume design: Albin Grau
Production company: Pan-Film, Berlin
Producers: Enrico Dieckmann, Albin Grau, Willy Seibold

Cast
Fritz Kortner: the count, a jealous husband
Ruth Weyher: his wife
Gustav von Wangenheim: his wife's lover
Eugen Rex: first cavalier
Max Gülstorff: second cavalier
Ferdinand von Alten: third cavalier
Fritz Rasp: first servant
Karl Platen: second servant
Lilly Harder: maid

Press preview: July 26, 1923, Berlin
Premiere: October 16, 1923, Berlin
First US screening: August 9, 1927, 55th Street Cinema, New York

Arthur (also: Artur) Robison
Born June 25, 1888, Chicago; died October 20, 1935, Berlin

Weimar films: *Zwischen Abend und Morgen. Der Spuk einer Nacht* (1923), *Pietro der Korsar* (1925), *Manon Lescaut* (1926), *Der letzte Walzer* (1927), *Looping the Loop* (1928)

What is reality? What is fantasy? Tortured by morbid jealousy, a count observes the guests at his festive table, at the center of which is his wife, surrounded by male admirers. He is appalled to see shadows of hands reaching, with evident desire, for her silhouette. Among the guests is a showman who recognizes the cause of the tense atmosphere; he hypnotizes everyone and, using shadow play, confronts them with their repressed feelings and desires.

"This film is billed as 'a nocturnal hallucination,' and that is a pity in one respect, for it takes away some of the surprise from the fantastic doings to come. The attentive viewer is informed too soon by this subtitle that the events are unreal. . . . What the scriptwriters and the director have achieved above all is . . . a blurring of the boundary between reality and unreality. It is marvelous how this boundary is bridged: the showman . . . shifts the light source that casts his silhouette on the wall. The shadows of the actual people in the play slide from the back of the set across the table, for a brief moment the clarity of the image is blurred, and out of the mistiness the people emerge again on the right side of the set table, just where they were seated at the beginning of the shadow play. Reality appears to continue as if there had

never been a showman at the table, and the coquettish woman, who threatened to turn away from her older, earnest husband to lend an ear to the cavaliers—this woman now experiences in a seemingly wakeful, sober state what will become of her if she continues her frivolous behavior. The film itself is without titles; the four acts, filled with movement without actual tension, are superbly explained by the simple picture sequence. . . . ¶So it turns out that the film *Schatten*, in essence a chamber piece . . . a product of pure artistry, is a courageous l'art pour l'art experiment in the genre of film. ¶It is to their credit that they [the director and scriptwriters] set aside today's far too familiar Expressionism in favor of the primary cinematographic medium of light. . . . The chiaroscuro captured on celluloid by the photographer Fritz Arno Wagner is one of the most balanced and meticulous achievements ever accomplished in a sustained visual medium."

J-s, *Film-Kurier*, no. 173 (July 27, 1923).

"This production has no titles, and after viewing it one concludes that captions, exasperating though they may be in some pictures, would be a blessing in this case."
Mordaunt Hall, *New York Times*, August 10, 1927.

Die Strasse 1923
The Street

Germany
Director: Karl Grune
Screenplay: Karl Grune, Julius Urgiss, from a story idea by Carl Mayer
Cinematography: Karl Hasselmann
Art direction: Karl Görge (execution), Ludwig Meidner (drafts)
Production company: Universum Film AG (UFA), Berlin

Cast
Eugen Klöpfer: the husband
Lucie Höflich: the wife
Aug Egede Nissen: the prostitute
Max Schreck: the blind man
Anton Edthofer: his son, the murderer
Sascha: the child
Leonhard Haskel: the man from the provinces

Premiere: November 29, 1923, Berlin
First US screening: September 1927, Fifth Avenue Playhouse, New York

Karl Grune (born Bertold Grünwald)
Born January 22, 1890, Vienna; died October 2, 1962, Bournemouth, England. Exile: 1933: went to England

Selected Weimar films: Menschen in Ketten (1919), Frauenopfer (1922), Schlagende Wetter (1923), Eifersucht (1925), Am Rande der Welt (1927)

An elderly official, tired of his wife of many years, breaks out of his day-to-day tedium. One evening during supper he bolts out of his apartment, lets himself be carried along by the stream of pedestrians on the street, and immerses himself in the exciting, dangerous nightlife of the metropolis. A conniving prostitute promises to satisfy his sexual desires. She lures him into a dance hall where her accomplices are conning an unsuspecting patron from the provinces with a crooked game for money. When the patron unexpectedly wins the game, he is killed. The prostitute's accomplices manage to pin the crime on her naive companion, and he is arrested; in his jail cell he attempts suicide but is unsuccessful. When a child identifies its own father as the murderer, the upright citizen is released. Frightened and repentant, he returns to his wife.

"Everything on the set lies still in the sober light of day. Workers are climbing on giant scaffolding, applying huge brushes to gigantic facades. . . . Riggers on tall light carriages are experimenting with electrical devices. Steamrollers pass across the asphalt once more. In between swarm policemen, passersby, ladies in elegant evening dresses, laughing girls, beggars, pairs of lovers, bicyclists. Automobiles, carriages, and trucks wait in a long row. ¶Commands ring out across the street. Atop a sandy hill, towering above it all, stands Karl Grune, the mind behind the picture and the one who controls it. Nothing escapes his critical director's gaze. . . . A command to the crowds on the far side of the wide square is swiftly relayed by bicyclists. . . . A whistle shrills through the night. Spotlights come on. The demonic street is brightly illuminated. Attention! Camera! The play begins. . . . And becomes reality. . . . I am no longer myself, but a medium that stumbles through the unleashed chaos of the street. Relaxed and driven by manifold yearnings for dance and delirium and play and love."

Eugen Klöpfer, "Nachtaufnahme," in UFA press material for Die Strasse, 1923, pp. 16–17. Schriftgutarchiv, Stiftung Deutsche Kinemathek, Berlin.

"Grune unleashes the monstrous chaos of the street with speeding cars, glowing advertising signs, people and animals running, makes the life in glittering dancehalls seethe, presses suffering into the nooks and corners, drips sympathy into all the hurried searching, drowns out the noise of the street with frantic screams, captures the fear and mortal terror in dark back stairwells, chases murder across slippery steps, follows shadows from the paving into middle-class rooms, sets skulls on the necks of slender girls, and turns everything into a monstrous kaleidoscope. . . . The director has become a poet of the night, of the inferno."

Deutsche Allgemeine Zeitung, December 2, 1923.

Isn't Life Wonderful   1924

USA

Director: D. W. Griffith

Screenplay: D. W. Griffith, from the short-story collection *Defeat* (1924) by Geoffrey Moss (born Geoffrey Cecil Gilbert McNeill-Moss)

Cinematography: Hendrik Sartov, Harold S. Sintzenich

Musical arrangement: Louis Silvers, Cesare Sudero

Production company: D. W. Griffith Productions, New York

Producer: D. W. Griffith

Cast

Carol Dempster: Inga
Erville Alderson: the professor
Neil Hamilton: Paul, son of the professor
Frank Puglia: Theodor, another son
Helen Lowell: grandmother
Marcia Harris: aunt
Lupino Lane: Rudolph, musician
Walter Plimmer, Jr.: American
Hans Adalbert Schlettow (in the US: Count von Schacht), Paul Rehkopf, Robert Scholz: hungry workers
Desha Delteil: cabaret dancer

Premiere: November 23, 1924, Rivoli, New York

D. W. (David Wark) Griffith

Born January 22, 1875, LaGrange, Kentucky; died July 23, 1948, Hollywood

After World War I, a professor and his family flee to Berlin from the newly established Poland. The impoverished, humiliated family includes the professor; his grown sons, Paul and Theodor; his adopted daughter, Inga; and the children's grandmother. They are all forced to share two tiny rooms in a tenement block. Each day is a fight for survival. While Theodor works as a waiter in order to continue his university studies, Paul has given up his studies to earn money at a shipyard. When he falls seriously ill, the self-sacrificing Inga takes care of him. The two are in love and wish to marry, but so long as she is unable to support the two of them, her grandmother refuses to allow it. Millions of people are suffering as a result of the hyperinflation that began in 1923; the family's privations are somewhat alleviated by the produce that Paul grows on his own plot in Köpenick, a Berlin suburb, and the food they are given by neighbors and a sympathetic American, but they are still barely surviving. On their way home from harvesting their first potatoes, Inga and Paul are attacked by starving workers, who steal their crop. Paul, beaten unconscious, only barely escapes death. But once they have gotten over the shock, they rejoice, for—despite everything—isn't life wonderful?

"Even though Griffith has treated this love story with great devotion and sensitivity, the issue of whether poverty can kill love was not his main concern. He concentrates all of his creative energies on the job of presenting a picture of the inflation catastrophe. He felt he could best do so by having everything in the film revolve around the one problem: food. Every motif in the action, for good or for bad, has to do with securing the most necessary foodstuffs . . . as the comments by the [American] press and the public show—Griffith fully achieves his goal, for the images are harrowing precisely because of their extreme simplicity, and arouse our sympathy."

Anonymous New York correspondent, "Griffiths Deutschlandfilm," *Film-Kurier*, no. 296 (December 16, 1924).

Film Notes:

There were no public screenings of the film in Germany during the Weimar Republic.

Der letzte Mann 1924

The Last Laugh

Germany
Director: F. W. Murnau
Screenplay: Carl Mayer
Cinematography: Karl Freund
Art direction: Robert Herlth, Walter
    Röhrig
Composer: Giuseppe Becce
Production company: Universum Film
    AG (UFA), Berlin
Producer: Erich Pommer

Cast
Emil Jannings: doorman
Maly Delschaft: his niece
Max Hiller: her fiancé
Emilie Kurz: his aunt
Hans Unterkircher: director
Olaf Storm: young guest
Hermann Vallentin: paunchy guest
Georg John: night watchman

Premiere: December 23, 1924, Berlin
First US screening: January 25, 1925,
Rialto Theatre, New York

F. W. Murnau
See page 90

It is clearly difficult for the elderly doorman at the Atlantic, a grand hotel, to fulfill his many duties: courteously greeting guests and seeing them off, carrying their heavy suitcases, whistling to alert taxi drivers to waiting customers. When he gets to work one morning he finds a younger doorman in a snappy uniform in his spot, and he is shocked when the hotel director informs him that he has been demoted to restroom attendant. On the very day that his niece is to be married he is forced to turn in his splendid uniform, which has been a source of pride for many years. To keep from disgracing himself at the wedding, he steals the uniform. During the ceremony he is admired, but when a silly coincidence exposes his deception, he is mocked. Deathly unhappy and without hope, he experiences the darkest moment of his life in the men's restroom. But he is surprised to inherit a large fortune from a grateful client and ends up as a guest in the hotel.

"Although we learn only with mixed feelings that a German film was shown in New York earlier than in Berlin, it is of the greatest importance to emphatically salute this first success of a German film in New York. Anyone familiar with America is aware of the almost insurmountable difficulties standing in the way of the presentation of any film expressly presented as 'made in Germany.'"

Lichtbild-Bühne, no. 144
(December 9, 1924).

"There was a telegram from Hollywood addressed to UFA, asking what camera we had used to shoot the film. It added that in the USA there was no such camera, and no town to compare with the one in our film. The Americans, used to a precise technique, didn't dream that we had discovered new methods with only the most primitive means at our disposal. ¶We had been helped by our use of perspective models, too. In order to make convincing the sequence where the man who thinks he is the most important person in the hotel whistles to summon motor-cars, the hotel behind him had to appear enormous, at least thirty stories high. . . . ¶The view, or rather 'background,' seen from the revolving door was managed by means of a perspective shot of a sloping street 15 meters high in the foreground diminishing to 5 in the 'distance.' The street ran between model skyscrapers as much as 17 meters high—this again caused Hollywood a good deal of astonishment. To make the 'perspective' work we had big buses and Mercedes cars in the foreground; in the middle ground middle-sized cars; and in the background small ones, with behind them again children's toy cars. Farthest away of all, in front of the shops, we had crowds of 'people' cut out and painted and moved across the screen on a conveyor belt."

Robert Herlth, "With Murnau on the Set,"
    in Lotte H. Eisner, *Murnau* (London:
    Secker & Warburg, 1973), p. 67.

Sylvester 1924

New Year's Eve

Germany
Director: Lupu Pick
Screenplay: Carl Mayer
Cinematography: Karl Hasselmann
(interiors), Guido Seeber (exteriors)
Art direction: Klaus Richter (drafts),
Robert A. Dietrich (execution)
Editing: Luise Heilborn-Körbitz
Production company: Rex-Film, Berlin
Producer: Lupu Pick

Cast
Eugen Klöpfer: tavern owner
Edith Posca: his wife
Frieda Richard: his mother
Also featuring: Karl Habacher, Julius E.
Herrmann

Premiere: January 3, 1924, Berlin

Lupu Pick
Born January 2, 1886, Jassy,
Romania; died March 7, 1931, Berlin

Selected Weimar films: *Tötet nicht
mehr!/Misericordia—Tötet nicht
mehr!* (1919), *Der Dummkopf* (1920),
Scherben (1921), *Eine Nacht in
London/A Night in London* (1928),
Gassenhauer (1931)

On New Year's Eve a tavern owner wishes to celebrate with his wife away from his guests. Suddenly his mother turns up. His wife reluctantly sets a third place at the table; the two women dislike each other, and he is able to calm his wife for only a short time before they erupt in a violent quarrel. Unable to face the conflict, he locks himself in a room. When his drunken guests break down the door, they are shocked to discover his corpse.

"In the subtitle, Carl Mayer calls *Sylvester* 'a light show.'" . . . He doubtless meant to show as well the light and darkness in man himself, in his soul. The eternal alternation of light and shadow in people's emotional relationships. At least this was what the subtitle suggested to me. When I read the script, I was captivated by the universality of the material. And I wanted to communicate to the viewer the feelings I had while reading it. . . . During the course of the production . . . I recognized more and more that here an eternal and universal subject is masterfully captured—at least in the script—in the events of a single hour. An hour that men spend in senseless celebration, oddly enough, instead of in self-reflection, which would be more logical. ¶As for the book itself: in my opinion it fulfills the prerequisites of a film script if only because in the reading it not only conveys purely visual sequences of images. To an even greater degree it triggers purely emotional sensations that move all of us. Watching the three people flay each other emotionally in their narrow quarters, one feels with each one the pain of wanting to be nice to the others, in truth, but being unable to."

Lupu Pick, foreword to Ernst Angel, ed., *Sylvester: Ein Lichtspiel* (Potsdam: Gustav Kiepenheuer, 1924), pp. 9–10.

"I saw *The Last Laugh* [F. W. Murnau, 1924] again the other day and it reminded me that here was a film of which I was, at the time it was made, quite frankly not a little proud. You see, it was I who had at first the scheme that the atmosphere of a film ought to be emphasized by the movement of the camera and that there should be no captions. It was done in the script of my film *Sylvester*, or *New Year's Eve*. . . . ¶In *Sylvester* I told the story of an hour before midnight on New Year's Eve, and the whole film took just one hour also to project. There was a clock in this film showing the time and this clock had to be made dramatic—it had to be the film, the central point around which went all the action. For this it was necessary that the camera should be mobile, able to move at will, smoothly, without fuss. All this I wrote into the script, and pointed it out to the director, Lupu Pick, and the cameraman, Guido Seeber. Between them, they constructed the primitive little trolley. . . . It worked! And as a result of the development of this idea the camera was able to move also in *The Last Laugh.*"

Carl Mayer, "I Remember . . . ,"
Sight and Sound, no. 28
(Winter 1938–39): 157.

Das Wachsfigurenkabinett 1924
Waxworks

Germany
Directors: Paul Leni, Leo Birinski (actors)
Assistant director: Wilhelm Dieterle
Screenplay: Henrik Galeen
Cinematography: Helmar Lerski
Art direction: Paul Leni (drafts), Fritz
    Maurischat (construction)
Props: Paul Dannenberg
Costume design: Ernst Stern
Production company: Neptun-Film,
    Berlin, on behalf of Universum Film
    AG (UFA), Berlin

Cast
Emil Jannings: Harun al-Rashid
Conrad Veidt: Ivan the Terrible
Werner Krauss: Jack the Ripper
Wilhelm Dieterle: the poet/Assad,
    pastry cook/Russian prince
Olga Belajeff: young girl/Maimume/
    Boyar
John Gottowt: waxworks owner

Premiere: November 13, 1924, Berlin
First US screening: (as *The Three Wax
    Works*) May 18, 1926, Cameo,
    New York

Paul Leni
See page 84

The owner of a waxworks hires a penniless writer to write stories about three of the exhibits—Harun al-Rashid, Ivan the Terrible, and Jack the Ripper—that will captivate the carnival public. Because the writer has fallen in love with the owner's daughter, he accepts the job.

"[In all three episodes] it is the demonic power of Eros, sensuality, that exposes the depths of inhumanity. What ties them together is the uniform stylization of forms into the sphere . . . the costumes of the Boyar women of the first act, bristling with gold, the arcaded architecture of the Kremlin, Ivan's stylized canopy bed, and in the third part Harun and his vizier and the palace cupolas and the audacious curve of the palace steps; only Ivan himself and the sages of Baghdad intrude into this spherical world with their Gothic stiffness. But the approaches are full of rhythmic mysteries . . . in several panoramas of the first act . . . the refinement of the close-ups à la Beardsley in the group of dancing Boyar women, the magical veils of Jack the Ripper's overlapping dream visions, and much else. Patterns from the realm of the graphic arts are frequently apparent."

W. L., *Film-Kurier*, no. 270
(November 14, 1924).

"There is scarcely anything weaker as literature than the script by Henrik Galeen: erratic, without inner cohesion, without dramatic development. . . . But what Paul Leni, the 'director,' and Leo Birinski, the 'codirector,' have managed to make from it! We are doubtless correct in assuming that Leni was responsible for the technical direction, Birinski the acting. We must also emphasize the hackneyed explanation that it is Leni the painter who imposes his stamp on this work. The whole production is an artist's whim, a graceful and spirited amusement, in which the picturesque is most important by far."

Dr. M-l [Dr. Georg Victor Mendel],
Lichtbild-Bühne, no. 134
(November 15, 1924).

Film Notes:

On November 16, 1922, Leni bought the world film rights for Gustav Meyrink's collection of stories *Wachsfigurenkabinett: Sonderbare Geschichten* (1908), but neither the film nor the screenplay had anything in common with the book. It is likely that Leni simply wanted to secure the rights for the title for his film.

At the premiere the episodes about Jack the Ripper and Harun al-Rashid followed that of Ivan the Terrible. After the second rejection by the Berlin censors, on November 12, 1924, the sequence was changed: instead of serving as the finale, Harun al-Rashid introduced the internal action. A fourth episode, about Rinaldo Rinaldini, was planned but never realized.

Varieté 1925
Variety

Germany
Director: E. A. Dupont
Screenplay: E. A. Dupont, from the
novel *Der Eid des Stephan Huller*
(1912) by Friedrich Hollaender
Cinematography: Karl Freund, Carl
Hoffmann
Art direction: Oskar Friedrich
Werndorff
Conductor at premiere: Ernö Rapée
Production company: Universum Film
AG (UFA), Berlin
Producer: Erich Pommer

Cast
Emil Jannings: Boss
Maly Delschaft: his wife
Lya de Putti: Bertha-Marie, stranger
Warwick Ward: Artinelli
Kurt Gerron: harbor worker
Georg John: sailor
Also featuring: Paul Rehkopt

Premiere: November 16, 1925, Berlin
First US screening: June 27, 1926,
Rialto Theatre, New York

E. A. Dupont
See page 93

After a long incarceration, Boss is able to leave prison early, thanks to his wife's successful appeal for clemency. But before the prison superintendent lets him go, he wants to know why Boss committed his crime. Boss has previously refused to reveal his motives, but now he relates them in detail. After an accident he was forced to give up his career as a trapeze artist. He subsequently operated a successful beauty contest in St. Pauli, Hamburg's harbor quarter. With his wife and small daughter, he lived a contented existence until a sailor entrusted to his care an orphan girl, Bertha-Marie. Boss engaged her as a dancer and fell under the sway of her charm. Boss took off with Bertha-Marie and went back to his former occupation, this time at Berlin's Winter Garden Varieté, where Artinelli, a famous aerialist, urgently required a replacement for his brother, who had died in an accident. Artinelli and Bertha-Marie began an affair, and when Boss learned of it, he wanted revenge and set a trap for his rival. Having arranged a last rendezvous between the lovers, Boss waited for Artinelli in his apartment, stabbed him, and turned himself in to the police.

"Little of Hollaender's original is left; only the basic idea. What Dupont has written is altogether his own, and a high-quality literary work. . . . ¶But the actual content seems only marginal compared to the rich and powerful description of these three characters who give the film its substance and direction. There is the young woman from who knows where, erotic down to her fingertips, libidinous and corrupt in her deepest soul. Lya de Putti gives her sparkling, hot-blooded life and the kind of exotic beauty that lets us know that she, like Omphale with Herakles, can wind a bull of a man around her little finger— for example the elegant, degenerate, and devil-may-care star performer that Warwick Ward portrays so convincingly, making him likable despite the fact that he is such a scoundrel. . . . ¶The bull we are speaking of is naturally Emil Jannings. This is perhaps not his very greatest performance. The fleshy colossus and muscled show-off is too much in the foreground; the intellectual element is forced to submit to it too much. And yet, how wonderfully he portrays the contrasts between the adoring father, the childishly naive, fiery, and submissive lover, and the brutal, savage god of vengeance! . . . ¶As a director, Dupont devotedly lingers over details in a way that often slows the pace."

Dr. M-l [Dr. Georg Victor Mendel],
Lichtbild-Bühne, no. 232
(November 16, 1925).

Die Verrufenen. Der fünfte Stand 1925
Slums of Berlin

Germany
Director: Gerhard Lamprecht
Screenplay: Luise Heilborn-Körbitz, Gerhard Lamprecht, from the verbal reports of Heinrich Zille
Cinematography: Karl Hasselmann
Art direction: Otto Moldenhauer
Production company: National-Film, Berlin
Producer: Franz Vogel

Cast

Bernhard Goetzke: Robert Kramer
Aud Egede Nissen: Emma, prostitute
Arthur Bergen: Gustav, her brother and pimp
Hildegard Imhof: Gerda
Frieda Richard: Frau Heinicke
Margarete Kupfer: barkeep
Eduard Rothauser: Rottmann, photographer
Mady Christians: Regine Lossen
Christian Bummerstedt: her brother, manufacturer
Paul Bildt: Robert's father, pensioner
Frigga Braut: Gustav's mother, washerwoman
Georg John: her husband
Rudolf Biebrach: livestock dealer

Premiere: August 28, 1925, Berlin
US premiere: late August 1926, San Francisco
First US screening: January 25, 1927, Cameo, New York

Gerhard Lamprecht
Born October 6, 1897, Berlin; died May 4, 1974, Berlin. No exile

Selected Weimar films: *Fliehende Schatten* (1922), *Buddenbrooks* (1923), *Die Unehelichen* (1926), *Der alte Fritz* (two parts, 1928), *Der schwarze Husar* (1932), *Spione am Werk* (1933 [banned 1935])

After three years spent in prison for perjury, the former engineer Robert Kramer is ruined, both socially and financially. His upper-middle-class father has rejected him, and his fiancée, Gerda, has long since left him to marry a stockbroker. Despite all his efforts to find employment, no one wants to give a former convict a chance. Robert's cell mate, Gustav, returns to his squalid, derelict family home. Although his mother earns a little money as a washerwoman, his father wastes most of her miserable income on drink. Profoundly disappointed and without hope of escape from his miserable living conditions, Robert wants to take his own life. Emma, a prostitute, herself despised, prevents him from doing so and takes care of him. Emma is Gustav's sister, which brings Robert together with his cell mate once again. Gustav, along with Emma and other accomplices, robs a wealthy livestock dealer, and when the victim resists, he is stabbed to death. The siblings convince Robert they are innocent, and he helps them flee. Finally, the open-minded manufacturer Lossen and his sister, Regine, give him a demanding task in their Düsseldorf branch. After completing the job successfully, Robert returns to Berlin, where he learns that Emma is dying. She confesses her love for him, and Robert mourns her death. Regine comforts him. The two have long felt more than mere friendship for each other.

"The name Zille, which looms above this film, is programmatic. It stands for the depiction of the proletarian psyche by way of art. This art does not judge. It pictures the proletarian as the product of his surroundings. . . . It presents a slice of the real world and is content to say: this is how it is. Its simple portrayal of reality amounts to harsher criticism of the status quo than any of the published diatribes. . . . Gerhard Lamprecht has managed to evoke the atmosphere of this world in a believable way. The characters become exponents of the milieu in which they live. . . . Lamprecht has achieved what is the ultimate goal of every film . . . namely that the world it pictures comes alive for the viewer."

Heinz Michaelis, *Film-Kurier*, no. 203 (August 29, 1925).

Film Notes:
Heinrich Zille was an illustrator known for his depictions of working-class Berliners.

Wege zu Kraft und Schönheit 1925
The Way to Strength and Beauty

Germany
Director: Wilhelm Prager
Screenplay: Nicholas Kaufmann
Scientific treatment: Nicholas
    Kaufmann
Cinematography: Friedrich Weinmann,
    Eugen Hrich, Friedrich Paulmann,
    Jacob Schatzow (slow motion),
    Erich Stöcker (slow motion)
Art direction: Hans Sohnle, Otto
    Erdmann, Jacques (also: Jack, born
    Jacek) Rotmil, Depenau, Gustav
    Hennig
Trick drawings: Hanns Büchel
Production company: UFA-
    Kulturabteilung, Berlin
Producer: Ernst Krieger

Featuring:
Ancient Greek gymnasium: Deutsche
    Hochschule für Leibesübungen,
    Berlin
Track and field: Paddock, H. H.
    Meyer, Murchison, Riley, Brown
Boxing: Erich Mielenz, Rocky Knight
Tennis: Helen Wills
Baseball: Babe Ruth
Additional athletic scenes filmed with
    Lloyd George, Minister Balfour, the
    Crown Prince of Norway, Benito
    Mussolini, and Gerhart Hauptmann

Premiere: March 12, 1925, Berlin

Wilhelm Prager
Born September 6, 1876, Augsburg,
Bavaria, German Empire; died April
20, 1955, Prien am Chiemsee, West
Germany. No exile

Weimar films: *In der Sommerfrisch'n*
(1921), *Der kleine Muck* (1921), *Die
Radio-Heirat* (1924), *Die Heimat des
Rentieres* (documentary, 1929), *Nach
Indien ins Tamilenland* (short documen-
tary, 1932)

"A Roman bath is reconstructed with historical accuracy. We witness the procedure in
which lovely female bodies are oiled and
salved before the bath. . . . The present-day
equivalent is set in a marshy landscape. . . .
When . . . suddenly hundreds of people of
both sexes appear, bathing in paradisical
freedom in light, air, sun, and water, we are
transported beyond prudery and accept the
scene as something altogether natural and
a matter of course. . . . ¶[The film] shows
middle-class people of all kinds, shows them
contemplating ancient works of art that
obviously celebrate the nude body—and it
presents the poor and hardworking people
whose labor at modern machines and in
offices leaves them in miserable shape, for
not so much out of laziness but because of
their unfavorable living conditions they are
unable to find any free time for physical
exercise. ¶In contrast to underdeveloped
young people, we see the representatives
of a new race for whom body culture is
uppermost, who know how to strengthen
themselves and stay robust."

Felix Hollaender, "*Wege zu Kraft und
Schönheit*," UFA advertising flyer, 1925,
pp. 5–6. Schriftgutarchiv,
Stiftung Deutsche Kinemathek, Berlin.

"In many cases the trick shots . . . make
extended explanatory text unnecessary, and
the generous use of stop-action photography
not only permits precise study of sequences
of movement normally unseen but is also jus-
tified aesthetically. Thanks to it, the jumper
flies and the dancer floats, seconds are
isolated, and one can actually appreciate
the many positions that make up a uniform
flow of movement. . . . ¶Both the intention
and execution of this UFA film are worthy of
praise. Although physical strength is by no
means the highest good, it is an essential
part of the well-rounded man."

Siegfried Kracauer, *Frankfurter Zeitung*,
May 21, 1925.

Zur Chronik von Grieshuus 1925
The Chronicles of the Gray House

Germany

Director: Arthur von Gerlach

Screenplay: Thea von Harbou, from the novella by Theodor Storm (1884)

Cinematography: Fritz Arno Wagner

Assistant camera: Carl Drews, Erich Nitschmann

Art direction: Robert Herlth, Walter Röhrig, Hans Poelzig (drafts for foreign designs)

Sculptures: Walter Schulze-Mittendorff

Costume design: Paul Gerd Guderian

Composers: Gottfried Huppertz, Hans Joseph Vieth (adaptation for small orchestra)

Production company: Universum Film AG (UFA), Berlin

Producer: Erich Pommer

Cast

Arthur Kraussneck: old Grieshuus
Paul Hartmann: Junker Hinrich, his son
Rudolf Forster: Junker Detlev, his brother
Rudolf Rittner: Owe Heiken
Lil Dagover: Bärbe, his daughter
Gertrud Welcker: Gesine, widowed Countess von Orlamünde
Gertrud Arnold: Matte, maid
Josef Peterhans: Junker Rolf
Hans Peter Peterhans: Enzio, Hinrich and Bärbe's son
Christian Bummerstedt: Christof

Premiere: February 11, 1925, Berlin
First US screening: (as *At the Gray House*) November 5, 1927, 55th Street Cinema, New York

Arthur von Gerlach

Born February 19, 1876, Berlin; died August 4, 1925, Berlin

In Weimar-era Germany, Gerlach directed only one other film, *Vanina* (1922), with Asta Nielsen in the leading role.

Despotic old Grieshuus has two sons: Hinrich prefers the simple country life and wishes to marry Bärbe, the daughter of a serf; Detlev, who craves the courtly glamour of the city, hopes to marry an avaricious countess. Grieshuus becomes so provoked by both sons' demands that he dies of a heart attack. Hinrich and Bärbe wed and assume ownership of the entire family estate. Detlev insists to Bärbe, now pregnant, that the family inheritance belongs to him and his aristocratic wife. The brothers engage in a merciless duel on the moors, which ends with Detlev's death and Hinrich fleeing the castle. Bärbe dies giving birth to a boy, Enzio. Ten years later Hinrich returns to the castle, unrecognized. Detlev's widow hates Enzio and has him abducted. Hinrich pursues the kidnapper and brings his son to safety but is mortally wounded in the process. He dies assured that Enzio knows who has saved his life.

"There [on the UFA studio lot in Potsdam-Babelsberg] Gerlach created the important parts: night shots by torchlight and with breathtaking movement. The abduction scene is extremely successful. And then when the fugitive father is put on the trail of the abductor by the spirit of the dead mother, which flashes up like a flame in the lonely heath, we are wholly captivated by the successive images."

C. Haensel, *Deutsche Allgemeine Zeitung*, February 14, 1925.

Film Notes:

After the Berlin premiere UFA issued two shorter versions of the film, under the titles *Um das Erbe von Grieshuus* and *Junker Hinrichs verbotene Liebe*. In the US a considerably shortened version of *Zur Chronik von Grieshuus* was distributed.

Die Brüder Schellenberg 1926
The Two Brothers

Germany
Director: Karl Grune
Screenplay: Willy Haas, Karl Grune,
   from the novel by Bernhard
   Kellermann (1925)
Cinematography: Karl Hasselmann
Trick camera: Helmar Lerski
Special effects: Ernst Kunstmann
Art direction: Karl Görge, Kurt Kahle
Musical arrangement for premiere:
   Werner Richard Heymann
Conductor at premiere: Ernö Rapée
Production company: Universum Film
   AG (UFA), Berlin
Producer: Erich Pommer

Cast
Conrad Veidt: Wenzel Schellenberg
   and Michael Schellenberg
Lil Dagover: Esther Raucheisen
Liane Haid: Jenny Florian
Henry de Vries: Raucheisen, factory
   owner
Werner Fuetterer: Georg Weidenbach
Bruno Kastner: Kaczinsky
Julius Falkenstein: Esther's first admirer
Wilhelm Bendow: Esther's second
   admirer
Erich Kaiser-Titz: Esther's third admirer
Paul Morgan: profiteer
Jaro Fürth: extortionist
Frieda Richard: impoverished widow

Premiere: March 22, 1926, Berlin

Karl Grune
See page 97

The Schellenberg brothers have conflicting natures: Wenzel ruthlessly pursues his own interests, and Michael feels morally obligated to serve the good of mankind. Both are employed at an explosives factory, Michael as a chief engineer, Wenzel as the owner's secretary. An explosion destroys the factory, and the death of a number of workers leaves Raucheisen, the owner, unmoved. All that matters to him is collecting the insurance. When he dismisses Wenzel for being late, Michael resigns in protest and subsequently devotes himself to housing for an unemployed workers' colony. Wenzel, on the other hand, acquires a fortune speculating on the stock exchange. His lover, Jenny Florian, is engaged to Georg Weidenbach, a worker who was hurt in the explosion. While Wenzel is promoting Jenny's acting career, Michael gives Georg work in the housing project. Wenzel soon grows tired of his lover and turns to Raucheisen's daughter, Esther. Even though she loves Kaczinsky, Wenzel forces her to marry him. When Jenny discovers her lover's betrayal, she attempts to take her own life but only succeeds in wounding herself badly. Michael takes care of her. Esther's affair with Kaczinsky drives Wenzel to madness, and he kills her. Jenny and Georg reconcile and decide to follow the alternative lifestyle that Michael has begun to realize.

"He says little, speaking slowly and with long pauses. His thinking is slow and deliberate. He has time, for he knows what he wants. . . . He has seen five hundred faces today: he fills each bit part himself. He is dead tired. But he is ready to discuss, for two hours, a small scene in the manuscript that has to be changed. . . . Like all truly logical men, he is outwardly sometimes illogical. He can never be talked into anything but can be swayed. If a scene is suggested to him and he can't picture it, he will reject it. But over the course of the day the author sees it with increasing clarity. The next morning he is able to perform it for him, in an awkward, dilettantish manner, of course. . . . Grune thinks for five minutes, ten minutes. Then he corrects this and that false nuance—and accepts the rest. I have the feeling that it was finally when working with Grune that I learned to create a scene that is authentic in every respect."

   Willy Haas, "Zusammenarbeit mit
   Karl Grune," *Film-Kurier*, no. 218
   (September 16, 1925).

Die Geschichte des Prinzen Achmed/ Die Abenteuer des Prinzen Achmed 1926

The Adventures of Prince Achmed

Germany

Director: Lotte Reiniger

Screenplay: Lotte Reiniger, based on tales from *One Thousand and One Nights*

Silhouettes and animation: Lotte Reiniger

Collaborators: Walther Ruttmann (moving backgrounds), Berthold Bartosch, Carl Koch (production manager), Alexander Kardan, Walter Türck, Lore Leudesdorff

Composer: Wolfgang Zeller

Production company: Comenius-Film, Berlin

Producer: Louis Hagen

Premiere: May 2, 1926, Berlin

First German screening: September 3, 1926, Berlin

First US screening: February 26, 1931, Town Hall, New York

Lotte (born Charlotte) Reiniger

Born June 2, 1899, Berlin; died June 19, 1981, Dettenhausen, West Germany. Exile: 1933–36: worked in France and Germany; 1936: went into exile in England; 1939: settled in Italy; 1944: moved briefly back to Berlin before returning to England; 1980: moved to Dettenhausen

Selected Weimar films: *Das Ornament des verliebten Herzens* (1919), *Aschenputtel* (1922), *Dr. Dolittle und seine Tiere* (three short films, 1928), *Zehn Minuten Mozart* (1930), *Harlekin* (1931)

Prince Achmed, the son of the high caliph, has saved his sister, Dinarsade, from an evil, predatory magician, who takes revenge by having a magic horse carry Achmed into the sky. The courageous prince manages to return to earth, and on the island of Wakwak he falls in love with the island's beautiful ruler, Paribanu, and takes her with him on a voyage. But the magician steals her to marry her off to the emperor of China. With the help of a good witch and Aladdin with his magic lamp, the prince manages to free Paribanu.

"The important thing is that Lotte Reiniger has built upon something old while creating something new. The shadow play, whose roots go back to the thirteenth century, has been brilliantly refashioned for our own time. The Romanticism of a poetic era that produced an Andersen and the Brothers Grimm has found a new champion in this woman, who in arduous, devoted labor has created the cinematic fairy tale. . . . The magical creatures and marvels of myth and the skaldic imagination have been revived: serpents, dragons, monsters, the Greek Hydra, the magician of romance, the German witch. . . . How delicate is Achmed's profile, how elegantly curved the body of the caliph's daughter. How lovingly the cut of the shoes, veils, and garments, how exquisite the colorful decor. Forests, mountains and landscapes, sky and sea are suggested in large strokes in the background. . . . Storm clouds, suddenly illuminated by lightning, sweep by, circles of fire flicker upward. In front of them we see the love-struck prince, his lamenting lover, the gruesome magician, the ugly witch. This romantic film, foreshadowed in Lotte Reiniger's scissor cuts, has created for itself the stylized stage."

Hans-Walther Betz, *Der Film*, no. 26 (September 15, 1926).

Film Notes:

This is the world's first full-length animated film (Ephraim Katz, *The Film Encyclopedia*, 5th ed. [New York: Collins, 2005], p. 1,173).

Between 1923 and 1926, two hundred and fifty thousand shots were made for this film; one hundred thousand were used, to create sixty-six minutes of running time. Fifty-two separate shots were required for two seconds of film.

The Pleasure Garden 1926

Irrgarten der Leidenschaft

Germany and Great Britain
Director: Alfred Hitchcock
Assistant director: Alma Reville
Editing: Alma Reville
Screenplay: Eliot Stannard, from
   the novel by Oliver Sandys (aka
   Marguerite Florence Barclay,
   1923)
Cinematography: Gaetano di
   Ventimiglia
Art direction: Ludwig Reiber
Production companies: Emelka,
   Munich; Gainsborough, London
Producer: Michael Balcon

Cast
Virginia Valli: Patsy Brand
Carmelita Geraghty: Jill Cheyne (British
   version), Jane Gill (German version)
Miles Mander: Levet (British version),
   Levett (German version)
John Stuart: Hugh Fielding (British ver-
   sion), Bill Brown (German version)
Ferdinand Martini: Mr. Sidey
Florence Helminger: Mrs. Sidey
Georg Heinrich Schnell: Oscar
   Hamilton
Karl Falkenberg: Prince Ivan

Premiere: January 8, 1926, Berlin
British release: January, 1927, London

Alfred Hitchcock
Born August 13, 1899, Leytonstone
(now London), England; died April 29,
1980, Los Angeles

Hitchcock worked on two other
German-British films during the years of
the Weimar Republic: he directed *The
Mountain Eagle/Der Bergadler* (1926)
and worked as the assistant director
and set designer, as well as on the
screenplay, for *The Blackguard/Die
Prinzessin und der Geiger* (Graham
Cutts, 1925).

The amicable dancer Patsy Brand is rehears-
ing her ensemble for the opening of a
revue in The Pleasure Garden, a London
theater. Jill Cheyne, an ambitious provincial dancer, gets a part in the production
with Patsy's support and even convinces the
director to give her a solo. The two women
share a sublet in the home of Mr. and Mrs.
Sidey. Jill's fiancé, Hugh Fielding, is about
to leave for an extended stay in the trop-
ics with his friend Levet. While they celebrate Jill's triumph as a dancer and Hugh's
departure in a luxurious restaurant, Jill flirts
with Ivan, a Russian prince. Patsy assures
Hugh that she will prevent Jill from doing
anything stupid while he is away, but Jill
leaves Hugh for the prince. Meanwhile,
Patsy and Levet become closer and soon
marry. After her husband departs, Patsy
hears little from him. In fact he has fallen
in love and shares his home with a lovely
native woman. Levet falls ill and writes
Patsy to tell her; she asks Jill for money for
ship passage, but Jill refuses. The Sideys
pay for her ticket. When Patsy finally
reaches Levet, she catches him with the
native woman who, out of despair, tries to
drown herself, but Levet, completely drunk,
drowns her with his own hands. Believing
himself persecuted by his victim's ghost,
Levet goes crazy. When he tries to kill
Patsy, he ends up shot by a local doctor.
Patsy recognizes that Hugh is the man she
really loves; Jill loses not only her job but
also her wealthy husband, Prince Ivan.

"[Alfred Hitchcock] has a sense of humor
and inserts into a number of serious scenes
some droll idea, so that one's attention is
diverted from the breaks and unevennesses
in the script. The film is directed with such
freshness and vitality, and so skillfully
avoids becoming tedious, that it is surely
among the best films produced by Film-
München so far."

-g, *Film-Kurier*, no. 8
(January 9, 1926).

Film Notes:
The Pleasure Garden was the first film Hitchcock directed.

Berlin. Die Sinfonie der Grossstadt 1927
Berlin: Symphony of a Great City

Germany
Director: Walther Ruttmann
Screenplay: Walther Ruttmann, Karl
 Freund, from a story idea by Carl
 Mayer
Cinematography: Reimar Kuntze,
 Robert Baberske, László Schäffer
Camera monitoring: Karl Freund
Art direction: Erich Kettelhut (hidden
 cameras)
Editing: Walther Ruttmann
Composer: Edmund Meisel
Symphonic themes: "Arbeitsmarsch,"
 "Maschinenrhythmen,"
 "Verkehrsrhythmen," "Mittagschoral
 der Grosstadt," "Sportrhythmus,"
 "Nachtrhythmus," "Berlin-Thema"
Production company: Deutsche-
 Vereinsfilm, Berlin, on behalf of Fox-
 Europa-Produktion, Berlin
Producer: Karl Freund

Premiere: September 23, 1927, Berlin
First US screening: (as *Berlin: A
Symphony of a Big City*) May 1928,
Fifth Avenue Playhouse, New York

Walther Ruttmann
Born December 28, 1887, Frankfurt
am Main; died July 15, 1941, Berlin.
No exile

Selected Weimar films: *Lichtspiel
Opus 1* (1921), *Deutscher Rundfunk*
(1928), *Feind im Blut* (1932); as
codirector: *Der Sieger. Ein Film in
Farben* (with Julius Pinschewer, 1922),
Hoppla, wir leben! (with Curt Oertel
and Erwin Piscator, 1927)

The course of a day in the German metropolis.

"Shooting began, and with it a long
period of physical strain and major tests
of patience for my cameramen and me.
Week after week we would convene at
four in the morning to film 'the dead city'
before dawn. . . . With infinite devious-
ness and prudery Berlin tried to escape my
penetrating lens. . . . Just when it seemed
that—let us say Scene 183 was ready
to shoot, everything changed, for Scene
297 had to be attacked. . . . Each day
the footage was developed, and very, very
slowly, only to me, the first act began to
take shape. After the trial cut I could see
what I still needed, here a picture for a
delicate crescendo, there an andante, a
tinny sound or a fluty tone, and afterward I
once again determined what needed to be
shot and what sorts of subjects I needed to
look for—I constantly changed my manuscript while we worked. . . . Soon enough
there was the problem of shooting at night
and inside. If the film was to become a uni-
fied whole, it was impossible to approach
these shots with the resources heretofore
employed (floodlights, light carriages, etc.).
I discussed these difficulties with my cameraman, Reimar Kuntze, and of necessity
he succeeded in sensitizing the film to the
point that we were not dependent on light
conditions."

> Walther Ruttmann, "Wie ich meinen
> Berlin-Film drehte," *Lichtbild-Bühne*,
> no. 241 (October 8, 1927).

"The novelty of this film is not, as is pro-
claimed, the fact that it has no plot, no
titles. Rather the way it is composed, edited,
pasted together. Its tempo, its rhythm. The
kaleidoscope of thousands of motifs. Not
its juxtapositions, sequences, but its inter-
weaving, blending. It presents, or means
to present, the totality of today's Berlin.
¶From the surge of the sea, across glisten-
ing rails through forests, past allotment gar-
dens, we arrive in the morning in the eerily
empty Anhalter Bahnhof. The symphony of
Berlin begins, swelling up out of motifs of
the early twilight; in ghastly gray streets,
parades of shutters, slinking cats, tangles of
paper slowly chased in the morning wind;
two workers, three workers, individuals
multiply into masses. Out of the streetcars,
subways, and streets, crowds of people
are herded into factories like (parallelism)
cattle into the slaughterhouse. . . . ¶This
is a magnificent, magnificently successful
film. All the more prize-worthy because it
is wholly without abstraction, wholly without stylization, wholly without symbolism.
. . . Nevertheless, films of this kind cannot
supplant feature films. . . . And here we
encounter the flaw in Ruttmann's film, the
flaw that stands in the way of its universal appeal: there is no humanity. Where,
in this tumult of images, is mankind? We
see too many images, too many facades,
too much simple movement. We see buildings, streets, vehicles, but not the people in
them, as they sleep, love, feel, work, hate,
get worn down. We see only technological
labor, no intellectual work, nobody who
reads, writes, conducts research. . . . We
glimpse the face of the city, but not the face
of humanity in its million permutations."

> Kurt Pinthus, *Das Tage-buch*, no. 42
> (October 15, 1927): 1,689–90.

FOX-Europa-Produktion   Berlin.
                                „Die Sinfonie der Großstadt."

„Dirnentragödie"

Dirnentragödie 1927
Tragedy of the Street

Germany
Director: Bruno Rahn
Screenplay: Ruth Goetz, Leo Heller, from the play by Wilhelm Braun (1920)
Cinematography: Guido Seeber
Art direction: Carl Ludwig Kirmse
Production company: Pantomim-Film, Berlin

Cast
Asta Nielsen: Auguste, old prostitute
Hilde Jennings: Clarissa, young prostitute
Oskar Homolka: Anton, pimp
Werner Pittschau: Felix, student
Hedwig Pauly-Winterstein: his mother
Otto Kronburger: his father
Hermann Picha: Kauzke, piano player
Eva Speyer: prostitute

Premiere: April 14, 1927, Berlin

Bruno Rahn (aka Alfons Berthier)
Born November 24, 1887, Berlin; died September 15, 1927, Berlin

Selected Weimar films: *Der Mann ohne Gnade* (1920), *Die Beute* (1925), *Frauen, die den Weg verloren* (1926), *Kleinstadtsünder* (1927), *Ehekonflikte* (1927)

The elderly prostitute Auguste leads a dreary life. When she discovers Felix, a student who has run away from his bourgeois parents' home, unconscious on the street, she takes him home with her. Her housemates are Anton, a pimp, and Clarissa, a younger prostitute. Auguste falls in love with Felix and wants to start a new life with him. She is determined to use her savings to buy a pastry shop they can run together. The pimp, fearing the loss of income, sets up Felix and Clarissa with each other. For revenge, Auguste incites Anton to kill Clarissa but recognizes at the last minute that she must not stand in the way of the young couple's happiness. She tries to prevent Anton from killing Clarissa, but in vain. The police arrest the murderer, and Auguste commits suicide. Shocked and ashamed, Felix returns to his family.

"Nielsen is still a great artist, but her subject matter is outworn. She plays the prostitute that she often has before, working in a red-light district that has been exhaustively explored by literature that is no longer contemporary. This points back to the Strindberg era, and as a social fact has lost its primacy among other social facts that are equally deplorable. Even so, Nielsen towers above the milieu, and even though she does not provide any new nuances, she commands her familiar ones masterfully. . . . She beautifully makes the transition from cynical prostitute to bashful girl in love. Even more profoundly moving is her depiction of disappointment. Her features sag, her suffering turns them into a death mask. . . . Homolka's pimp is of the same stature. He is a consummate blend of vulgarity, dumb loyalty, and infantility. That he succeeds is clear from the fact that his character manages to preserve a certain appeal. Borrowing from earlier models, the directing has managed to evoke the dreary atmosphere with undeniable sensitivity. The architecture is too obviously fake. A scene in which an encounter on the street is indicated solely with the movement of legs is exquisitely executed."

Siegfried Kracauer, *Frankfurter Zeitung*, May 4, 1927.

Der Fürst von Pappenheim 1927
The Masked Mannequin

Germany

Director: Richard Eichberg

Screenplay: Robert Liebmann, from the operetta by Franz Robert Arnold and Ernst Bach, with a score by Hugo Hirsch (1923)

Cinematography: Heinrich Gärtner, Bruno Mondi

Art direction: Jacques (born Jacek) Rotmil

Production company: Eichberg-Film, Berlin, on behalf of Universum Film AG (UFA), Berlin

Producer: Richard Eichberg

Cast

Curt Bois: Egon Fürst
Mona Maris: Princess Antoinette
Dina Gralla: Diana, called Diddi
Lydia Potechina: Camilla Pappenheim, owner of a fashion salon
Hans Junkermann: Prince Ottokar, Antoinette's uncle
Werner Fuetterer: Sascha, Prince of Gorgonia
Julius von Szöreghy: Count Katschkoff
Albert Paulig: prince's adjutant

Premiere: September 7, 1927, Berlin

Richard (born Richard Albert) Eichberg

Born October 27, 1888, Berlin; died May 8, 1952, Munich. Exile: 1933: became Swiss citizen and worked on films in Austria; 1934–36: made films in France and Germany; 1937: made films in India; 1938: emigrated to the US; 1949: returned to Germany

Selected Weimar films: *Sklaven fremden Willens* (1920), *Monna Vanna* (1922), *Fräulein Raffke* (1923), *Die Kleine vom Bummel* (1925), *Die unsichtbare Front* (1932)

Princess Antoinette's family wishes her to marry Prince Sascha of Gorgonia, whom she does not know; instead she has fallen in love with an unknown man who brazenly kissed her in a park. Refusing to marry someone she does not love, Antoinette runs away from home. On the train she meets Egon Fürst (his surname means "prince"), an employee at a Berlin fashion salon owned by Camilla Pappenheim. Fürst von Pappenheim, as Egon is called, is traveling with his former lover, Diddi, and her new admirer, Count Katschkoff. When Antoinette resists Egon's advances, he turns again to Diddi. Katschkoff, who is very jealous and rather aggressive, immediately challenges Egon to a duel; Egon loses and is obliged to kill himself within twenty-four hours, but he does everything he can to circumvent his obligation. Meanwhile he has helped Antoinette to secure a position at the salon, where she disguises her identity by using the name Toni. The mysterious man from the park tracks her down and tells her he is a car salesman; he finds her a delightful, but poor, shopgirl. At the insistence of Prince Sascha, Antoinette's uncle, Prince Ottokar, searches for her with the help of his friend Camilla. Egon, fearing upcoming complications, convinces Diddi to pretend to be Antoinette. Happy to get rid off the annoying Katschkoff, Diddi travels with Ottokar to his castle, where she is presented to an adjutant of Prince Sascha as the princess he is eager to marry. Camilla organizes a glamorous fashion show in Baden-Baden, a famous German spa, to present her extravagant new collection to a wealthy public, and Ottokar, Diddi, and Katschkoff are in the audience. Egon and Toni are afraid they will be recognized and decide to change genders: Toni wears a tailcoat and a mask while Egon wears a female suit. Ottokar finds this "girl" very attractive and arranges a date. At his castle all the confusion is cleared up: Prince Sascha and Princess Antoinette learn that the other is the anonymous person they fell in love with in the park and can finally marry.

"A couple of gorgeous young women are on hand, also the reliable assortment of film comics, and the audience accepts with salvos of laughter each attempt to inject a bit of cheer into its life. The pace is fast, and there is plenty of atmosphere. The cutting is skillful: the director, holding all the threads firmly in hand, never once gives his audience time to reflect. . . . The 'prince' in the Pappenheim firm is played by Curt Bois. A Berlin specialty. . . . Full of beans, always ready to place himself in the foreground; always, even in the largest ensemble scenes, the small, fun-loving soloist."

Hans Feld, *Film-Kurier*, no. 212 (September 8, 1927).

„Der Fürst von Pappenheim"

Der Himmel auf Erden 1927

Germany
Director: Alfred Schirokauer
Artistic supervision: Reinhold Schünzel
Screenplay: Reinhold Schünzel, Alfred
    Schirokauer, from the play *Der
    Doppelmensch* (1910) by Wilhelm
    Jacoby and Arthur Lippschitz
Cinematography: Edgar S. Ziesemer
Art direction: Oskar Friedrich
    Werndorff
Production company: Reinhold
    Schünzel-Film, Berlin
Producer: Reinhold Schünzel

Cast

Reinhold Schünzel: Traugott Bellmann
Charlotte Ander: Juliette
Adele Sandrock: morality president
Otto Wallburg: Louis Martiny
Ida Perry: Frau Martiny
Erich Kaiser-Titz: Dr. Dresdner
Paul Morgan: Herr Kippel
Ellen Plessow: Frau Kippel
Szöke Szakall: manager

Premiere: July 25, 1927, Berlin

Alfred Schirokauer

Born July 13, 1880, Breslau, German
Empire (now Wroclaw, Poland); died
October 27, 1934, Vienna. Exile:
1933: went into exile in the Netherlands;
1934: collaborated on the screenplay
for *De Familie van mijn Vrouw* (Jaap
Speyer, 1934) and spent the last
months of his life in Vienna

During Weimar-era Germany, Schirokauer
was active mainly as a screenwriter in
such films as *Der Stolz der Kompanie*
(Georg Jacoby, 1925) and *Kadetten*
(Jacoby, 1931); as director: *Die Faust
des Schicksals* (1921), and *Mutter
und Sohn* (1924); as codirector:
Der Sprung ins Dunkle (with Ernst
Reicher, 1920)

The archconservative parliament member Traugott Bellmann is faced on his wedding day, of all days, with a grave decision, a crucial test of conscience: should he accept an inheritance of five hundred thousand marks in cash and the nightclub Heaven on Earth, under the proviso that he personally tend to the guests—or decline it in accordance with the moral harangues he has presented in parliament? He does not hesitate very long; he accepts the inheritance but does not tell his wife what occupies him from dusk to dawn every night since their disappointing wedding night. His father-in-law, the nightclub's longtime supplier of bubbly, is astonished to see a person bearing an amazing resemblance to his son-in-law. To keep anyone from recognizing him, Traugott dresses as a woman. When his father-in-law begins to flirt with him, Traugott finds himself in an almost hopeless position. Suddenly his wife appears in the club. When one of the guests begins to pester her, jealousy forces Traugott to reveal his true identity. It is only thanks to unexpected news from the executor of the estate—that the nightclub has been sold—that peace in the family is restored.

"Once again Schünzel plays one of those unlucky fellows who blend a schlemiel-like helplessness with a dose of roguishness and cunning. And it is nice that this time Schünzel, the actor, has not laid on his special color too thick. Used sparingly, it has an even greater effect. In general, the ensemble playing in this Schünzel film is more successful."

H. W-g [Hans Wollenberg], *Lichtbild-
    Bühne*, no. 177 (July 26, 1927).

Die Hose 1927

A Royal Scandal

Germany
Director: Hans Behrendt
Screenplay: Franz Schulz, from the
play by Carl Sternheim (1911)
Cinematography: Carl Drews
Art direction: Heinrich Richter, Franz
Schroedter
Production company: Phoebus-Film,
Berlin

Cast
Werner Krauss: Theobald Maske, town
clerk
Jenny Jugo: Luise Maske, his wife
Christian Bummerstedt: prince
Rudolf Forster: Scarron, court poet
Veit Harlan: Mandelstam, barber
Olga Limburg: spinster neighbor
Joop von Hülsen (aka Joop van
Hulzen): adjutant

Premiere: August 20, 1927, Berlin
First US screening: September 23,
1929, 55th Street Playhouse,
New York

Hans Behrendt
Born September 28, 1889, Berlin; died
probably at the end of August 1942,
Auschwitz concentration camp, Poland.
Exile: 1933: because Jewish, and
therefore unable to work in Germany,
went into exile in Spain, where
he made two films but left the country
before the outbreak of the Civil War;
1936: settled in Austria but unable
to continue his film career; 1938–40:
lived in Belgium after German occupation until arrested by the Belgian
police; sent to the French internment
camp Saint-Cyprien under auspices of
the Vichy government; August 1940:
Paul-Emil Janson, the liberal Belgian
minister of justice, tried in vain to free
Behrendt; 1941: sent to Gurs camp
in February and then Les Milles, near
Marseille, in June; efforts by supporters
like Marlene Dietrich fail to gain him
(continued)

Something horribly embarrassing happens to Luise, the young wife of Theobald Maske, the respectable, considerably older town clerk, as she is leaving church. In the middle of the square, in front of the assembled bourgeoisie, her underpants drop to her ankles. Among the fascinated spectators is the bon vivant Scarron, who works in the service of a prince. Two rooms are for rent in the Maske house, and Scarron jumps at the chance to seduce Luise. With her consent he moves in. Theobald, however, without his wife's knowledge, has promised the two rooms to Mandelstam, the barber. The conflict is resolved with each applicant taking a room. Luise allows herself to be courted by the charming, witty, and elegant Scarron, and finally even agrees to a secret rendezvous with him, largely because her husband has scolded her for her scandalous behavior. Her spinster neighbor removes Luise's last doubts, helping her invent an excuse that allows her to commit adultery undisturbed and without arousing suspicion. Luise shows Theobald a forged letter from her mother, asking her to come visit for a day. Unsuspecting, Theobald agrees to let her go, under the condition that he take her to the train himself. Luise's new accomplice, together with Scarron, is able to remove this obstacle as well. She finally arrives at the isolated meeting place, but to her disappointment Scarron has brought along the prince, who is quite taken with her. Scarron, his vanity wounded, leaves them and gets drunk with Theobald in Theobald's favorite pub.

Mandelstam has seen through Luise and finally opens her naive husband's eyes. Theobald is about to break out in a fit of rage when Luise comes home. He is immediately calmed by the unexpected news that the prince is promoting him to chief clerk and awarding him a decoration.

"Krauss does not hold back. He is uneconomical, a spendthrift. But this acting genius can afford it. Although the entire role is played fortissimo, there is a downpour of inspired ideas. Generations of vassals are summed up by his swollen chest, his goose step. Generations of sentimental philistines skewered when Krauss sings "Die Lorelei." In this role everything is vanity and groveling. When Krauss sits in his office, a tin god, a specter of power—millions of subaltern officials are ridiculed. Krauss sits and does nothing, files piled up all around him. At twelve o'clock he unwraps his sandwich and devours it, each swallow reflected in his fat face. . . . 'The face of the ruling class'—Werner Krauss draws it after George Grosz."
Herbert Ihering, *Berliner Börsen-Courier*,
August 22, 1927.

"If only the German film industry would strike now, we suddenly have a German satirical film comedy that for once will be able to match the American grotesque."
Willy Haas, *Film-Kurier*, no. 197
(August 22, 1927).

entry to the US; August 14, 1942:
deported from Drancy camp in Paris
to Auschwitz and presumably gassed
shortly after arrival

Selected Weimar films: *Alt-Heidelberg*
(1923), *Die Schmugglerbraut von
Mallorca* (1929), *Danton* (1930), *Der
Herr Bürovorsteher* (1931); as codirec-
tor: *Die Regimentstochter* (with H. B.
Parkinson, 1928)

Sunrise: A Song of Two Humans   1927
Sonnenaufgang—Ein Lied zweier Menschen

USA

Director: F. W. Murnau

Screenplay: Carl Mayer, from the story "Die Reise nach Tilsit" (1917) by Hermann Sudermann

Cinematography: Charles Rosher, Karl Struss

Assistant camera: Stuart Thompson, Hal Carney

Special effects: Frank D. Williams

Art direction: Rochus Gliese

Assistant art direction: Edgar G. Ulmer, Alfred Metscher

English intertitles: Katherine Hilliker, H. H. Caldwell

Editing: Harold D. Schuster

Composer, musical score for New York premiere: Hugo Riesenfeld

Composer, musical score for Los Angeles premiere: Carli Elinot

Composer, musical score for Berlin premiere: Willy Schmidt-Gentner

Production company: Fox Film Corporation, Los Angeles

Producer: William Fox

Cast

George O'Brien: the man

Janet Gaynor: the woman

Margaret Livingston: the woman from the city

Bodil Rosing: the maid

J. Farrell MacDonald: the photographer

Ralph Sipperley: the hairdresser

Jane Winton: the manicurist

Arthur Housman: the obtrusive gentleman

Eddie Boland: the obliging gentleman

Premiere: September 23, 1927, Times Square Theatre, New York

First German screening: November 17, 1927, Berlin

F. W. Murnau
See page 90

A femme fatale from the metropolis attempts to destroy the marriage of a young peasant couple. She is coolly calculating and attractive; the husband falls for her, and she incites him to murder his unsuspecting wife. He plans to kill her on a boat trip across a lake from the village to the city. The husband has hidden a bundle of rushes on their rowboat to use as a kind of life preserver, so that the crime will appear to be an accident. As soon as the skiff leaves the shore, the wife suspects what he plans to do because of his odd behavior. Intimidated by her horrified look, he fails to follow through. When the boat arrives at the city, the wife runs away, but he catches up and with words and gestures tries to calm her. They have a good cry in a city café, then attend the church wedding of an unknown couple. These experiences lead them to a gradual reconciliation. On the return trip their boat is caught in a storm and capsizes. The husband manages to tie the rushes onto his wife's body before losing sight of her. He reaches the shore unhurt, but after a long nocturnal search his wife is given up for lost. Since the femme fatale believes her lover has committed the murder as planned, she lures him to the shore of the lake. Beside himself with rage, he pounces on her with the intention of throttling her. But she is saved by the news that his wife has been rescued after all; all that matters to the jubilant husband now is his beloved wife.

"In the future, when debating whether film can be art, people will point to Murnau's *Sonnenaufgang*. . . . With photographed contours of objects and people plus complexes of images flowing rhythmically into and next to each other, it is therefore possible to reveal what resonates between objects and between people: the soul of life, a view of the world's soul."

H. W-g [Hans Wollenberg], *Lichtbild-Bühne*, no. 276 (November 18, 1927).

"Much more clearly than Mayer, the film's author, Murnau reveals how poorly he has managed to create a satisfying synthesis between German and American tastes. He makes a crucial mistake in atmosphere: after the man's frightening murder attempt on his wife, after all the gloomy mood painting of the first part, the tone and acting in the city suddenly shifts to pure comedy: arms around each other, the man and wife cross a wide square, kiss for so long on the street that a huge traffic jam results. . . . In itself, this is very funny, it is just that it belongs in a Harold Lloyd or Buster Keaton film. . . . With this far too swift, far too intense, and (after the altogether kitschy scene in church) far too happy reconciliation, the film's tension is virtually completely erased as early as the second act. The viewer asks himself: So the two are reconciled, now what?

H. P. [Heinz Pol], *Vossische Zeitung*, November 20, 1927.

Film Notes:

Murnau plays an uncredited bit part as a vacationer on a boat (Lucy Fischer, *Sunrise: A Song of Two Humans* [London: British Film Institute, 1998], p. 73).

Die Carmen von St. Pauli 1928
Docks of Hamburg

Germany
Director: Erich Waschneck
Screenplay: Bobby E. Lüthge, Erich
Waschneck, from an idea by
Lüthge
Cinematography: Friedl Behn-Grund
Art direction: Alfred Junge
Production company: Universum Film
AG (UFA), Berlin

Cast
Jenny Jugo: Jenny, called Carmen of
St. Pauli
Willy Fritsch: Klaus, petty officer
Fritz Rasp: Doctor
Wolfgang Zilzer (in the US: Paul
Andor): Nipper
Tonio Gennaro: gentle Heinrich
Otto Kronburger: Karl, the pilot
Walter Seiler: randy Alfred
Charly Berger: Captain
Fritz Alberti: Rasmussen, shipowner
Max Maximilian: Hein, Rasmussen's
old servant
Betty Astor: Maria, Klaus's fiancée

Premiere: October 10, 1928, Berlin
First US screening: July 7, 1930, 8th
Street Playhouse, New York

Erich Waschneck
Born April 29, 1887, Grimma,
German Empire; died September 22,
1970, Berlin. No exile

Selected Weimar films: *Regine. Die
Tragödie einer Frau* (1927), *Die
geheime Macht* (1928), *Skandal in
Baden-Baden* (1929), *8 Mädels im
Boot* (1932), *Hände aus dem Dunkel*
(1933 [banned 1936])

On a freighter lying at anchor in Hamburg's harbor, Klaus, a young seaman, is on night watch. Suddenly he discovers a suspicious figure on board, dressed in men's clothing and dripping wet. When changing clothes, the stranger is revealed to be a young woman. Jenny belongs to a gang of smugglers and has come on board to escape being pursued by the police. She begs Klaus not to let the police know where she is hiding, and he does what she asks. Later, on shore leave, Klaus encounters Jenny in front of a seedy bar. Inside, they flirt under the envious gazes of the smugglers, who plunder the ship's freight to revenge themselves on Klaus. He is dismissed by the shipowner and signs on with a transoceanic steamer. Shortly before it sails, Jenny convinces him not to leave her. He moves out of his parents' house and moves in with her in her room in a harbor bar. On his release from prison, the head

of the gang of smugglers picks a fight with Klaus. The police end the brawl and arrest the hoodlum. Klaus escapes but is taken into custody a short time later under suspicion of having murdered a new, wealthy admirer of Jenny's. But one of Klaus's comrades confesses to the deed, and Klaus is released. Meanwhile Jenny has distanced herself from the crooks. Their happiness can begin.

"St. Pauli is known worldwide . . . and any film that promises to present the story of a Carmen in this unusual place sounds appealing. . . . The Carmen is Jenny Jugo. She brings with her a sensual, relaxed expressiveness; she has a frivolous kind of charm, a bewildering erotic playfulness. But the role is flawed: this wild, seductive Carmen is actually a Maid of Orléans. One can hardly believe that she has maintained her purity in the midst of these wild thugs, these aggressive crooks. But it is true. And this forces the actress to hold back when she should actually let herself go."
P. M., *Lichtbild-Bühne*, no. 245
(October 11, 1928).

Film Notes:
The film was banned by censors on May 28, 1928; on July 25, 1928, after required cuts, it was released for adult viewing.

Geschlecht in Fesseln 1928
Sex in Fetters

Germany
Director: Wilhelm Dieterle
Screenplay: Herbert Juttke, Georg C.
    Klaren
Cinematography: Walter Robert Lach
Art direction: Max Knaake, Fritz
    Maurischat
Production company: Essem-Film,
    Berlin

Cast
Wilhelm Dieterle: Franz Sommer,
    engineer
Mary Johnson: Helene Sommer, his wife
Gunnar Tolnæs: Steinau
Paul Henckels: privy councilor,
    Helene's father
Hans Heinrich von Twardowski: Alfred
Gerd Briese: public prosecutor
Hugo Werner-Kahle: member of
    parliament
Carl Goetz: prisoner

Premiere: October 24, 1928, Berlin

Wilhelm (in the US: William) Dieterle
Born July 15, 1898, Ludwigshafen
am Rhein, German Empire; died
December 9, 1972, Ottobrunn, West
Germany. Exile: 1930: emigrated to
the US, directed German-language
versions of films for First National
Pictures, a subsidiary of Warner Bros;
1933: ended a seven-year contract
with Warner Bros; 1941–42: director
of the William Dieterle Production
Company at RKO; 1945 onward:
directed films for studios including
MGM, Selznick, and Paramount;
1958: returned to Germany as an
American citizen; produced mainly
stage and television plays

Selected Weimar films: *Der Mensch
am Wege* (1923), *König für einen
Tag* (1927), *Die Heilige und ihr Narr*
(1928), *Ludwig der Zweite, König von
Bayern* (1930), *Eine Stunde Glück*
(1930)

The impoverished, unemployed engineer Franz Sommer is sentenced to a year and a half in prison for accidentally killing someone while trying to protect his wife, Helene, a bar waitress, from an importunate patron. In prison Franz gets to know Steinau, another prisoner awaiting trial, who has been wrongly denounced as a smuggler. Steinau is shocked by the psychological damage caused by inmates' forced sexual abstinence; on his release he reports the inhumane conditions in the prison to a member of parliament. He also takes care of Helene, just as he promised Franz he would. She obtains from Steinau a position in his firm, and the two fall in love. Despite guilty consciences, they finally give in to their desires. Meanwhile, Franz has sex with a younger inmate. When he is released and returns to Helene, the envious Steinau recognizes that the two still love each other. Nevertheless, their respective infidelities stand in the way of an untroubled, happy relationship. Distraught over their seemingly hopeless situation, Franz and Helene commit suicide.

"A film that does not make for banal conversation. . . . A work written with the iron stylus of seminal realism, captured by the camera as though with the human eye, which is accustomed to seeing things objectively and unadorned. Sexual needs, things that one otherwise tends to dismiss in a whisper, have been handled with seriousness and honesty, though with the necessary discretion, so freely and openly that one has to have strong nerves to be able to follow the plot. ¶Dieterle in the main role. Dieterle as director. Two artistic triumphs, two peak performances. The portrayal of rare simplicity, with no posturing, unstarlike, and precisely for that reason so effective, so shattering."

Welt am Montag, October 29, 1928.

Heimkehr 1928

Homecoming

Germany
Director: Joe May
Screenplay: Fred Majo (aka Joe May), Fritz Wendhausen, from the novel *Karl und Anna* (1927) by Leonhard Frank
Cinematography: Günther Rittau
Second camera: Konstantin Irmen-Tschet
Art direction: Julius von Borsody (drafts), Artur Schwarz (construction)
Art advisor: Alexander Arenstam
Editing: Joe May
Production company: Universum Film AG (UFA), Berlin
Producer: Erich Pommer

Cast
Lars Hanson: Richard
Dita Parlo: Anna, Richard's wife
Gustav Fröhlich: Karl
Also featuring: Theodor Loos, Philipp Manning

Premiere: August 29, 1928, Berlin
First US screening: November 17, 1928, Paramount Theatre, New York

Joe May (born Julius Otto Mandl)
Born November 7, 1880, Vienna; died April 29, 1954, Hollywood. Exile: 1934: went into exile in the US with his wife, the actress Mia May

Selected Weimar films: *Fräulein Zahnarzt* (1919), *Das indische Grabmahl* (two parts, 1921), *Der Farmer aus Texas* (1925), *Ihre Majestät die Liebe* (1931), *. . . und das ist die Hauptsache* (1931)

Two German soldiers, Richard and Karl, have been captured by the Russians during World War I. As prisoners of war on the steppes of Siberia, Richard talks to Karl about Anna, whom he loves more than anything, and soon Karl knows as much about her as her husband does. They decide to escape across the steppes and back to Hamburg. The journey is endless. Karl carries the exhausted Richard on his back, but when the Cossacks turn up, he leaves Richard helpless in the wilderness in order to save himself. Karl makes his way to Hamburg, where Anna takes him in, and over time they develop a deep affection for each other. Richard manages to return to Anna and feels deceived by her and Karl. Richard considers shooting Karl but fails to follow through, recognizing that they love each other sincerely, but Karl surrenders Anna to his comrade.

"How many principles and theories had to fall before air and working space could be created for the new form of the international German film, which is finally here! Complete separation from the avant-garde, no concession to the experts, rejection of overelaborate sets. . . . The anguish of a universal subject; since Pommer has not yet discovered civilian beauty, he once again called on the uniform. And the world war—this indispensable background in front of which the individual fate takes on such clear outlines. . . . The Chinese, the Americans, the Russians, the Austrians, the English—they are all driven by yearning for the wives back home. All people understand this. Also marriage troubles, the Enoch Arden who comes home too late, the need of the woman who chooses a new bed partner. They will also understand Anna and Karl. The Coolies, the Yankees, the Japanese, the Berliners. . . . Joe May—without giving full rein to his individualism—has accomplished the gigantic task of making his characters understandable to a collective soul. The ticking of the clock, the water dripping in the drain—he takes these as seriously as the distant but powerful visions of the lead mines, the harbor life, the train-station bustle. . . . The camera is aimed at the head. But what matters is the heart. . . . An astounding range of light and shadow effects is seen in almost every new scene: the background for the light—is darkness. . . . Wholesome eroticism—healthy dalliance. One breathes freely. The suffocating air of excessive German psychology, the oppressive sultriness has been banished from the studio. Pommer brought this breath of fresh air from America. It is the most remarkable aspect of the whole affair. Between the girl and the lady there is still a middle creature: the woman."

Ernst Jäger, *Film-Kurier*, no. 207 (August 30, 1928).

Zuflucht 1928
Refuge

Germany
Director: Carl Froelich
Screenplay: Friedrich Raff, from an
    idea by Walter Supper
Cinematography: Gustave Preiss
Art direction: Franz Schroedter
Production company: Universum Film
    AG (UFA), Berlin
Producers: Henny Porten, Carl
    Froelich, Wilhelm von Kaufmann

Cast
Henny Porten: Hanne Lorek
Franz (in the US: Francis) Lederer:
    Martin Falkhagen
Max Maximilian: old Schurich
Margarete Kupfer: his wife
Alice Hechy: their daughter
Carl de Vogt: Kölling, butcher's
    apprentice
Mathilde Suffin: Frau Falkhagen
Bodo Bronsky: Bodo Falkhagen
Lotte Stein: Marie Jankowsky

Premiere: August 3, 1928, Berlin

Carl Froelich
Born May 5, 1875, Berlin; died
February 12, 1953, Berlin. No exile

Selected Weimar films: *Die
Liebschaften der Käthe Kruse* (1919),
Die Brüder Karamasoff (1920), *Irrende
Seelen* (1921), *Die Nacht gehört uns*
(1929), *Luise, Königin von Preussen*
(1931)

Martin, a communist, fled to Bolshevist Russia following the German Revolution of 1918–19. Years later he returns to Berlin, his hometown, disillusioned and in poor health. Because of a falling-out with his upper-middle-class parents before he left for Russia, he spends the night in the shed of an allotment garden instead of asking them for a place to stay. The garden's owner, Frau Schurich, and her lodger Hanne Lorek discover him there and immediately take to the exhausted, needy intruder. He is later arrested during a raid in the allotment garden, but Frau Schurich manages to get him released. She takes him in, but her husband and another lodger let him know that he is unwelcome. He leaves, and Hanne promptly leaves as well, and they both move in with her girlfriend Marie Jankowsky. Hanne works hard in the market halls but also, with great self-sacrifice, takes care of the uncommunicative Martin. They gradually become deeply fond of each other. Martin finds a job at a building site, and Hanne becomes pregnant, but their happiness is short-lived: he becomes incurably ill with consumption. At Hanne's urging he reconciles with his mother, but he dies in the hospital on the day they are to be married. His well-to-do mother and proletarian lover are left to raise the baby together.

"Carl Froelich has had the courage to display what he has learned from current Russian filmmaking. . . . There are hardly any traditional formulas, there is no coy prettifying, no one acts 'cute'; indeed, the outstanding Henny Porten is not afraid to transform herself into a self-effacing Cinderella. This sounds callous, but it is a relief from the traditional teasing of so many film divas, so many directors. ¶The attempt at realism, the presentation of beauty and ugliness as they are, is not yet altogether successful; at times there is a tendency—probably unconscious—to underline too much. But even so: the film is a ray of hope. Despite the plentiful tears on the screen and in the theater."

-i-, *Berliner Lokal-Anzeiger*,
September 1, 1928, evening edition.

"This film deserves credit for giving us a new lover: Franz Lederer. Here we see the unfolding of a great gift, one that gets away from the conventional film-beau formula and combines the intense feeling and masculine ruggedness that we value in [gentleman-hero actor] Ronald Colman. We have nothing like him [in Germany]; here is a talent to cultivate."

Film-Echo, supplement to *Berliner Lokal-Anzeiger*, September 3, 1928.

Asphalt 1929

Germany
Director: Joe May
Screenplay: Fred Majo (aka Joe May), Hans Székely, Rolf E. Vanloo, from a story by Vanloo
Cinematography: Günther Rittau
Assistant camera: Hans Schneeberger
Art direction: Erich Kettelhut, Walter Röhrig, Robert Herlth
Costume design: René Hubert
Production company: Universum Film AG (UFA), Berlin
Producer: Erich Pommer

Cast
Albert Steinrück: chief constable Holk
Else Heller: his wife
Gustav Fröhlich: constable Holk, their son
Betty Amann: Else Kramer
Hans Adalbert Schlettow: gangster, her accomplice
Hans Albers: thief
Hermann Vallentin: examining magistrate
Rosa Valetti: bar owner
Also featuring: Paul Hörbiger

Premiere: March 11, 1929, UFA-Palast am Zoo, Berlin
US premiere: May 3, 1930, 55th Street Playhouse, New York

Joe May
See page 132

Investigating a theft from a jeweler's shop, Holk, a policeman, promptly recognizes that the seductive Else Kramer is the culprit, although she swears she is innocent. To avoid being taken to the police station, Else lures Holk to her apartment, under the pretense that she needs to get her identity card, and then seduces him. On the way home to his parents Holk is plagued by feelings of guilt. The next day he receives from the thief a package containing cigars, a letter of thanks, and his identification, which he had left at her place. Angered by this obvious bribe, Holk returns the package to Else, to whom he is so sexually enslaved that she is easily able to calm him. Suddenly Holk is confronted with Else's criminal friend and kills him in a fight. He confesses the whole affair to his father, a policeman himself, who turns him over to the authorities. The trial ends in Holk's acquittal. He is judged to have acted in self-defense, and Else is given a stiff sentence.

"[In *Asphalt*] several very important scenes take place on a very large thoroughfare. One of my jobs as the film's architect was building this huge set. . . . The large, exemplary studios at UFA . . . gave me the idea of breaking with previous convention and setting up the whole complex structure, despite its size, in the studio. What mattered was that from experience I knew that building a set inside requires fewer and more lightweight materials, since there is no worry about rain and wind. . . . It was . . . to create the greatest possible mobility for the cameraman and his equipment. This was achieved with a mobile camera tower. This complicated structure consists of a lower framework on rubber tires that is easily steered, atop which is mounted a tower standing on a turntable. This tower holds a lift in which the cameraman sits with his camera."

Erich Kettelhut, "Dekoration,"
Reichsfilmblatt, no. 10
(March 9, 1929): 12.

Die Büchse der Pandora 1929
Pandora's Box

Germany
Director: G. W. Pabst
Assistant directors: Mark Sorkin, Paul
  Falkenberg
Screenplay: Ladislaus Vajda, from
  the plays *Erdgeist* (1895) and *Die
  Büchse der Pandora* (1904) by
  Frank Wedekind
Cinematography: Günther Krampf
Art direction: Andrej Andrejew,
  Gottlieb Hesch (born Bohumil Heš)
Costume design: Gottlieb Hesch
Editing: Joseph R. Fieseler
Conductor at premiere: Willy
  Schmidt-Gentner
Production company: Nero-Film, Berlin
Producer: Seymour Nebenzahl

Cast
Louise Brooks: Lulu
Fritz Kortner: Dr. Schön
Franz (in the US: Francis) Lederer:
  Alwa Schön
Carl Goetz: Schigolch
Krafft Raschig: Rodrigo Quast
Alice Roberts: Countess Geschwitz
Daissy d'Ora: Dr. Schön's fiancée
Michael von Newlinksi: Marquis
  Casti-Piani
Siegfried Arno: stage manager
Gustav Diessl: Jack
Also featuring: Hans Casparius, Paul
  Falkenberg

Premiere: February 9, 1929, Berlin
First US screening: December 1,
1929, New York

G. W. (Georg Wilhelm) Pabst
Born August 27, 1885, Raudnitz,
Bohemia, Austria-Hungary (now
Roudnice nad Labem, Czech Republic);
died May 29, 1967, Vienna. Exile:
1910–14: worked as actor at the
Deutsches Theater in the Irving Place
Theatre, New York; 1932–33:

(continued)

Lulu, a music-hall dancer, is irresistible to men. Dr. Schön and his son, Alwa, both desire her. She urges Dr. Schön to leave his fiancée and marry her, which he does. The marriage promptly ends in catastrophe when Lulu kills Dr. Schön in a struggle. She is tried and sentenced to prison, but a fire alarm is set off by Schigolch, her confidant, her music-hall partner Rodrigo Quast, and the lesbian Countess Geschwitz. During the ensuing panic in the court, Lulu escapes. She returns to her dead husband's house and finds Alwa there. He prevents her from phoning the prosecutor to give herself up and convinces her to flee with him to Paris. On the train the couple meets the Marquis Casti-Piani, who urges them to follow him on a different voyage by boat, where they are joined by Schigolch, Geschwitz, and Quast. On the ship Alwa gambles, loses all his money, and ends up—thanks to

Lulu—arrested for being a card sharp. Rodrigo is murdered by Geschwitz. Before the police arrive, Lulu flees with Alwa to London. To survive, she takes up prostitution and is murdered by Jack the Ripper.

"The director Pabst (or his firm) has fetched from Hollywood a Lulu who would have captivated [Frank] Wedekind if he could have seen her: a Lulu who is young, pretty, and innocent, no demon, as early literature critics made her out to be, and no vamp, but a female, a sexual animal who, desirable and desiring, destroys men and is destroyed by them without any evil intent, simply by following her destiny. ¶It is Louise Brocks [*sic*] as Lulu that makes the film a success—to the director's credit he used her correctly, so that one sees a creature functioning as it must. The weakness of the film, in its first half, is mainly that Kortner, as Dr. Schön, opposes the naturalism of his partner with the most labored theatricality, so that two irreconcilable styles collide."

Ludwig Reve, *Berliner Morgenpost*,
February 11, 1929.

directed films in France and England; 1933–34: filmed *A Modern Hero* for Warner Bros. in Hollywood and planned various projects that were never realized; 1936: returned to France, directed a number of films; 1939: took family business trip to Austria (at the time annexed by Germany) and decided to work for the National Socialist film industry

Selected Weimar films: *Der Schatz* (1923), *Die freudlose Gasse* (1925), *Geheimnisse einer Seele* (1926), *Die Liebe der Jeanne Ney* (1927), *Westfront 1918* (1930)

Die Frau, nach der man sich sehnt 1929

Three Loves

Germany
Director: Kurt Bernhardt
Screenplay: Ladislaus Vajda, from the novel by Max Brod (1927)
Cinematography: Curt Courant, Hans Scheib
Art direction: Robert Neppach
Composer: Edward Kilenyi
Songs: "Stascha," "Bist du das Glück, nach dem ich mich gesehnt?"
Production company: Terra-Film, Berlin

Cast
Marlene Dietrich: Stascha
Fritz Kortner: Dr. Karoff
Frieda Richard: Frau Leblanc
Oskar Sima: Charles Leblanc, her son
Uno Henning: Henri Leblanc, his brother
Bruno Zierer: Philipp, servant to the Leblancs
Karl Etlinger: old Poitrier
Edith Edwards: Angèle, his daughter

Premiere: April 28, 1929, Berlin
First US screening: (as *The Woman Men Yearn For*) September 8, 1929, 55th Street Playhouse, New York

Kurt (in the US: Curtis) Bernhardt
Born April 15, 1899, Worms, German Empire; died February 22, 1981, Pacific Palisades, California. Exile: 1933: went into exile in France and England; 1939: moved to the US

Selected Weimar films: *Namenlose Helden* (also titled *Infanterist Scholz*, 1924), *Qualen der Nacht* (1926), *Schinderhannes* (1928), *Die letzte Kompanie* (1930); as codirector: *Der Rebell. Die Feuer rufen* (with Luis Trenker, 1932)

To avert the threatened bankruptcy of the family business, Henri and Charles Leblanc, the firm's directors, see only one way out. Henri, the younger of the two, declares his willingness to marry Angèle, whom he does not love but who is the daughter of a wealthy industrialist. On their honeymoon trip by train to the Riviera, Henri meets the mysterious Stascha and feels immediately drawn to her. She informs him that she despises her companion, Dr. Karoff. Henri succumbs to the attractive stranger, and Angèle witnesses his betrayal of their marriage vows. After the train leaves Stascha and Karoff at the next station, Henri stops the train by pulling the emergency brake and follows them to their hotel. Karoff, who on Stascha's behalf has murdered her husband, threatens to report Stascha to the police if she leaves him for her new lover. Chastened, she abandons her plan and stays with her accomplice, who beats up Henri. When the police arrive to arrest Karoff and Stascha in the hotel, Karoff shoots Stascha and kills her. He is arrested, and Henri ruefully returns to his wife.

"It was a good idea to fill the roles with Marlene Dietrich and Kortner. Kortner did all he could with it, but his part was not forthcoming. Dietrich would be an enchanting actress in America, full of unforced charms. Here she is supposed to play Garbo, whom the German film calls for. Done up with confusing magic. Pity. But in fact as though made for the film."

Ernst Blass, "Filme, nach denen man sich nicht sehnt," *Berliner Tageblatt*, May 5, 1929.

"Garbo presents such a strong narcotic of femininity that it can be bewitching even in smaller doses. Nevertheless: Marlene Dietrich does not try to imitate her, she even anxiously avoids it. There is no question but that she shares with the former a kind of primal affinity."

Frank Maraun [Erwin Goelz], *Deutsche Allgemeine Zeitung*, May 4, 1929.

Fräulein Else 1929

Germany
Director: Paul Czinner
Screenplay: Paul Czinner, based on
the novella by Arthur Schnitzler
(1924)
Dramaturgy: Carl Mayer
Cinematography: Karl Freund, Adolf
Schlasy, Robert Baberske
Art direction: Erich Kettelhut
Production company: Poetic-Film,
Berlin
Producer: Paul Czinner

Cast
Elisabeth Bergner: Fräulein Else
Albert Bassermann: Dr. Alfred Thalhof,
her father
Else Haller: his wife and Else's mother
Adele Sandrock: Aunt Emma
Jack Trevor: Paul, her son
Albert Steinrück: Herr von Dorsday, art
dealer
Grit Hegessa: Cissy Mohr

Premiere: March 7, 1929, Berlin

Paul Czinner
Born May 30, 1890, Budapest;
died June 22, 1972, London. Exile:
1932: went with Elisabeth Bergner
to London (where they were married
the following year) to direct a film,
for producer Alexander Korda, that
was never realized; 1933: remained
in exile in the UK; 1938: obtained
British citizenship; 1939: moved with
Bergner to the US; 1940: worked as a
theater director and producer in New
York after a brief stint in Hollywood;
1950: returned to London

Selected Weimar films: *Opfer der
Leidenschaft* (1922), *Der Geiger von
Florenz* (1926), *Doña Juana* (1928),
Ariane (1931), *Der träumende Mund*
(1932)

Dr. Alfred Thalhof, a Viennese attorney, has speculated on the stock market with borrowed money and has lost everything. Meanwhile his daughter, Else, is in St. Moritz enjoying winter sports with her aunt and her cousin, Paul. In a letter from her mother, Else learns that her father is in desperate need of money to cover his large debts and keep him out of prison. Her mother urges her to beg Herr von Dorsday, an art dealer and old friend of the family staying in the same hotel, to help. Dorsday is willing to pay the required sum under one condition: Else must let him see her naked. Torn between obligation and shame, Else sees no way out but to take an overdose of sleeping pills. Half-unconscious and wearing only a fur coat, she searches for Dorsday in the hotel, discovers him surrounded by guests, fulfills his wish, then falls unconscious and dies.

"Since *Der Geiger von Florenz*, since [Czinner's previous films] *Nju* [1924] and *Liebe* [1927], Elisabeth Bergner has developed a film style of her own. But her effectiveness on screen has been far surpassed by her major stage successes. Why? Elisabeth Bergner did not pose for the camera. She walked, she pranced around it. . . . ¶In this sense *Fräulein Else* . . . marks a pleasant turn for the better. . . . Bergner no longer draws away from the camera, she acts. . . . There is still a trace of understatement, a residual anxiety about the role in this psychologically subtle profile of a young woman, a hesitancy, a reserve, but it is precisely this passivity that lends the figure something strangely veiled and detached. The sixteen-year-old's sense of erotic crisis is prepared in discreet, spare outlines: the transition from enthusiastic athleticism to neurotic nightmare, to hysteria, to suicide. A gradual slipping over, a clouding, a fading. *Fräulein Else* is Elisabeth Bergner's first truly professional achievement in film."

Hans Sahl, *Der Montag Morgen*,
March 11, 1929.

„Jenſeits der Straße"

Jenseits der Strasse 1929
Harbor Drift

Germany
Director: Leo Mittler
Assistant director: Julius Oblatt
Screenplay: Jan Fethke, Willy Döll
Cinematography: Friedl Behn-Grund
Art direction: Robert Scharfenberg,
    Carl Haacker
Production company: Prometheus-Film,
    Berlin
Producer: Willi Münzenberg

Cast
Lissi Arna: prostitute
Paul Rehkopf: beggar
Fritz Genschow: unemployed man
Siegfried Arno: fence
Friedrich Gnass: sailor
Margarete Kupfer: hostess

Premiere: October 10, 1929, Berlin

Leo Mittler
Born December 18, 1893, Vienna;
died May 16, 1958, Berlin. Exile:
1930: began work as director
for Paramount in Paris; 1935–36:
directed two British films, and shortly
afterwards went into exile in the US;
1951: returned to Germany

Weimar films: *Serenissimus, der
Vielgeliebte, und die letzte Jungfrau*
(1928), *Es gibt eine Frau, die dich
niemals vergisst* (1930), *Der König
von Paris* (1930); as codirector: *In der
Heimat, da gibt's ein Wiedersehen*
(with Reinhold Schünzel, 1926)

An old beggar finds a pearl necklace that a rich woman has dropped in the street and puts it in his pocket. A young prostitute watches him with envy, follows him, and discovers where he sleeps at night. Although she does not yet have the necklace, she haggles over its price with a fence at a dodgy harbor dive. There she meets an unemployed man, and they sleep together. As it happens, he lives with the beggar on a boat; urged by the prostitute, he tries to steal the necklace. After a scuffle, the beggar flees, falls into the water, and drowns. A newspaper article about a corpse found in the water reveals that a necklace of fake pearls was found on the body.

"Friedl Behn-Grund harbor scenes, boats, bridges, iron girders, alleyways, canals, mills, chiaroscuro shrubbery photographed from nature, framed, felt, made impressive, make *Jenseits der Strasse* . . . a landscape film of the first order. . . . ¶The action is not important enough and is only vaguely related to the settings. ¶Even so, Leo Mittler's directing is remarkably skilled. He is still just beginning and often wants too much. He follows Russian models, most of all the good master of *Der lebende Leichnam* [1929], [Fedor] Ozep—in the landscape pictures and goblin reality. . . . ¶Lissi Arna very interesting when she flirts, when she smiles, when she simply sits there: like a Pola Negri with touches of [social critic and illustrator Heinrich] Zille. You could almost hear her speak (Berlinish)."

Ernst Blass, *Berliner Tageblatt*,
October 13, 1929.

"In the last third of the film . . . [Leo Mittler] introduces the famous 'short cutting' of the Russians. In the flight of a young man who has murdered an old one, he splices in night scenes with no figures, a bush, for example, that sways in the wind in front of a dark background. . . . The end of the film is marvelous; there is nothing like it in recent German film production. After an episode of lovemaking with the young unemployed man, the prostitute goes back on the street. A fat, friendly man speaks to her, gallantly places her on his right side, and walks down the street with her: his fat belly thrusting in front of the girl's figure."

Hanns G. Lustig, *Tempo*, no. 238
(October 11, 1929).

Der Kampf der Tertia 1929
The Battle of the High School

Germany
Director: Max Mack
Screenplay: Axel Eggebrecht, Max Mack, from the story by Wilhelm Speyer (1927)
Cinematography: Emil Schünemann
Special effects: Alexander von Lagorio, Leon Malachowski
Art direction: Hans Jacoby
Production company: Terra-Film, Berlin

Cast
Karl Hoffmann: the Great Elector
Fritz Draeger: Reppert
August Wilhelm Keese: Otto Kirchholtes
Gustl Stark-Gstettenbauer: Borst
Ilse Stobrawa: Daniela
Aribert Mog: first teacher
Hermann Neut-Paulsen: second teacher
Rudolf Klein-Rohden: mayor of Boestrum
Max Schreck: Benno Biersack, town councilman
Fritz Richard: Falk, town-hall attendant
Fritz Greiner: patrolman Holzapfel
Twenty-five high school seniors and other students

Premiere: January 18, 1929, Berlin

Max Mack
Born October 21, 1884, Halberstadt, German Empire; died February 18, 1973, London. Exile: 1933: being Jewish, went into exile in Prague and then Paris; 1935: moved permanently to London

Selected Weimar films: *Sündiges Blut* (1919), *Die Fledermaus* (1923), *Das Mädchen mit der Protektion* (1925), *Ich hatte einst ein schönes Vaterland* (1928), *Tausend für eine Nacht* (1933)

The students and teachers of a high school on an island in the North Sea are experimenting with a self-determined, communal form of living and learning that is in stark contrast with that of traditional schools. The only girl, the athletic and artistically talented outsider Daniela, is in competition with the Great Elector for the office of class spokesman but loses because she prefers dogs to cats. Offended, Daniela distances herself from her classmates. On the mainland, just across from the island, lies the small town of Boestrum. There, a shady dealer in cat pelts, Biersack, manages to get a regulation passed in the town council, to which he belongs. Henceforth all stray cats are to be killed, and for every pelt Biersack will pay a bounty. The island's students refuse to let this happen.

"The Daniela is taken straight from the book: . . . an austere Amazon among contemporary boys. This sets up the relationship to our time. When in recent years has one seen a German film with such a definite worldview? . . . The younger generation struggling for liberalization. Championing a self-governing parliamentary system that attracts self-reliant, self-confident people. Collaboration between students and teachers. Taking a common stand against the older generation. . . . ¶The commitment of the youth of tomorrow will necessarily be to protest a present that has to a great extent preserved the school of the past."

Hans Feld, *Film-Kurier*, no. 18 (January 19, 1929).

"The bourgeois press is enthusiastic about this 'progress.' A liberal student community . . . which undertakes to rescue endangered cats in the neighboring small town. No erotic conflict, no rebellion on the part of the young people against the tyranny of their teachers: simple shenanigans and games of well-situated youths who cannot even be boyish, like the splendid American scamps, but only as though drilled in the barracks courtyard. A pointless piece of make-believe."

Sozialistische Bildung, no. 2 (February 1929): 62–63.

Der lebende Leichnam (Das Ehegesetz) 1929
The Living Corpse, Zhivoi trup

Germany and USSR
Director: Fedor Ozep
Screenplay: Boris Gusman, Anatoli
    Marienhof, from the play by Leo
    Tolstoy (1913)
Cinematography: Anatoli Golovnja,
    Piel Jutzi
Art direction: Sergej Koslovski, Viktor
    Simov
Editing: Fedor Ozep, Vsevolod
    Pudovkin
Conductor and musical arrange-
    ment for Berlin premiere: Werner
    Schmidt-Boelcke
Production companies: Meshrabpom-
    Film, Moscow; Prometheus-Film,
    Berlin; Länderfilm, Berlin
Producer: Willi Münzenberg

Cast
Vsevolod Pudovkin: Fedja Protasov
Maria Jacobini: Lisa Protasov
Gustav Diessl: Viktor Karenin
Viola Garden: Sasha, Lisa's sister
Julia Serda: Anna Pavlovna
Nato Vachnadze: Masha, gypsy
Vera Maretzkaya: prostitute
Dimitri Vvedensky: Artemev, the
    "good spirit"
Vladimir Uralsky: Petushkov
Boris Barnet: pickpocket

Premiere: February 14, 1929, Berlin
First USSR screening: March 26,
1929, Moscow
US premiere: January 10, 1931, 8th
Street Playhouse, New York

Fedor Ozep (born Fyodor Otsep)
Born February 9, 1895, Moscow;
died June 20, 1949, Beverly Hills.
Exile: 1933: emigrated to Paris; 1940:
before the arrival of German troops in
June, fled by ship from Nice, intending
to go to the US, but was interned in
Morocco by the Vichy government;
August 1941: arrived in New York

(continued)

Fedja Protasov wishes to divorce his wife, Lisa, because she loves another man, but the Russian Orthodox Church refuses to allow it. In order to be able to leave her in accordance with the rigid laws governing marriage during the czarist era, Fedja arranges to have hired witnesses see him commit adultery with a prostitute. But at the last moment he recoils from such a humiliating situation. He attempts to commit suicide but is unsuccessful. Instead, he resorts to a plan conceived by his lover, Masha, a gypsy. He will feign suicide and go underground in a slum as a "living corpse." Lisa declares her husband dead and marries Karenin. But when it turns out that Fedja is still alive, both he and Lisa are accused of bigamy. Fedja shoots himself in the courtroom before the final verdict, which rules that their shattered marriage cannot be dissolved.

"My only major acting role was that of Fedja in *The Living Corpse*, which I was not directing. . . . ¶I remember a scene where I stand, peeping from behind the stove, revolver in hand, displaying the half-crazed face of a man on the verge of suicide. I remember that to prepare for that scene I hid myself behind the stove, out of sight of the camera, and, pressing the revolver to my heart, I endlessly repeated the words of Kirillov in Dostoyevsky's *The Possessed*: 'At me, at me, at me. . . .' I thus drove myself into a near frenzy and then peeped out from around the corner. . . . ¶The organic inner coherence was constructed not by suppressing myself but by directly revealing myself. In each individual fragment I was myself in the most literal sense of the word. If there was anything

new or different about me, it was created purely as a result of the montage."
    Vsevolod Pudovkin, "The Actor in Film," 1933–34, in Pudovkin, *Selected Essays*, Richard Taylor, ed. (Calcutta: Seagull Books, 2006), pp. 294–95.

"The Pudovkin case—Fedja amounts to a stylistic revolution. A revolt against the star performer. Pudovkin is a man who simply plays himself. . . . In his case there are only real emotions to photograph, nothing contrived, no deliberately inflated gestures, no psychologizing fluttering of eyelashes, no close-ups heavy with meaning—he does not want to be an actor playing a character. He simply reveals facets of his own psyche."
    Ernst Jäger, *Film-Kurier*, no. 41 (February 15, 1929).

"The film shows much more clearly than Tolstoy, or at least much more clearly than [Max] Reinhardt's staged version, the struggle against the old Russian marriage laws. . . . The gypsy scenes are composed and intercut so vividly that they virtually anticipate the sound film. The way movement becomes audible, the way the grand interior shots, the massed groupings intensify the sound, the way the single detail shots mute it, the way movements away from and in toward the motif, that is to say spatial dispositions, are perceived acoustically—all this is phenomenal.
    Herbert Ihering, *Berliner Börsen-Courier*, February 15, 1929.

Film Notes:
Other US versions of Tolstoy's *The Living Corpse* include *The Weakness of Man* (Barry O'Neil, 1916), *Atonement* (William Humphrey, 1919), and *Redemption* (Fred Niblo, 1930).

Weimar films: *Der Mörder Dimitri Karamasoff* (1931), *Grossstadtnacht* (1932, German version of *Mirages de Paris* [1932])

Melodie der Welt

Melodie der Welt 1929
Melody of the World

Germany
Director: Walther Ruttmann
Cinematography: Reimar Kuntze
    (in Germany), Rudolf Rathmann,
    Wilhelm Lehne, Paul Holzki
Art direction: Erich Czerwonsky
Sound: Guido Bagier (production
    director), Karl Brodmerkel, Adolf
    Jansen
Editing: Walther Ruttmann, Erna Hölzel
Composer: Wolfgang Zeller
Music: Bernhard Etté Dance Orchestra
Production companies: Tonbild-
    Syndikat (Tobis), Berlin, with
    Hamburg-Amerika Linie (HAPAG),
    Hamburg

Cast
Iwan Kowal Samborski: seaman
Renée Stobrawa: woman
Grace Chiang: Japanese woman
O. Idris: Malay temple dancer
Wilhelm Cuno: as himself, general
    director of HAPAG
Also featuring: Juliska D. Ligeti

Premiere: March 12, 1929, Berlin

Walther Ruttmann
See page 118

An ocean journey with stops in numerous countries illustrates the similarities and differences between cultures.

"One needs to recognize that the sound film, owing to the way it is made, cannot be anything but counterpoint. That is to say that pictures cannot be enhanced by parallel sound. Such an attempt will only weaken them, just like asserting something twice or trying to reinforce a lame excuse with two different arguments. In the counterpoint that makes a sound film the two forms of expression are played off against each other—images and sounds in a meaningful combination. For example: you hear: an explosion—and see: a woman's horrified face. You see: a boxing match—and hear: the roaring crowd. You hear: a plaintive violin—and see: one hand tenderly stroking another. ¶You hear: a word—and see: the effect it has in the other person's face. ¶Only in this way can these two wholly different things, sound and image, enhance each other. If they run parallel, the result is: panopticon."

Walther Ruttmann, "Tonfilm?"
advertising flyer for *Melodie der Welt*, n. d. Schriftgutarchiv, Stiftung Deutsche Kinemathek, Berlin.

"Here, in fact, is a vision of the nature and growth of the world, of the similarity and simultaneity of everything earthly achieved by way of the simple viewing of pictures.

With startling objectivity Walther Ruttmann exposes the rhythmic repetition of the same customs in people's lives: work, commerce, sports, war, theater—a series of juxtaposed motifs of movement that have been pursued from New York to Tokyo, from Berlin to Ceylon, around the whole world, and composed in the manner of a symphony. A triumph of photomontage, of inspired editing, of silent film music. A sound film? Ruttmann uses it only when it arises directly out of what we are seeing: the noise of the ship's motors, of the anchor chains and sirens, the clatter, pounding, and bumping on deck—one gets a sense of the sound film as newsreel, as an instrument of reportage. It is here that its future possibilities lie."

Hans Sahl, *Der Montag Morgen*,
March 18, 1929.

Film Notes:

This documentary with a plot was largely shot in 1928 during a voyage around the world on the HAPAG steamship *Resolute*, departing from and returning to New York, with the camera operated by Heinrich Mutzenbecher. Ruttmann did not go along. This silent material was supplemented with a sound track and interior shots directed by Ruttmann in the studio. The coproducers and several German critics hailed *Melodie der Welt* as the first German feature-length sound film, but others disputed this, pointing to Ruttmann's previous film *Deutscher Rundfunk*.

Mutter Krausens Fahrt ins Glück   1929
Mother Krause's Journey to Happiness

Germany
Director: Piel Jutzi
Screenplay: Willy Döll, Jan Fethke, in collaboration with Otto Nagel, based on the verbal reports of Heinrich Zille
Cinematography: Piel Jutzi
Art direction: Robert Scharfenberg, Carl Haacker
Musical arrangement and conductor at premiere: Paul Dessau
Artistic patronage: Käthe Kollwitz, Hans Baluschek, Otto Nagel
Production company: Prometheus-Film, Berlin
Producer: Willi Münzenberg

Cast
Alexandra Schmitt: Mother Krause
Ilse Trautschold: Erna, her daughter
Holmes Zimmermann: Paul, her son
Gerhard Bienert: night lodger
Vera Sacharowa: Friede, prostitute
Friedrich Gnass: Max, construction worker
Fee Wachsmuth: child

Premiere: December 30, 1929, Berlin

Piel (born Philipp; since 1931 known as Phil) Jutzi
Born July 22, 1896, Altleiningen, German Empire; died May 1, 1946, Neustadt an der Weinstrasse, West Germany. No exile

Selected Weimar films: *Bull Arizona, der Wüstenadler* (1919), *Um's tägliche Brot* (1929), *Blutmai 1929* (documentary, 1929), *Was gibt's Neues heut'?* (short film, 1932); as codirector: *Kindertragödie* (with Karl Lutz, 1928)

Old Mother Krause shares a tiny apartment in a Berlin housing block with her daughter, Erna, and her son, Paul, along with a pimp and Friede, a prostitute who works for him and has a child. The pimp makes advances on Erna, and although she rebuffs them, her lover, Max, becomes jealous; they quarrel and separate. In order to supplement her small income, Mother Krause delivers newspapers. Paul helps her once, but then he squanders the day's income on drink. The pimp, exploiting Paul's need for money, gets him to join a gang committing a break-in. The police surprise the robbers, and Paul lands in jail. Mother Krause sees only one way out. She turns on the gas, killing herself and Friede's child.

"The director Piel Jutzi is promising. Not because he has once again, assisted by the 'Wedding [a proletarian district in Berlin] painter' Otto Nagel, exploited the milieu. . . . Many types are too typical, and the exaggerated gluttony of the wedding guests is a mistake. Also, in his excess devotion to detail Jutzi does not yet understand the art of omission. But he has not simply borrowed the externals from the Russians, as others have, but truly learned from them. His shots of streets, buildings, and courtyards are magnificent, his transitions logically motivated."
    Siegfried Kracauer, "Wedding im Film," *Frankfurter Zeitung*, January 28, 1930.

"We heartily thank Piel Jutzi for fulfilling our old demand that nonactors be placed in front of the camera. Genuine types when picturing a particular area. The Russians have discovered the human face, and this director also works, à la Zille, without makeup, he takes his camera into the housing blocks of East Berlin, he visits the gin palaces, and brings an amazing degree of reality to the screen. . . . It is difficult for professional actors to hold their own against this backdrop. But Alexandra Schmitt manages to—she is staggering, the little old woman with a rounded back. . . . Gerhard Bienert also manages to empathize with the milieu in an extraordinary way; not so Herr Gnass, who can only express his emotions by constantly baring his teeth. As an actor Ilse Trautschold is still somewhat tense . . . but she will be fine once she learns to 'act' as little as possible. . . . Even so, Piel Jutzi's work could have become a textbook example of the honest film (in Berlin!)—if he were not an imitator of the Russians even in the awkward ideology of the intertitle, a follower of the second Moscow film generation; the [political] bias is pasted in with distressing naïveté, an almost touching lapse in taste."
    Hanns G. Lustig, "Tragischer Zille-Film," *Tempo*, no. 2 (January 3, 1930).

Film Notes:
Banned by National Socialist censors on April 22, 1933.

In the early 1920s Philipp Jutzi called himself Piel Jutzi; after the director and actor Harry Piel sued him over the use of the name in 1931, he chose to be called, in subsequent films, Phil.

154

Die wunderbare Lüge der Nina Petrowna 1929

The Wonderful Lies of Nina Petrovna

Germany
Director: Hanns Schwarz
Screenplay: Hans Székely
Cinematography: Carl Hoffmann, Hans Schneeberger
Art direction: Robert Herlth, Walter Röhrig
Artistic consultant: Alexander Arnstam
Costume design: René Hubert
Production company: Universum Film AG (UFA), Berlin
Producer: Erich Pommer

Cast
Brigitte Helm: Nina Petrovna
Franz (in the US: Francis) Lederer: Michael Andrejevitch Rostov, cadet
Warwick Ward: Cossack colonel
Lya Jan: peasant girl

Premiere: April 15, 1929, Berlin
First US screening: May 1930, 55th Street Playhouse, New York

Hanns Schwarz (born Ignatz Schwarz, also: Hans Schwartz [in Great Britain] and Howard Shelton [in the US after the start of World War II])
Born February 11, 1888, Vienna; died October 27, 1945, Hollywood. Exile: 1934: went into exile in the US; 1937: after three years of no activity directed the British film *Return of the Scarlet Pimpernel;* 1938: returned to Hollywood and filmed, for Paul Kohner, *Two Humans in Mexico,* the sound-film remake of *Zwei Menschen* (1923), his German directorial debut; 1944: engaged by the film department of the Office of Strategic Services (OSS)

Selected Weimar films: *Nanon* (1924), *Ungarische Rhapsodie* (1928), *Melodie des Herzens* (1929), *Bomben auf Monte Carlo* (1931), *Das Mädel vom Montparnasse* (1932)

In St. Petersburg at the time of the czars, Nina Petrovna leaves a wealthy Cossack colonel in order to live with Michael, a cadet she loves. It is increasingly difficult for them to make ends meet. Michael risks his last money playing cards at the officer's casino and loses it all to the colonel; the colonel then catches Michael cheating and forces him to confess his guilt in writing. With this admission, which could ruin Michael's military career, the colonel makes Nina return to him. She lies to Michael and tells him that she has been using him for a brief dalliance. At his villa the colonel discovers Nina's dead body.

"The choice of material shows what the producer cares about: drama in its most primal form. . . . A timeless romance is [shifted] far away from modern times. Emphasis on the historical setting is what makes the work so effective. . . . ¶Whether a US import or a German export—the biggest hits appeal to a mass audience. The romanticism of coquettish sentimentality is accepted everywhere. Sardou on film, Dumas illustrated—these are welcomed wherever people seek to forget their day-to-day troubles. . . . The Pommer film has already gone far beyond the typical American smash hit. There, at best, a script is realized with technical perfection in the smallest details, built around the star. Erich Pommer does more: with the collaboration of his writers, his production apparatus, and his actors he has produced a piece of intimate theater on film.

. . . ¶An ensemble film with leads instead of a star production . . . Lederer plays the innocent cadet; the shyness with which he approaches his first sex is altogether believable, with no trace of cuteness. . . . Brigitte Helm plays Petrovna. Now, finally, without convulsions. She is like a lovely, animated picture, dazzling in costumes made to accentuate her figure. When have we ever seen her smile this way, genuinely, charmingly, without the fake undercurrent of vampishness?"

Hans Feld, *Film-Kurier,* no. 90 (April 16, 1929).

"The film exploits all the technical advances, but is deathly boring nevertheless. . . . Every once in a while, the director guides us through some imaginative visual, but for the most part has his actors do only what is called for. When something distressing happens, Brigitte Helm mechanically raises her eyelids the way we raise the blinds when the sun comes up. Out of laziness or a fear of damaging her career, Brigitte Helm, whose movements are the most fluid of film music, and who managed to achieve great things as an anemic creature of the night with a touch of ancient Greece in fantastic, stylized films—think of *Metropolis*—has been forced into the Greta Garbo mold."

Rudolf Arnheim, "Lust- und Unlustkurven," *Die Weltbühne,* no. 18 (April 30, 1929): 677.

Abschied   1930
Farewell

Germany
Director: Robert Siodmak
Screenplay: Emmerich Pressburger,
   Irma von Cube
Cinematography: Eugen Schüfftan
Art direction: Max Knaake
Sound: Erich Leistner
Composer: Erwin Bootz
Musical arrangement: Herbert
   Lichtenstein
Lyrics: Gerd Karlick
Songs: "Reg' dich nicht auf, wenn mal
   was schief geht," "Wie schnell ver-
   gisst man, was einmal war"
Production company: Universum Film
   AG (UFA), Berlin
Producer: Bruno Duday

Cast
Brigitte Horney: Hella, salesgirl
Aribert Mog: Peter Winkler, vacuum-
   cleaner salesman
Emilia Unda: Frau Weber, boarding-
   house owner
Konstantin Mic: Bogdanoff
Frank Günther: Neumann, master of
   ceremonies
Edmée Symon, Gisela Draeger,
   Marianne Mosner: the three Lennox
   sisters
Erwin Bootz: Bootz, musician
Martha Ziegler: Lina, maid
Vladimir Sokoloff: Bàron

Premiere: August 25, 1930, Berlin

Robert Siodmak
Born August 8, 1900, Dresden; died
March 10, 1973, Locarno, Switzerland
Exile: 1933: went to Paris; 1939:
arrived in New York in September
with his wife, Bertha; 1951: returned
to Europe to direct British and French
films; 1954: moved to the Federal
Republic of Germany and worked on
behalf of the producer Artur Brauner
and his company, CCC

(continued)

The illustrious guests in Frau Weber's second-class Berlin boardinghouse include lovers Hella and Peter (a salesgirl and a vacuum-cleaner salesman), the musician Bootz, the deadbeat Bàron, the more financially secure Bogdanoff, the talkative master of ceremonies Neumann, and three dancers, the Lennox sisters. Hella is outraged when she learns from the landlady that Peter intends to move to Dresden the next day for the sake of a new job. She confronts him. Peter assures her that nothing has been decided yet and in fact he was hoping to surprise her with the better-paid position. To his surprise, she advises him to accept the position, leading him to suspect her of deceiving him with another man; on over-hearing Hella on the telephone, he misinterprets her conversation as lover's banter with a rival. Peter's worst fears appear to be confirmed when he discovers a strange man's calling card in Hella's address book. He promptly packs up his belongings and leaves. Hella, desperately unhappy, cannot understand why Peter has left her. Her fellow boarders comfort her. Bàron gives her the engagement ring he found while searching Peter's room. Inside it is the inscription "Wear it always, forget me never."

"Robert Siodmak . . . has understood better than all previous directors how greatly and in what way the sound film differs from the silent film and the theater. The mood music of this sound film from Pressburger and Cube is not an arbitrary addition, but during the hour-and-a-half duration of the film and the plot a young composer, the actual composer for the film, E. Bootz, can be heard improvising at the piano. ¶The people are mercilessly presented in photographic and acoustic close-ups . . . [for example] close-ups of the jealous young man, who asks 'How often have you been unfaithful to me in the last three years?' And one hears, without at first seeing her, her voice: 'One, two, three, four' . . . then the camera pans to the girl, who is packing laundry into her friend's suitcase, and continues, 'five—there was supposed to be another shirt here.'"
   K. P. [Kurt Pinthus], *8 Uhr-Abendblatt*, August 26, 1930.

Film Notes:
The version that UFA brought out a year after the premiere included an epilogue that was not directed by Siodmak (the director is unknown).

Selected Weimar films:
Stürme der Leidenschaft (1931),
Voruntersuchung (1931), *Quick*
(1932), *Brennendes Geheimnis*
(1933), *Le Sexe faible* (1933)

Der blaue Engel 1930

The Blue Angel

Germany
Director: Josef von Sternberg
Assistant director: Sam Winston
Screenplay: Robert Liebmann, Carl
   Zuckmayer and Karl Vollmoeller,
   from the novel *Professor Unrat, oder
   Das Ende eines Tyrannen* (1905)
   by Heinrich Mann
English dialogue: Josef von Sternberg,
   Carl Winston
Cinematography: Günther Rittau, Hans
   Schneeberger
Art direction: Otto Hunte, Emil Hasler
Costume design: Tihamer Varady, Karl-
   Ludwig Holub
Sound: Fritz Thiery, Herbert Kiehl
Editing: Sam Winston
Composer: Friedrich Hollaender, using
   compositions by other musicians
Lyrics: Friedrich Hollaender, Robert
   Liebmann, Richard Rillo
Music: Weintraubs Syncopaters
Songs: "Ich bin von Kopf bis Fuss auf
   Liebe eingestellt" ("Falling in Love
   Again"), "Ich bin die fesche Lola"
   ("They Call Me Naughty Lola"),
   "Nimm dich in Acht vor blonden
   Frauen" ("Beware of Blonde
   Women"), "Kinder, heut' abend
   such' ich mir was aus" ("Children,
   This Evening I Gotta Get a Man,
   Just a Man, a Real Man")
Production company: Universum Film
   AG (UFA), Berlin
Producer: Erich Pommer

Cast
Emil Jannings: Professor Immanuel Rath
Marlene Dietrich: Lola Lola
Kurt Gerron: Kiepert, magician
Rosa Valetti: Guste, his wife
Hans Albers: Mazeppa
Reinhold Bernt: clown
Eduard von Winterstein: school
   director
Rolf Müller: Angst, high school student

Immanuel Rath is an eccentric, aging bachelor who teaches at a small-town high school. Some of his students have been going to see the well-known singer Lola Lola at an obscure club, the Blue Angel, every night; Rath is determined to visit the club and find out why his students are so crazy about her. He discovers one of his students there and, in chasing him, ends up in Lola's dressing room. The student, hiding in the dressing room, witnesses his teacher's quick surrender to Lola Lola's sex appeal. The next morning Rath's class mocks him vociferously, calling him Professor Unrat (Professor Garbage). The school's director silences the clamor and demands an explanation, in the presence of the students, from Rath. When an embarrassed Rath announces that he will soon marry his beloved Lola, he is dismissed from his position. Rath joins his new wife's ensemble and leaves his hometown for a yearlong tour. The marriage swiftly collapses. To earn his living Rath is forced to offer photos of Lola Lola to the public and then serve as an assistant to the troupe's director, a magician. A performance in his hometown, in which he appears as a clown, ends in scandal when Rath notices his wife deceiving him backstage with the actor Mazeppa. He wants to throttle her but is forcibly prevented from doing so and ends up in a straightjacket, raving mad. He is released once he has calmed down and immediately returns to his school; his corpse is discovered in his classroom by the janitor.

"Never before has one seen so clearly how the sound film can be developed into a genre of its own, in many respects by combining or contrasting the methods of theater and film beyond theater and film. For example: . . . The professor humbles himself before the singer, and she says, almost to herself: 'Na, ja!' [Whatever!]. But after the silent acting that precedes it, this single, loaded comment would have had to be replaced by a number of sentences in stage dialogue, or in a silent film by any number of gestures to capture her complex feminine feelings: triumph, sympathy, indifference, obtuseness. A kind of sound-film dialogue is being developed in which nothing more is said to show that something can be said, but in which, in fact, in that brief phrase something that defines the character or drives the plot has to be said. . . . With the sound film *Der blaue Engel*, German production is therefore beginning to match worldwide production, after its absurd musicals so alien to film in their stiffness and after the soldier-filled sound films based in Hungary and other operetta settings, with both its technical and . . . intellectual qualities, namely its motifs descriptive of character, its depiction of setting."

Kurt Pinthus, *Das Tage-Buch*, no. 14
   (April 5, 1930): 546–47.

Roland Varno: Lohmann, high school
    student
Karl Balhaus: Ertzum, high school
    student
Robert Klein-Lörk, Goldstaub, high
    school student
Karl Huszar-Puffy: innkeeper
Wilhelm Diegelmann: captain
Gerhard Bienert: policeman
Ilse Fürstenberg: Rath's housekeeper
Friedrich Hollaender: piano player
Weintraubs Syncopaters: musicians

Premiere: April 1, 1930, Berlin
British trade preview: July 3, 1930,
London
First British screening: August 2,
1930, Regal Theatre, London
First US screening: December 5,
1930, Rialto Theatre, New York

Josef von Sternberg (born Jonas
Sternberg)
Born May 29, 1894, Vienna; died
December 22, 1969, Hollywood.
No exile

Der blaue Engel is Sternberg's only
German film.

Cyankali 1930

Germany
Director: Hans Tintner
Screenplay: Hans Tintner, from the play
Cyankali Paragraph 218 (1929)
by Friedrich Wolf
Cinematography: Günther Krampf
Art direction: Franz Schroedter
Composer: Willy Schmidt-Gentner
Production company: Atlantis-Film, Berlin

Cast
Grete Mosheim: Hete Fent
Nico Turoff: Paul, her fiancé
Herma Ford: her mother
Claus Clausen: Max, Paul's friend
Louis Ralph: Prosnik, building
 superintendent
Josefine Dora: Frau Klee
Else Heller: Frau Witt
Margarete Kupfer: Madame Heye
Ludwig Andersen: Dr. Moeller
Paul Henckels: Dr. Meyer
Paul Kemp: Kuckuck
Alexander Murski: Witt
Hermann Vallentin: commissioner
Blandine Ebinger: courtyard singer
Hella Hartwich: lady

Premiere: May 23, 1930, Berlin

Hans Tintner
Born November 28, 1894, Vienna;
died September 28, 1942, Auschwitz
concentration camp, Poland. Exile:
1920s: worked for the Fox-Europe production service in Berlin; 1927: wrote
the screenplay *Das Wochenende. Ein
Film von Licht und Schönheit*, which
was never realized; 1928: coauthored
the screenplay *Heut' spielt der Strauss*
(*Der Walzerkönig*), directed by Robert
Wiene; early 1930s: returned to
Austria and went into exile in France;
July 19, 1942: deported to Auschwitz

Weimar films: *Die Jugendgeliebte*
(1930), *Kaiserliebchen* (1931)

Hete and her lover, Paul, are both looking forward to the birth of their child. They are employed in the same Berlin firm, but following the crash of 1929 the couple and their coworkers are locked out after striking for higher wages. Paul and a friend steal food from the firm's canteen and are arrested. Hete fears that she will no longer be able to nourish her growing baby, so with a heavy heart she decides to terminate the pregnancy (forbidden under Paragraph 218 of the penal code). She turns to a building superintendent who will only help her in exchange for sex. A doctor refuses to execute the illegal abortion, so Hete is forced to seek out a backstreet abortionist who gives her potassium cyanide. Poisoned by the overdose, Hete suffers terrifying pains, which her mother tries in vain to relieve. Hete dies, and her mother goes to jail for assisting with the abortion.

"The film is silent. But in two scenes at the end one suddenly hears the screams of Grete Mosheim, clinging to life with all her strength, finally growing silent as she succumbs to death. These cries of despair, suddenly bursting forth from the silent screen, move us more profoundly than all the sound-film effects we have heretofore experienced."

H. P. [Heinz Pol], *Vossische Zeitung*,
May 27, 1930.

Film Notes:

In April 1930 *Cyankali* was cleared for public screening (but not for minors) by the Berlin censors. The Bavarian government successfully challenged this decision before Berlin's superior film board, and, beginning in late August, the film could not be shown anywhere in the country. After major cuts, the film was released for public screening in mid-December 1930, but it was never shown again in Bavaria.

Die Drei von der Tankstelle 1930
Three from the Filling Station

Germany
Director: Wilhelm Thiele
Screenplay: Franz Schulz, Paul Frank
Cinematography: Franz Planer
Art direction: Otto Hunte
Editing: Viktor Gertler
Sound: Hermann Fritzsching
Composer and conductor: Werner
 Richard Heymann
Music: Lewis Ruth Band
Lyrics: Robert Gilbert
Songs: "Ein Freund, ein guter
 Freund," "Erst kommt ein grosses
 Fragezeichen," "Hallo, du
 süsse Frau," "Liebling, mein
 Herz lässt dich grüssen," "Das
 Lied vom Kuckuck (Lieber Herr
 Gerichtsvollzieher)," "Womit kann
 ich Ihnen dienen?"
Production company: Universum Film
 AG (UFA), Berlin
Producer: Erich Pommer

Cast
Lilian Harvey: Lilian Cossmann
Willy Fritsch: Willy
Oskar Karlweis: Kurt
Heinz Rühmann: Hans
Fritz Kampers: Cossmann, consul
Olga Tschechova: Edith von Turoff
Kurt Gerron: Dr. Kalmus, attorney
Gertrud Wolle: his secretary
Felix Bressart: marshal
Comedian Harmonists
Lewis Ruth Band

Premiere: September 15, 1930, Berlin
First US screening: (as Three Good
Friends) June 19, 1931, UFA
Cosmopolitan, New York

Wilhelm (in the US: William) Thiele
(a.k.a. Wilhelm Isersohn)
Born May 10, 1890, Vienna; died
September 7, 1975, Woodland Hills,
California. Exile:1933: went into exile
to the US by way of England and
Austria

(continued)

Three friends—Willy, Kurt, and Hans—return from a trip and are faced with the harsh consequences of the ongoing economic crisis: they are deeply in debt, and everything in their house has been impounded, except for their dog and their car. They sell the car and use the money to buy a gas station. One of their customers is the ravishing Lilian Cossmann, the spoiled young daughter of a wealthy consul general. All three compete for her affection without telling each other, but their rivalry is accidentally exposed. At the urging of Edith von Turoff, a friend of her father, Lilian gathers her three admirers together in a dancing bar, the Kit Cat Club, in order to finally make the choice she has long postponed. Willy, the one she chooses, ought to be happy, but he reacts in anger, thinking that Lilian has been toying with them. Edith deflects the threatened falling-out between the men with a clever trick: she gets Consul Cossmann to promote them to directors of Gas Stations, AG, a company he has founded, with a new secretary who just happens to be Lilian. Kurt and Hans decline their exalted positions, and Willy personally dictates his resignation to Lilian and signs it. But in fact what he has signed is a marriage contract.

"A sound-film operetta, logically enough complete with song and dance. . . . One can definitely speak of it as a new type of film. . . . Even in the brief musical prelude the composer W. R. Heymann provides a surprise. He introduces the shawm into sound-film music, and thereby into light music in general. . . . ¶The writer Robert Gilbert is in large part responsible for the film's success; his lyrics not only tie in with the dialogue, for the most part, but enliven it, introduce it, continue it, act as a bridge, always in deference to the music, whose unsentimental, lively, and melodic quality satisfies even a cultivated ear."

ps., *Lichtbild-Bühne*, no. 222
(September 16, 1930).

Selected Weimar films: *Das Totenmahl auf Schloss Begalitza* (1923), *Orientexpress* (1927), *Liebeswalzer* (1929), *Die Privatsekretärin* (1931); as codirector: *Die letzte Nacht* (with Reinhold Bauer, 1920)

Lohnbuchhalter Kremke   1930

Germany
Director: Marie Harder
Screenplay: Herbert Rosenfeld
Cinematography: Franz Koch, Robert Baberske
Art direction: Carl Ludwig Kirmse
Editing: Oleg Woinoff
Production company: Naturfilm Hubert Schonger, Berlin
Producer: Hubert Schonger

Cast
Hermann Vallentin: Kremke, payroll clerk
Anna Sten: Lene, his daughter
Ivan Kowal-Samborski: Erwin, young laborer
Wolfgang Zilzer (in the US: Paul Andor): student

Premiere: September 15, 1930, Berlin

Marie (born Marie Margarethe) Harder
Born March 27, 1898, Schleswig-Holstein, German Empire; died March 26, 1936, Popocatépetl, Mexico, in a plane crash. There is no information about Harder's movements during the Weimar era, about why she left Germany or whether she went into exile in Mexico.

Harder directed one other Weimar-era film, Der Weg einer Proletarierin (short film, 1929).

After twenty years with the same firm, Kremke, a payroll clerk, loses his job as a result of the worldwide economic crisis; his manual labor will be replaced by bookkeeping machines. Finding a new position proves to be hopeless. After working briefly as a salesman, the bourgeois Kremke, like millions of the proletarians he looks down upon, is forced to claim unemployment assistance. Although his daughter, Lene, is employed in a department store and earns her own money, she cannot meet the expenses of their two-person household. Lene is in love with a student, but when he happens to learn that a bill collector is after her father, he leaves her. Kremke sternly rejects her new boyfriend, Erwin, a laid-off truck driver now eking out a living as a window washer. When Lene and Erwin want to get engaged, the father and daughter quarrel, and Lene moves out. Kremke is destitute. While handing out advertising flyers, he catches sight of a former colleague and runs away from him in shame, throws away the flyers, and forfeits his pay. Alone and desperate, Kremke finally takes his own life.

"Lohnbuchhalter Kremke proves that everyday events are fully as dramatic as invented fables with emotional catastrophes, jazz, and other fashionable doings. Three earlier films have pointed in this same direction: Mutter Krausens Fahrt ins Glück [Piel Jutzi, 1929], Cyankali [Hans Tintner, 1930], and Der Mensch der Masse [King Vidor, 1928]. . . . But even in these films the novelistic entanglements of the plot predominated, whereas Lohnbuchhalter Kremke presents none of the customary suspenseful film moments. . . . ¶Here social and economic grievances are just as important as the suffering of an individual. The film becomes a portrait of the times, and simultaneously, despite the strictly matter-of-fact presentation, an indictment of an absurd economic system."

F. Sch. [Felix Scherret],
Vorwärts, September 5, 1930,
evening edition.

"Hermann Vallentin plays Kremke, the upright, tradition-bound bourgeois who keeps his soldier's cap hanging in a place of honor in his parlor, who stands at attention when he hears military music, and who, as long as his life follows its accustomed course, wishes to have nothing to do with politics and parties, a man who becomes derailed when his life strikes a curve. (He would have voted for the National Socialists last Sunday.)"
Georg Herzberg, Film-Kurier, no. 219
(September 16, 1930).

Film Notes:
In the parliamentary election of September 14, 1930, the NSDAP (National Socialist party—or Nazis), with eighteen percent of the vote, became the second-strongest party behind the SPD (Social Democratic party), with twenty-five percent. Vorwärts was the newspaper of the SPD.

Harder directed the German Social Democratic Film Office (distributors and producers), situated in Berlin, from 1929 to 1932.

Menschen am Sonntag 1930
People on Sunday

Germany

Directors: Robert Siodmak, Edgar G. Ulmer

Screenplay: Billie (in the US: Billy) Wilder, after a report by Kurt Siodmak

Cinematography: Eugen Schüfftan

Camera assistants: Fred Zinnemann, Ernst Kunstmann

Editing: Robert Siodmak

Artistic director: Moriz Seeler

Musical arrangement and conductor at premiere: Otto Stenzeel

Production company: Filmstudio 1929, Berlin

Producers: Heinrich Nebenzahl, Moriz Seeler

Cast

Erwin Splettstösser: Erwin, taxi driver

Brigitte Borchert: Brigitte, gramophone record–seller

Wolfgang von Waltershausen: Wolfgang, wine salesman

Christl Ehlers: Christl, model

Annie Schreyer: Annie, girl who stayed home

Kurt Gerron, Valeska Gert, Ernö Verebes, Heinrich Gretler: passersby

Premiere: February 4, 1930, Berlin

Robert Siodmak
See page 156

Edgar G. (Georg) Ulmer
Born September 17, 1904, Vienna; died September 30, 1972, Woodland Hills, California. Exile: 1924: began to work in the US as an assistant director at Universal under Carl Laemmle; 1926: married the American dancer Josephine Warner; 1926–27: worked as assistant art director on F. W. Murnau's *Sunrise*;

(continued)

A young wine salesman and a model become briefly acquainted in the center of Berlin. They agree to spend the next day, a Sunday, together at a lake in the city's outskirts. The model appears at the rendezvous with a female friend who sells records, the wine salesman brings along his own friend, a taxi driver. Although the taxi driver's girlfriend announced that morning that she would join them later, she sleeps all day. The men and women get to know each other on the beach and in the water. Finally they play cat and mouse in the surrounding woods. The play becomes serious. One couple disappears, and in an isolated spot they make love. The two others wait for them impatiently; the girl left behind is jealous. After their return to the hectic metropolis the four agree to do something together the next Sunday. But later it occurs to the two men that they would prefer to do something more important: watch a soccer game.

"An experiment! A film without actors. . . . Is that Berlin? Berlin's young people? No question but that the film comes incredibly close to reality! . . . The acting is not altogether convincing, which is after all more challenging than appearing in so-called reportage or documentary films. . . . It is the atmospheric flavor that matters. And in this respect Siodmak and Ulmer, who directed the film, and the cameraman Schüfftan have succeeded in creating images of astonishing vividness. One could say that no one has ever captured more attractive landscape pictures from the environs of Berlin. No less effective is the bustle of the metropolis. Gratifying that the quick cutting is only used where it was a matter of presenting speed and movement. Superb some of the pictures of the sleeping city on Sunday."

n., *Lichtbild-Bühne*, no. 31 (February 5, 1930).

Film Notes:

The film's opening credits tell us, of the actors, "These five people faced a camera for the first time in their lives. Today they are all pursuing their careers. Erwin Splettstösser drives the taxi IA 10088. Brigitte Borchert has sold 150 copies of the record 'In einer kleinen Konditorei' in the past month. Wolfgang von Waltershausen, officer, farmer, antiquarian, professional dancing partner, wine salesman. Christl Ehlers wears out her shoes as a film extra. Annie Schreyer, a model."

1929: returned to Germany to direct
Menschen am Sonntag then returned
to the US; 1933: granted asylum in
the US

Ulmer's only documented directorial
work during the Weimar Republic
was *Menschen am Sonntag*. He
claimed to have collaborated on
the set design and art direction of
Murnau's *Nosferatu. Eine Symphonie
des Grauens* (1922) and *Der letzte
Mann* (1924), but this has never been
confirmed.

167

Berlin-Alexanderplatz 1931

Germany
Director: Phil Jutzi
Dialogue director: Karlheinz Martin
Screenplay: Alfred Döblin, Hans
   Wilhelm, from Döblin's 1929 novel
Cinematography: Nikolaus Farkas
Camera: Erich Giese
Art direction: Julius von Borsody
Costume design: Richard and Alma
   Timm
Editing: Géza Pollatschik
Sound: Fritz Seeger
Composer: Allan Gray (born Josef
   Zmigrod)
Musical supervision: Artur Guttmann
Songs: "Adieu Berlin" (lyrics: Alfred
   Döblin), "Alexanderplatzmarsch,"
   "Liebe kommt, Liebe geht,"
   "Lied des Franz Biberkopf,"
   (lyrics: Erik Ernst Schwabach),
   "Über den Dächern von Berlin"
   (lyrics: Schwabach), "Ich hatt'
   ein Kameraden" (lyrics: Ludwig
   Uhland), "Piep, piep, piep, der
   Piepmatz spielt"
Production company: Allianz-Tonfilm,
   Berlin
Producer: Arnold Pressburger

Cast
Heinrich George: Franz Biberkopf
Maria Bard: Cilly
Margarete Schlegel: Mieze
Bernhard Minetti: Reinhold
Gerhard Bienert: Karl the Plumber
Albert Florath: Pums
Paul Westermeier: Henschke,
   innkeeper
Jakob Tiedtke: guest
Hans Deppe: guest
Julius Falkenstein: wheeler-dealer
Also featuring: Käte Haack

Premiere: October 8, 1931, Berlin
First US screening: May 10, 1933,
Vanderbilt Theatre, New York

Phil Jutzi
See page 152

On his release from a Berlin prison, Franz Biberkopf swears he will become an honest man. He meets Cilly, and they fall in love. Cilly is torn between wanting to help him lead a decent life and her commitment to Reinhold, the brutal leader of a gang of criminals. Reinhold successfully uses Cilly as a decoy to involve the naive Franz in a break-in. While being chased by the police, Reinhold shoves Franz out of the moving car, and as a result Franz's arm has to be amputated. Reinhold perversely kills Franz's new girlfriend, Mieze. Thanks to a tip from a member of the gang, the police arrest both the murderer and Franz before Franz can take revenge. The court sentences Reinhold; Franz, free again, sells roly-poly toys on Alexanderplatz.

"No attempt was made to follow the original [novel], which is already half film script. It takes from it only a self-contained underworld plot of the sort that every high-quality entertaining novel offers. . . . If only the producers had resolutely confessed to making propaganda! At the same time, they commit the second error and are to some extent embarrassed about the concessions. . . . In order to satisfy so-called higher standards, they subsequently try to incorporate some of the novel's epic associations. . . . I am thinking of Biberkopf's endless tram ride into the city from prison, and above all the interminable photographs of Alexanderplatz. . . . The film's inadequacy is in large part the result of its being a definite star vehicle. . . . I do not question George's great acting ability; but he does not carry the role, he adapts it to himself. Biberkopf is not George, he only takes on George's features."
   Siegfried Kracauer, *Frankfurter Zeitung*,
      October 18, 1931.

Die 3 Groschen-Oper 1931
The Threepenny Opera

Germany and USA
Director: G. W. Pabst
Assistant directors: Mark Sorkin,
    Herbert Rappaport
Screenplay: Leo Lania, Ladislaus
    Vajda, Béla Balázs, from the play
    by Bertolt Brecht, with a score by
    Kurt Weill (1928)
Cinematography: Fritz Arno Wagner
Assistant camera: Carl Moeller, Walter
    Hrich
Second camera: Robert Baberske
Art direction: Andrej Andrejew
Costume design: Max Pretzfelder
Editing: Hans Oser
Sound: Adolf Jansen
Composer: Kurt Weill
Musical director: Theo Mackeben
Orchestra: Lewis Ruth Band
Lyrics: Bertolt Brecht
Songs: "Die Moritat von Mackie
    Messer," "Das Hochzeitslied
    für ärmere Leute," "Lied von der
    Unzulänglichkeit menschlichen
    Strebens," "Barbarasong," "Lied der
    Seeräuber-Jenny," "Kanonensong"
Production company: Nero-Film, on
    behalf of Tobis-Tonbild-Syndikat
    (Tobis), Berlin, and Warner Brothers
    Pictures, New York
Producers: Seymour Nebenzahl (Nero-
    Film), Gus Schlesinger (Warner
    Brothers), Guido Bagier (Tobis)

Cast
Rudolf Forster: Mackie Messer (Mack
    the Knife)
Carola Neher: Polly Peachum
Reinhold Schünzel: Tiger-Brown, police
    chief
Fritz Rasp: Peachum, king of the
    beggars
Valeska Gert: Miss Peachum
Lotte Lenya: Jenny, prostitute
Hermann Thimig: pastor
Ernst Busch: street singer
Vladimir Sokoloff: Smith

Mackie Messer (Mack the Knife), the leader of a criminal gang feared by all of London, marries the lovely Polly. Her father, the beggar king Peachum, has designated his daughter as his successor and is against the marriage. Peachum demands that the police chief Tiger-Brown arrest his disagreeable son-in-law and threatens that the beggars he commands will ruin the queen's coronation. Mackie Messer, warned of the arrest by Tiger-Brown, entrusts Polly with the direction of his criminal affairs and hides in a bordello. Jenny, a prostitute and Mackie Messer's former lover, denounces him to the police, but a short time later she sees to it that he is set free. Polly has meanwhile opened a bank with Mackie Messer's gang, and Mackie Messer himself is appointed bank director. Although Tiger-Brown has changed his mind and wants to arrest him, the ragged beggars can no longer be prevented from creating chaos at the ceremonial procession in honor of Her Majesty. Tiger-Brown loses his job, but Mackie Messer offers him—and Peachum—a lucrative position at the bank.

"The *Dreigroschenoper* film is not a success. And I doubt that it could have been without a lawsuit between the authors of the work and Tobis-Warner. For even Brecht would not have been able to make this opera, which thrives in the theater, a piece for the sound film. It has a style that requires the stage, because it creates its own reality, which cannot be achieved by realistic means."

Siegfried Kracauer, *Frankfurter Zeitung*,
February 23, 1931.

Paul Kemp, Gustav Püttjer, Krafft
    Raschig, Oskar Höcker: Mackie
    Messer's gang
Herbert Grünbaum: Filch
Silvia Torff: madam

Premiere: February 19, 1931, Berlin
First US screening: May 17, 1931,
Warner Theatre, New York

G. W. Pabst
See page 138

Emil und die Detektive 1931
Emil and the Detectives

Germany

Director: Gerhard Lamprecht
Screenplay: Billie (in the US: Billy) Wilder, Paul Frank, from the novel by Erich Kästner (1929) and a story idea by Kästner and Emmerich Pressburger
Script consultant: Carl Mayer
Artistic supervision: Carl Meinhardt
Cinematography: Werner Brandes
Assistant camera: Karl Drömmer, Werner Krien
Art direction: Werner Schlichting
Sound: Hermann Fritzsching, Carlheinz Becker
Composer: Allan Gray (born Josef Zmigrod)
Production company: Universum Film AG (UFA), Berlin

Cast

Käte Haack: Frau Tischbein, hairdresser
Rolf Wenkhaus: Emil Tischbein, her son
Fritz Rasp: Grundeis
Rudolf Biebrach: Constable Jeschke
Olga Engl: Emil's grandmother
Inge Landgut: Pony Hütchen
Hans Joachim Schaufuss: Gustav with the Horn
Hubert Schmitz: Professor
Hans Richter: Flying Stag
Hans Löhr: Little Tuesday
Ernst-Eberhard Reling: Gerold
Waldemar Kupczyk: Mittenzwey

Premiere: December 2, 1931, Berlin
First US screening: December 20, 1931, UFA Cosmopolitan, New York

Gerhard Lamprecht
See page 109

To the distress of Jeschke, a policeman in a provincial town, the brash young Emil Tischbein is always playing practical jokes. One day Emil is responsible for a large sum of money: his mother asks him to take all her savings to his grandmother in Berlin. Emil finds himself alone in a train compartment with Grundeis, an older, overly friendly passenger, who gives Emil a bonbon that causes him to fall asleep. When he arrives in Berlin he has a rude awakening: all his mother's money is gone! By chance, Emil meets Gustav with the Horn, the leader of a gang of boys, and describes the theft to him. Immediately Gustav volunteers to help get the money back. Along with the gang, Emil and Gustav set out in search of the thief and finally recognize him as a guest in a hotel. Emil's cousin, Pony Hütchen, assists in the investigation. Emil searches the thief's wallet. When Grundeis leaves the hotel, more than a hundred children follow, and his attempts to flee are hopeless. Emil is able to prove to a policeman that Grundeis has stolen his money. It turns out that Grundeis is wanted for bank robbery, and Emil receives a reward. Now he can afford to fly back home. When his plane lands, the whole town greets him and celebrates him as a hero.

"It was not intended to be a film only for children. It was meant to appeal to the larger cinema public. And I feel it will manage to do so, if only because it places them, without any sentimentality or cuteness, in a world they experience themselves every day."

Gerhard Lamprecht, "Kinder spielen einen Film für Erwachsene," *Film-Kurier*, no. 279 (November 28, 1931).

„Emil und die Detektive"

Der Hauptmann von Köpenick (Ein deutsches Märchen) 1931

The Captain from Köpenick

Germany
Director: Richard Oswald
Screenplay: Carl Zuckmayer, Albrecht Joseph, from the play by Zuckmayer (1931)
Cinematography: Ewald Daub
Art direction: Franz Schroedter
Costume design: Walter Leder
Sound: Hans Grimm
Film and sound editing: Max Brenner
Production companies: G.P. [Gabriel Pascal] Films, Berlin, and Roto-Film, Berlin, on behalf of Südfilm, Berlin
Producers: Richard Oswald, Gabriel Pascal

Cast
Max Adalbert: Wilhelm Voigt
Ernst Dernburg: release official
Willi Schur: Kallenberg, called Kalle
Paul Wagner: Captain von Schlettow
Hermann Vallentin: A. Wormser, tailor
Emil Wabschke: Wabschke, pattern cutter at Wormser's
Peter Wolff: Willy, Wormser's son
Fritz Beckmann: master shoemaker
Arthur Mainzer: Manager Knoll
Heinrich Marlow: district commissioner
Heinz Sarnow: Dr. Jellinek
Edith Karin: consumptive prostitute
Gerhard Bienert: grenadier of the guards
Albert Florath: prison superintendent
Max Gülstorff: Dr. Obermüller
Käte Haack: Frau Obermüller
Martha Ziegler: Fanny, the Obermüllers' maid
Ilse Fürstenberg: Marie Hoprecht, Voigt's sister
Friedrich Kayssler: Friedrich, her husband
Leonard Steckel: Krakauer, junk dealer

Premiere: December 22, 1931, Berlin
First US screening: January 16, 1933, Europa Theatre (formerly UFA Cosmopolitan), New York

Richard Oswald
See page 72

During the reign of Kaiser Wilhelm II, Wilhelm Voigt, a cobbler, is released after twenty-three years in jail. Since the Prussian state refuses to give him a passport, he is unable to begin an ordinary life at home or to emigrate. He tries to steal a passport from a police station but is captured and has to go to jail for another ten years. During his incarceration, he studies military ranks and regulations. Once freed, Wilhelm faces the same absurd dilemma: without official documents he has no hope of leaving Prussia. But this time he chooses another way to get his hands on the indispensable passport. He buys a handsome uniform and a saber from a junk dealer, dresses up as a captain, and commands a handful of soldiers to occupy the town hall in Köpenick, near Berlin. On his orders the mayor and the town's finance director are arrested. He had not realized that no passports are issued at the town hall, but he manages to gather all the cash on hand and disappear with it. News of the German cobbler who tricked his uniform-worshiping countrymen spreads around the world. Even the kaiser laughs at the doings of this clever subject. After the shoemaker has confessed and served another brief prison sentence, the kaiser pardons him, and on his release Voigt is granted the passport he has sought for so long.

"Carl Zuckmayr [sic] fashioned this film fable after his stage play, but not slavishly. . . . [Richard Oswald] had . . . the brilliant idea of letting the amusing story end with laughter, which builds as it circles the globe. One person picks up the laugh from another, so to speak, first people in the street, then people in offices, then military officers, then His Majesty, and finally the whole world. The local caper appears in giant headlines on the world's newspapers as they roll through the presses."
    Ernst Lothar, *Neue Freie Presse* (Vienna), January 14, 1932.

56

Ihre Hoheit befiehlt 1931

Germany
Director: Hanns Schwarz
Assistant director: Carl Winston
Screenplay: Robert Liebmann, Paul
  Frank, Billie (in the US: Billy) Wilder
Cinematography: Günther Rittau
Assistant camera: Otto Baecker
Art direction: Erich Kettelhut
Costume design: Leopold Verch
Editing: Willy Zeyn, Jr.
Sound: Hermann Fritzsching
Composer: Werner Richard Heymann
Singers: Comedian Harmonists
Lyrics: Ernst Neubach, Robert Gilbert
Song titles: "Frag nicht wie, frag nicht
  wo," "Du hast mir heimlich die
  Liebe ins Haus gebracht," "Bisschen
  dies und bisschen das," "Trara!—
  Jetzt kommt die Marschmusik!"
Production company: Universum Film
  AG (UFA), Berlin

Cast

Käthe von Nagy: Princess Marie
  Christine
Willy Fritsch: Lieutenant Carl von
  Conradi
Reinhold Schünzel: Count Herlitz,
  minister of state
Paul Hörbiger: Pipac, detective
Paul Heidemann: Prince von
  Leuchtenstein
Michael von Newlinski: cavalry
  captain
Eugen Tiller: major
Karl Platen: valet
Erich Kestin: friend of Conradi
Erik Schütz: singer
Kenneth Rive: König
Attila Hörbiger: watchman
Comedian Harmonists: cooks

Premiere: March 3, 1931, Berlin
First US screening: November 6,
1931, UFA Cosmopolitan, New York

Hanns Schwarz
See page 155

"The story, which furnished the excuse for a great deal of excellent photography, many jokes, and considerable catchy music, tells how Marie Christine, just returned to the palace after having been at school in England, goes to a servants' ball incognita, encounters Lieutenant Conradi, also in disguise, dances and drinks comradeship with him, makes a date for the following evening and then steals home to throw all the ancient court etiquette into confusion in her determination about her love affairs. And much happens before the light, tangled web of near intrigue is unraveled and the inevitable happy end attained."
  H. T. S. [Harry T. Smith], *New York
    Times*, November 7, 1931.

"Especially in *Ihre Hoheit befiehlt* it seemed essential to bring out the musical element in the operetta more emphatically. I was able to find in Werner Richard Heymann, our musical director and composer, a cheerful and understanding coworker. We intended to push the music more into the foreground through humorous illustrations and through rendering the dialogue within the operetta's action as much as possible in music. . . . It no longer interests the public where the music that carries the film forward suddenly comes from. The music can serve as illustration in only the very fewest cases. To my thinking, it has to be organically motivated in the total work, just like the pictures. Accordingly, work on a sound-film operetta requires extreme rhythmic and musical precision, of a kind that is only possible with the sophisticated recording technique developed in the Neubabelsberg sound-film studio."
  Hanns Schwarz, "Operette und Tonfilm,"
    UFA-Feuilleton, no. 13
    (April 1, 1931): 8.

Kameradschaft 1931
La Tragédie de la mine

Germany and France
Director: G. W. Pabst
Consultant for the French scenes:
Robert Beaudoin
Assistant director: Herbert Rappaport
Screenplay: Ladislaus Vajda, Karl
Otten, Peter Martin Lampel, from a
story idea by Otten
French dialogue: Léon Werth
Cinematography: Fritz Arno Wagner,
Robert Baberske
Art direction: Ernö Metzner, Karl
Vollbrecht
Editing: Hans Oser
Sound: Adolf Jansen
Composer: G. von Rigelius
Production companies: Nero-Film,
Berlin; Gaumont-Franco-Film-Aubert,
Paris
Producer: Seymour Nebenzahl

Cast
Alexander Granach: Kasper
Fritz Kampers: Wilderer
Ernst Busch: Wittkopp
Elisabeth Wendt: his wife
Gustav Püttjer: Kaplan
Oskar Höcker: Obersteiger
Fritz Wendhausen: German mine
overseer
Daniel Mendaille: Jean Leclerc
Andrée Ducret: Françoise Leclerc
Marcel Lesieur: Albert
Heléna Manson: Rose, Albert's wife
Alex Bernard: Grandfather Jacques
Georges Charlia: Émile
Georges Tourreil: Vidal, engineer
Marguerite Debos: Jean's mother
Pierre-Louis (aka Pierre Amourdedieu):
Georges, Jacques's grandson

Premiere: November 17, 1931, Berlin
French premiere: January 29, 1932,
Paris
First US screening: November 8,
1932, Europa Theatre (formerly UFA
Cosmopolitan), New York

G. W. Pabst
See page 138

It is 1931, and the inhabitants on either side of the German-French border regard each other in light of their respective national prejudices. It is a fraught relationship, with unemployed German miners trying in vain to get work in a French coal mine. Three German friends, Wilderer, Kasper, and Kaplan, attend a miners' ball on the other side of the border. Wilderer asks Françoise, a Frenchwoman, to dance. Because she does not know his language, she does not understand what he wants from her. He, in turn, misinterprets her reaction as rejection and feels validated in his anti-French resentment. The next day there is a massive explosion in the mine, and countless workers are trapped. A German, working with a French rescue team, is able to save a number of them. Kasper, Kaplan, and Wilderer, working on their own, clear an underground path to the miners still trapped. To get to them, the trio dismantles a grate in the tunnel marking the boundary between the two countries. Since the three helpers become trapped in the mine as well, along with the old miner Jacques and his grandson, they, too, have to be freed. While the miners from two nations, supposedly archenemies, are fraternizing above ground, German and French police install a new grate below.

"Nothing is shown but a mining accident, firedamp, flames, gas, water in the shaft . . . and yet the result is the most moving and best German sound film in terms of technique. . . . ¶The visual effects are supplemented and heightened acoustically by short sentences, creaking and crashing in the tunnels, the gurgling and rushing of the water, echoing cries, knocking, dripping. . . . ¶Profoundly harrowing when, in the mind of the Frenchman nearly asphyxiated from the gas, the approaching hammering that promises help becomes the sound of machine guns, so that he takes the German rescuer in a gas mask to be the enemy he has to overpower. . . . ¶The artlessness of the actors is so extraordinary that it is no longer possible to make out which are the actors and which are extras, stattage from the real life of the mines."

Kurt Pinthus, *8 Uhr-Abendblatt*,
November 19, 1931.

Film Notes:
The film is a fictional treatment of a 1906 mine disaster in Courrières, in northern France near the Belgian border, in which more than a thousand men died. A team of German miners came to the aid of the victims.

"Kameradschaft"
Regie G. W. Pabst

Die Koffer des Herrn O. F.
Ein Märchen für Erwachsene   1931
The Trunks of Mr. O. F.

Germany
Director: Alexis Granowsky
Assistant director: Jacob Gärtner
Screenplay: Leo Lania, Alexis
 Granowsky, from a story idea by
 Hans Hömberg
Cinematography: Reimar Kuntze,
 Heinrich Balasch
Art direction: Erich Czerwonsky
Costume design: Edward Suhr
Make-up: Karl Holek, Bruno
 Cieslewicz
Editing: Paul Falkenberg, Curt von Molo
Sound: Hans Grimm, Hans Bittmann
Composer: Karol Rathaus
Music: Barnabas von Géczy and His
 Orchestra, Lewis Ruth Band
Musical supervision: Kurt Schröder
Lyrics: Erich Kästner
Song titles: "Cabaretsong,"
 "Barcarole," "Die kleine
 Ansprache," "Hausse-Song,"
 "Schlusssong"
Production company: Tobis, Berlin
Producer: Ernst Nölle

Cast
Alfred Abel: mayor
Hedy (born Hedwig Eva Maria) Kiesler
 (in the US: Hedy Lamarr): Helene,
 his daughter
Peter Lorre: Stix, newspaperman
Harald Paulsen: Stark, architect
Ludwig Stoessel: Brunn, hotelier
Ilse Korseck: secretary and, later, wife
 of the mayor
Margo Lion: Viola Volant, cabaret star
Liska March: Eve Lune
Gaby Karpeless: Eve Lune's assistant
Hadrian Maria Netto: Jean, barber
Hertha von Walther: his wife
Franz Weber: Dorn, tailor
Maria Karsten: his wife
Fred Döderlein: Alexander, mayor's son
Bernhard Goetzke: Professor Smith
Josefine Dora: Jean's mother-in-law
Friedrich Ettel: pharmacist
Meinhardt Mauer: doctor
Aribert Mog: architect's assistant

(continued)

In the middle of the world financial crisis, thirteen suitcases bearing the puzzling initials O. F. arrive, with no owner, in the sleepy provincial German town of Ostend. At the same time, six rooms are reserved in a hotel in town. Stix, a newspaperman, starts a rumor with far-reaching consequences: a billionaire by the name of Oscar Flott will soon arrive and will invest fantastic sums of money in the backwater town. A speculative fever breaks out among the citizens. Ostend develops into a modern metropolis. International scholars attempt to explain the fantastic boom. Stix manages to prevent his lie from being discovered. The actual cause of the economic upswing is soon forgotten: because an address was written incorrectly, thirteen suitcases belonging to the actress Ola Felden were sent to Ostend, Germany, instead of Ostend, Belgium.

"In an fanciful example it is effectively demonstrated what sorts of factors can trigger an 'economic miracle.' When faith in future profits is greater than doubt about them, people are once again willing to invest the money they have put aside into future opportunities like buildings. . . . Naturally all this is only a humorous and somewhat fantastic commentary on the seriousness of the present situation, but at least it is a film that deals with our time intelligently, without any clichés."

 Heinrich Braune, *Hamburger Echo*,
 June 11, 1932.

Film Notes:
On September 23, 1933, the film's title was changed by the National Socialist censors to *Bauen und Heiraten*; Erich Kästner's song lyrics were removed, and the names of Jewish actors and production workers were deleted. Kästner's literary works had been destroyed in public book burnings in May and June in Berlin and other cities.

Aenne Görling: Beck, landlady
Rudolf Hofbauer: film director
Arthur Mainzer: film producer

Premiere: December 2, 1931,
Mozart-Saal, Berlin

Alexis Granowsky (born Alexej Granowskij)

Born 1890, Moscow; died March 11,
1937, Paris. Exile: 1919: founded
and directed the Jewish Theatre Studio
in St. Petersburg; 1920: moved
Jewish Theatre Studio to Moscow
and renamed it the Jewish Chamber
Theatre, still under his direction; 1925:
appointed director and producer of
the Jewish Academic Theatre GOSET
in Moscow; 1928: while on a foreign
tour with the company, remained in
Germany; 1933: went into exile in
France

Granowsky directed only one other
film in Germany, *Das Lied vom Leben*
(1931).

Der Kongress tanzt 1931

Congress Dances

Germany
Director: Erik Charell
Assistant director: Paul Martin
Screenplay: Norbert Falk, Robert
    Liebmann
Cinematography: Carl Hoffmann
Trick photography: Theodor Nischwitz
Art direction: Robert Herlth, Walter
    Röhrig
Costume design: Ernst Stern
Sound: Fritz Thiery
Editing: Viktor Gertler
Composer and musical director:
    Werner Richard Heymann, using
    old Viennese compositions
Lyrics: Robert Gilbert (aka Robert
    Winterfeld)
Songs: "Das gibt's nur einmal," "Das
    muss ein Stück vom Himmel sein,"
    "Schön ist das Leben, wenn die
    Musik spielt"
Other music: German Dances (Franz
    Schubert), "Saber Dance" from the
    ballet *Gayane* (Aram Katchaturian)
Choreography: Boris Romanoff
Production company: Universum Film
    AG (UFA), Berlin
Producer: Erich Pommer

Cast
Lilian Harvey: Christel Weinzinger,
    salesgirl in a glove shop
Willy Fritsch: Czar Alexander of
    Russia/Uralsky
Otto Wallburg: Bibikov, adjutant to
    the czar
Conrad Veidt: Prince Metternich
Carl Heinz Schroth: Pepi, Metternich's
    private secretary
Lil Dagover: the countess
Alfred Abel: King of Saxony
Eugen Rex: Swabian ambassador
Adele Sandrock: princess
Margarete Kupfer: duchess
Julius Falkenstein: finance minister
Max Gülstorff: mayor of Vienna
Paul Hörbiger: singer at a Vienna
    Heuriger (wine tavern)

In 1814, during the Congress of Vienna, the shopgirl Christel and the Russian czar Alexander fall in love. For the commoner it is a fairy tale come true: she leads the life of an aristocrat, is introduced to prominent European statesmen, attends splendid balls, and is a guest in one of the czar's palaces. But Christel's good fortune is short-lived. After Napoleon resumes power during the Hundred Days, the congress quickly adjourns. Alexander returns to Moscow, leaving her, saddened, behind.

"We see nothing of the city of Vienna, only crowds of people in splendid costumes in grandiose movement. . . . Charell has learned a lot from Lubitsch. But he outdoes his teacher, at least in the best sequence: when the girl drives from her shop in the czar's carriage through all of the districts of Vienna. She sings rapturously, and the other girls, the passersby, the buyers and sellers at the market, the washerwomen at the stream, the equestrians on the elevated riding path through the meadow—all of them sing along, taking up the song's rhythm and imitating the gestures of Lilian Harvey, who moves with a dancer's grace and has never before been so endearing. . . . Without any added sentimentality or silliness, this is the most animated, most buoyant German mass-audience film yet produced, an intoxicating showpiece."

Kurt Pinthus, *8 Uhr-Abendblatt*,
October 24, 1931.

Premiere: September 29, 1931,
Vienna
First German screening: October 23,
1931, Berlin
First US screening: May 12, 1932,
Rivoli Theatre, New York

**Erik Charell (born Erich Karl
Löwenberg)**
Born April 8, 1894, Breslau, German
Empire (now Wroclaw, Poland); died
July 15, 1974, Zug, Switzerland.
Exile: 1932–36: went into exile in
London, Hollywood, New York, south-
ern France, and Switzerland; 1937:
emigrated to the US after trying in vain
to be granted asylum in Switzerland;
1938: taught at the New School for
Social Research, New York; 1948:
worked as a director in Paris and
Switzerland; 1949: directed films
and plays in the Federal Republic of
Germany and in Austria

Der Kongress tanzt was Charell's only
Weimar-era film.

Liebeskommando 1931

Germany
Director: Géza von Bolváry
Screenplay: Fritz Grünbaum,
    Alexander Roda Roda, Walter
    Reisch
Cinematography: Willy Goldberger
Art direction: Andrej Andrejew, Robert
    Dietrich
Sound: Fritz Seeger
Film editing: Hermann Haller
Composer: Robert Stolz
Lyrics: Robert Gilbert, Armin Robinson
Choreography: Tibor von Halmay
Songs: "Kamerad, wir sind die
    Jugend," "Im Traum hast du mir
    alles erlaubt," "Ich möcht' einmal
    wieder verliebt sein," "Eine kleine
    Freundschaft mit dir"
Production company: Super-Film, Berlin
Producer: Julius Haimann

Cast
Dolly Haas: Antonia Scanagatti
Walter Edthofer: Francesco, her
    brother
Livio Pavanelli: Count Giuseppe
    Scanagatti, their father
Gustav Fröhlich: Count von Lorenz, first
    lieutenant
Anton Pointner: commandant of the
    military academy
Yvette Rodin: Elisabeth, his daughter
Tibor von Halmay: Schreck von
    Schreckenstein, first lieutenant
Marcel Wittrich: singer
Harry Hardt: First Lieutenant Reisinger
Fritz Odemar: archduke
Gerhard Ritterband: Mehlmaier
Paul Morgan: regimental doctor

Premiere: November 10, 1931, Berlin
First US screening: April 27, 1932,
Europa Theatre (formerly UFA
Cosmopolitan), New York

Géza von Bolváry
Born December 27, 1897, Budapest;
died August 10, 1961, Altenbeuern,
West Germany. No exile

(continued)

Antonia undergoes military training at the Royal Cadet Academy in Vienna in place of her brother, Francesco, who wishes to study music. Dressed as a man, she behaves far more courageously than her classmates, passes all the examinations effortlessly, and is decorated for her outstanding achievements. She reveals her secret only to Elisabeth, the daughter of the commandant. In time the notorious womanizer Count von Lorenz, the lieutenant who trains future officers, realizes that his best and most impudent student is a charming young woman. But when the academy directors finally learn the truth, Antonia's stiff punishment is waived. Instead, she is discharged into civilian life with her military honors. She returns to her father in Trento, where Count Lorenz happens to have been transferred in punishment.

"In this cadet milieu . . . a young woman as a man, a woman as soldier. The discovery of the trouser role for a sound film. . . . One is convinced by Dolly Haas, in both her cadet uniform and boyish face. . . . Her eyes enchant, though she does not have to flutter them with playful nuances, she is simply there, marches past, simpers and obeys, plays jokes and sulks—with astonishing instinct she bypasses the ambiguity. . . . It is a singular triumph for Dolly Haas."
-ger, *Film-Kurier*, no. 265
(November 11, 1931).

"If one were to pull out the separate 'numbers' from this film, one would be doing an injustice to the composer Robert Stolz. Wholly infused with music like few other films, it swings along and touches feelings in us that a military humoresque can hardly elicit: a mellow mood is evoked by Stolz's subtly orchestrated melodies and by Dolly Haas's energetic little-girl's voice. His basic ideas are simple and therefore ultimately singable; he modulates them in harmonically traditional intervals and thereby achieves that 'inner sing-along' on the part of the listener that is a sure sign that a musical nerve has been struck."
H. A., *Lichtbild-Bühne*, no. 270
(November 11, 1931).

Selected Weimar films: *Mutterherz* (1923), *Der fesche Husar* (1928), *Der Erzieher meiner Tochter* (1929), *Zwei Herzen im 3/4 Takt* (1930), *Ich will nicht wissen, wer du bist* (1932)

„Das Lied vom Leben"   „Film-Kunst A.-G."

Das Lied vom Leben 1931
The Song of Life

Germany
Director: Alexis Granowsky
Screenplay: Victor Trivas, H. Lechner
Dialogue: Walter Mehring
Cinematography: Viktor Trinkler, Heinrich Balasch
Sound production director: Hans Conradi
Sound: Hans Bittmann, Ernst Schulz
Sound editing: Hans Oser
Composer: Franz Wachsmann (in the US: Franz Waxman)
Orchestra: Weintraubs Syncopaters
Singers: Ernst Busch, Leo Monosson, Greta Keller
Songs: "Arbeitslied" (music: Friedrich Hollaender, lyrics: Günther Weisenborn, Leo Hirsch), "Paradiessong" (music: Hollaender, lyrics: Walter Mehring), "Anrede an ein neugeborenes Kind" or "Song vom ersten Schrei" (music: H. Adam [Hanns Eisler], lyrics: Mehring), "Wiegenlied" or "Baby, wo ist mein Baby?" (music: Hollaender, lyrics: Mehring), "Über das Seefahren" or "Matrosensong" (music: Eisler, lyrics: Mehring), "Kesselsong" (music: Eisler, lyrics: Mehring)
Production companies: Tonbild-Syndikat (Tobis), Berlin; Film-Kunst, Berlin

Cast
Margot Ferra: Erika Walter, young girl
Elsa Wagner: her mother
Aribert Mog: Igor, engineer
Wilhelm Liepmann: doctor
Ernst Busch, Leo Monosson, Greta Keller: singers

Premiere: April 24, 1931, Berlin

Alexis Granowsky
See page 181

During her engagement party Erika leaves her wealthy fiancé, whom she does not love. A worker she does not know prevents her from committing suicide. They get to know each other, become lovers, and marry. Erika becomes pregnant and survives a complicated birth. Her little boy grows up, learns a profession, and leaves his parents. Aboard an ocean steamer he discovers the world.

"Granowsky provides a perfect example of how everything surreal and symbolic in a feature film fails to heighten the effect but rather weakens it. . . . ¶Granowsky's work is altogether characteristic of the peculiar way the Russian filmmakers overlay splendid sensual observation with a tendency toward theoretical constructs. . . . Just as in the silent film they [the Russians] are not content with their admirable skill in the observation of reality but rather attempt to insert 'ideas' by means of montages of symbolic images, they see the essence of the sound film as asynchronism, that is, the juxtaposition of sounds and scenes that do not belong together. . . . ¶On the other hand, the experiments with melodies made up of noises [in *Das Lied vom Leben*] struck me as very promising, for example when machine noises of different pitches are assembled one after the other like notes in a melody. It also provides a few instructive examples for the use of background music: the trumpet call of a nursing infant. . . . ¶The photography is altogether exemplary. From this film one can show how the strong emphasis on black-and-white values is not merely a luxurious touch, an indulgence, but a necessary prerequisite to the realization of the artistic idea. The whole effect of the long operation scene, for example, derives from the striking contrast between the white coats, white linens, and white cotton wadding and the black rubber gloves and instruments and faces."
Rudolf Arnheim, "Granowsky probiert,"
Die Weltbühne, no. 18
(May 5, 1931): 654–55.

Film Notes:
On March 18, 1931, the Berlin censorship board ruled that the film could be shown only at closed events to doctors and other medical professionals. The original version, sixty-six minutes long, was repeatedly shortened as a result of additional demands from the censors. On April 27, 1932, the censors finally approved a forty-minute version.

M 1931

Germany
Director: Fritz Lang
Screenplay: Thea von Harbou, Fritz Lang
Cinematography: Fritz Arno Wagner
Assistant camera: Karl Vass
Second camera: Robert Baberske
Art direction: Emil Hasler (drafts), Karl Vollbrecht (construction)
Sound: Adolf Jansen
Sound editing: Paul Falkenberg
Score: based on a motif from Edvard Grieg's *Peer Gynt*
Production company: Nero-Film, Berlin
Producer: Seymour Nebenzahl

Cast
Peter Lorre: Hans Beckert, murderer
Ellen Widmann: Frau Beckmann
Inge Landgut: Elsie, her daughter
Gustav Gründgens: safecracker
Friedrich Gnass: burglar
Fritz Odemar: card sharp
Paul Kemp: pickpocket
Theo Lingen: con man
Ernst Stahl-Nachbaur: police chief
Otto Wernicke: Chief Inspector Lohmann
Theodor Loos: Inspector Groeber
Franz Stein: minister
Gerhard Bienert: criminal secretary
Georg John: blind beggar
Rudolf Blümner: defense lawyer
Karl Platen: night watchman
Rosa Valetti: Beckert's landlady

Premiere: May 11, 1931, Berlin
First US screening: March 31, 1933, Mayfair, New York (a two-week run followed, with the German version with English intertitles showing for the first week, and a dubbed version showing for the second)

Fritz Lang
See page 88

A child murderer is terrorizing Berlin, and little Elsie Beckmann is his most recent victim. Because the police are searching for him, organized crime also feels threatened. Led by a safecracker, the gangsters team up to find the murderer. A blind beggar identifies the wanted man from his characteristic whistle, and the crooks capture him. They conduct a kangaroo court. Before he can be lynched, the police intervene and arrest the accuser along with the defendant.

"Gero Gandert: How did you hit upon the subject matter of *M*? Was it topical in 1931? ¶Fritz Lang: I am an unusually attentive newspaper reader. . . . I have been interested in a thousand things in my life, and out of this interest in a thousand things arose my chief interest: man. And not only what he does—for good or bad—but what motivates him, what makes him tick! . . . ¶In *M* I was not only concerned with investigating what drives a man to such a horrible crime as murdering a child but also laying out the pros and cons of the death sentence. The point of the film is not the conviction of the murderer but the warning to mothers: 'One has to keep closer watch over the children.' This human accent was especially important to my wife at that time, the writer Thea von Harbou; she helped me with the scripts for almost all my German films before 1933. . . . ¶Gandert: The use of sound as a dramatic tool in *M* has frequently been praised. . . . ¶Lang: *M* was my first sound film. At that time in Germany we had barely seen more sound films than you could count on the fingers of one hand. . . . At that time I came to the recognition that it is not only possible to use sound as a dramatic element but absolutely necessary. In *M*, for example, when the stillness of the streets . . . is suddenly shattered by police whistles or the unmelodic, recurring whistling of the child murderer, it serves as a wordless expression of his compulsion. I also feel that in *M* I was the first to have the sound, a sentence, for example, lap over from the end of one scene to the beginning of the next, which not only speeds up the tempo of the film but also underscores how the two scenes relate to each other. ¶Also, for the first time the dialogue of two contrapuntal scenes . . . was treated in such a way that the total dialogue to some extent forms a whole. When one of the criminals begins a sentence, for example, that is then logically completed by one of the criminal investigators. And vice versa. Later both methods were commonly employed."

Gero Gandert, "Fritz Lang über *M*: Ein Interview," in *Cinemathek*, vol. 3, *M—Protokoll* (Hamburg: Marion von Schröder Verlag, 1963), pp. 123–26.

Film Notes:

In 2001 the film was restored by the Nederlands Filmmuseum in collaboration with the Bundesarchiv/Filmarchiv (Berlin/Koblenz), KirchMedia Munich), and ZDF/Arte.

Mädchen in Uniform 1931
Girls in Uniform

Germany
Director: Leontine Sagan
Artistic supervision: Carl Froelich
Screenplay: Christa Winsloe, F. D.
   Andam, from Winsloe's play
   Gestern und Heute (1930)
Cinematography: Reimar Kuntze,
   Franz Weihmayr
Art direction: Fritz Maurischat,
   Friedrich Winkler-Tannenberg
Sound: Karl Brodmerkel, Fritz Stiller
Editing: Oswald Hafenrichter
Composer: Hansom Milde-Meissner
Production company: Deutsche Film-
   Gemeinschaft, Berlin
Producer: Friedrich Pflughaupt

Cast
Hertha Thiele: Manuela von
   Meinhardis
Ellen Schwanneke: Ilse von Westhagen
Ilse Winter: Marga von Rasso
Charlotte Witthauer: Ilse von Treischke
Erika-Margo Biebrach: Lilli von Kattner
Margarete (Ethel) Reschke: Oda von
   Oldensleben
Ilse Vigdor: Anneliese von Beckendorf
Dora Thalmer: Mariechen von Ecke
Gertrud de Lalsky: Manuela's aunt, Her
   Excellency von Ehrenhardt
Dorothea Wieck: Fräulein von
   Bernburg, teacher
Emilia Unda: Fräulein von Nordeck zur
   Nidden, headmistress
Marte Hein: duchess, the school's
   patron
Hedwig Schlichter: Fräulein von
   Kesten, teacher
Lene Berdolt: Fräulein von Gaerschner,
   teacher
Lisi Scherbach: Mademoiselle Oeuillet,
   teacher
Margory Bodker: Miss Evans, teacher
Erika Mann: Fräulein von Atems,
   teacher
Else Ehser: Elise, wardrobe mistress
(continued)

In a Potsdam boarding school for daughters of the aristocracy, iron discipline and rigid frugality are the rule. The new student Manuela von Meinhardis finds it especially difficult to adhere to the countless regulations. All her schoolmates adore the understanding teacher Fräulein von Bernburg, but Manuela feels far more for her. The other teachers and the extremely strict headmistress reject Fräulein von Bernburg's liberal teaching methods. Although it is forbidden, she gives Manuela a blouse she desperately needs. Manuela plays the title role in a school performance of Friedrich Schiller's *Don Carlos* and performs a love scene so well that even the headmistress is impressed. At a student party afterward the tipsy Manuela, miserably in love, toasts Fräulein von Bernburg and reveals who gave her the garment. She is severely punished by the headmistress and is shunned by students and teachers. When Fräulein von Bernburg informs the desperate girl that it would be best if they no longer saw each other, catastrophe follows.

"A film that pictures only women. It is gripping, for this film concerns everyone, because it broaches a humane subject unsentimentally, aside from the individual issues. It has to do with humanity, with the history of a system. A world of the past? It is past and present; it threatens to rise up again, to overrun what healthy modern education is attempting to do. . . . ¶Young creatures, hungry, anemic, and afflicted by awakening desires, they are defenselessly subjected to a tradition nourished by the iron bath of war and imagines it is cultivating the mothers of heroes for new conflicts. They are fed high-flown words about self-sacrifice and iron discipline for their rumbling stomachs; their every step is monitored: this is what education looks like in the shadows of the garrison city [Potsdam]. The robust survive, the more sensitive ones fall apart—natural selection aided by the broom of discipline. ¶The inevitable results of such boarding school confinement are apparent: one searches for the other; mutual suffering leads to mutual affection at the age of awakening desire. Confusions of puberty or same-sex feelings—the film leaves this open, and rightly so. . . . ¶[It] is not a star film. The actors work together, led to the most measured line readings by Leontine Sagan's sympathetic direction of the dialogue, the smallest detail of their gestures controlled, altogether true to life."
   Lotte H. Eisner, *Film-Kurier*, no. 279
   (November 28, 1931).

Film Notes:
Filmjournal 7, February 12, 1933, describes a trial over rights to the film's dialogue. What was at issue was whether the rights acquired by the American distributor were only for the original version or also for the German-language version with English subtitles shown in the United States. Mordaunt Hall wrote in the *New York Times* on September 21, 1932, that "the New York State Board of Censors at first frowned upon the suggestion in this film of the 'Captive' theme, but recently they reconsidered their refusal to grant it a license." *Mädchen in Uniform* was selected by the *New York Times* as one of the ten best films of 1932.

Mädchen in Uniform

Premiere: November 27, 1931, Berlin
First US screening: February 20, 1932, Criterion Theatre, New York

Leontine Sagan (born Leontine Schlesinger)
Born February 13, 1889, Budapest; died May 20, 1974, Pretoria, South Africa. Exile: 1932: directed *Men of Tomorrow* in London; 1933: after the National Socialist takeover in Germany, remained in England (it was too dangerous for a Jewish woman to return), touring South Africa and the US as a theater director; 1939: moved to South Africa

Mädchen in Uniform was the only film Sagan directed in Weimar-era Germany.

Der Mann, der seinen Mörder sucht   1931

Germany
Director: Robert Siodmak
Screenplay: Ludwig Hirschfeld,
 Kurt Siodmak, Billie (in the US:
 Billy) Wilder, Robert Siodmak
 (uncredited), from an idea by Ernst
 Neubach, based on the novel *Les
 Tribulations d'un Chinois en Chine*
 (1897) by Jules Verne
Cinematography: Konstantin Irmen-
 Tschet, Otto Baecker
Art direction: Robert Herlth, Walter
 Röhrig
Sound: Fritz Thiery
Composer: Friedrich Hollaender
Musical direction: Franz Wachsmann
 (in the US: Franz Waxman)
Lyrics: Billie Wilder
Songs: "Am Montag hab' ich leider
 keine Zeit," "Wo gibt's noch
 Männer voller Biederkeit," "Wenn
 ich mir was wünschen dürfte"
Production company: Universum Film
 AG (UFA), Berlin
Producer: Erich Pommer

Cast
Heinz Rühmann: Hans Herfort
Lien Deyers: Kitty
Raimund Janitschek: Otto Kuttlap,
 burglar
Lans Leibelt: Adamowski, general
 director
Hermann Speelmans: Jim
Friedrich Hollaender: president of the
 White Vest society
Gerhard Bienert: policeman
Also featuring: Franz Fiedler, Eberhard
 Mack, Erik Schütz, Rolant Varno,
 Wolfgang von Waltershausen,
 Hermann Blass, Fritz Odemar

Premiere: February 5, 1931, Berlin

Robert Siodmak
See page 156

"Siodmak's . . . grotesquerie is rooted in reality, preserves a sense of time and space. The Great Crash serves as the background and Berlin as the clearly identified setting. A wild automobile chase toward the end of the film passes by the city's sights and pictures such landmarks as the Kaiser-Wilhelm-Gedächtniskirche. A graphic explicitness previously impossible in Weimar Crash films permitted that excess, a requirement of the genre. The hero is a ruined young man, hopelessly in debt, who wants to take his own life. But thanks to his great love for Kitty, whom he gets to know by chance in a bar, his self-destructive melancholy is cured, and he is restored to life at the last minute."

Wolfgang Jacobsen, "Kann ich mal das Salz haben," in Jacobsen and Hans Helmut Prinzler, eds., *Siodmak Bros. Berlin–Paris–London–Hollywood* (Berlin: Stiftung Deutsche Kinemathek and Argon Verlag, 1998).

"In his sound-film grotesquerie *Der Mann, der seinen Mörder sucht* Robert Siodmak employs every imaginable stylistic element from Buster Keaton to *Einbrecher* [Hanns Schwarz, 1930]. He uses them, but he also makes them his own. He experiments with them, tests them, and incorporates them where they serve his purpose. . . . ¶Siodmak is already a great master. There is rarely a lapse. Everything is effortlessly exaggerated. A major step forward in terms of film, one that cannot be praised enough."

Herbert Ihering, *Berliner Börsen-Courier*, February 6, 1931; quoted in Ihering, *Von Reinhardt bis Brecht: Vier Jahrzehnte Theater und Film*, vol. 3 (Berlin: Aufbau, 1961).

"Laughter and more laughter . . . a good start for the first German sound-film grotesquerie. At the same time yet another indication of the determination with which Erich Pommer is expanding his production from one film to the next. . . . ¶Serious folks, like the contingent of German moviegoers, also want to know the why behind it, even while laughing. The grotesquerie, the end point of an artistic genre, which aims for nothing more than to relax and amuse, hides its meaning in the abundance of nonsense. . . . ¶Visual jokes and punch lines in the dialogue complement each other. Even in the sidelights, which are added touches and yet so crucial to the overall impression, the familiar Pommer splendor is obvious: the translation of a hit not only in visual terms, but even more, its fully organic development out of the dialogue."

Hans Feld, *Film-Kurier*, no. 31 (February 6, 1931).

"Unfortunately, Siodmak had no chance to make another film as brazen as this one, which so breezily traverses the precisely captured worlds of the bourgeois apartment, the bar, the underworld hangouts. He impudently caricatures the popular genres of the time: the innocuous Crash comedies, the fatal thrillers, the love stories. With cacophonous sounds, choral voices, and bizarre song inserts he makes fun of the conventions of the sound film that were fixed even then."

Jacobsen, "Kann ich mal das Salz haben."

Film Notes:

"*Der Mann, der seinen Mörder sucht* . . . survives only in a shortened forty-minute version under the title *Jim, der Mann mit der Narbe* [Jim, the man with the scar]. It is no longer possible to determine whether Siodmak had a hand in these changes. Curiously, they do not lessen the effect. Instead, they show up its experimental quality and set this production apart from the other UFA sound films more clearly."

Jacobsen, "Kann ich mal das Salz haben."

Niemandsland 1931
No Man's Land

Germany
Director: Victor Trivas
Screenplay: Victor Trivas, from an idea
by Leonhard Frank
Cinematography: Kamera-Kollektiv
Alexander von Lagorio, Georg
Stilianudis
Art direction: Arthur Schwarz
Sound: Carl-Erich Kroschke, Gustav
Brinkmann
Composer: Hanns Eisler
Musical direction: Kurt Schröder
Songs: "Arbeitssong," "Unterstandssong"
(music and lyrics: Leo Hirsch),
"Kriegssong" (music and lyrics:
Günther Weisenborn)
Military advisors: Major von Rutke,
Major von Erkert
Production company: Resco-
Filmproduktion, Berlin
Producer: Anton Resch

Cast
Ernst Busch: Ernst Kohler, German
Vladimir Sokoloff: Lewin, Russian
Hugh Stephens Douglas: Charles
Brown, Englishman
Louis Douglas: Joe Smile, African
Georges Péclet: Charles Durand,
Frenchman
Renée Stobrawa: Frau Kohler
Zoe Frank: Mrs. Brown
Rose Mai: Durand's sweetheart
Elisabeth Lennartz: woman from any-
where in the world, Lewin's bride

Premiere: December 10, 1931, Berlin
First US screening: January 29, 1934,
Acme Theatre, New York

**Victor (born Viktor Aleksandrovich)
Trivas**
Born July 9, 1896, St. Petersburg; died
April 12, 1970, New York. Exile:
1925–60: worked as a scriptwriter,
set designer, and director in Germany,
France, and the US

Weimar films: *Aufruhr des Blutes*
(1929), *Dans les rues* (1933)

"Five soldiers of different nationalities find themselves in a destroyed trench in the no-man's-land between the fronts, and in their misery they discover that they are separated only by language, by uniforms, but that otherwise they have the same thoughts, the same feelings. Why are they enemies? They are laborers, craftsmen, officials. War has driven them apart, made them mad. So declare war on war! At the end, they march like a symbol of the struggle for peace, united against their common enemy: war."

Felix Scherret, "Ein Film gegen den Krieg," *Vorwärts*, December 10, 1931, evening edition.

"In *Niemandsland* I was not concerned with exposing the horrors of war, but rather its cruel senselessness. If enemies, having fled from the atmosphere of mass insanity, will only come together in some spot between the fronts, they will also discover the common language of simple human feelings. This would doubtless be the most revelatory denunciation of war."

Victor Trivas, press material for French version, n.d.; reprinted in Hans-Michael Bock and Wolfgang Jacobsen, eds., *Filmmaterialien 9: Victor Trivas* (Hamburg: CineGraph; Berlin: Deutsche Kinemathek, 1996), pp. 4–5.

"A war film that sees the subject from a new perspective. What is important here is not the action but the translation of the idea into images, a process in which the director Trivas has fully succeeded. . . . ¶The technique of rapid cross-dissolves and montage, as mastered by the Russian silent film, has here been applied to the sound film. Trivas places greatest importance on the image. Words, noises, and music only serve as background and interpretation. The film is primarily film, not photographed theater. To be sure, Trivas has not yet achieved ultimate artistic cohesion, for at the end it becomes broadly naturalistic and loses momentum."

Scherret, "Ein Film gegen den Krieg."

Film Notes:
This film was banned by National Socialist censors on April 22, 1933.

32

„Niemandsland"

Der weisse Rausch.
Neue Wunder des Schneeschuhs   1931
The White Ecstasy

Germany
Director: Arnold Fanck
Screenplay: Arnold Fanck
Cinematography: Richard Angst, Kurt
   Neubert (outdoors), Hans Karl
   Gottschalk, Bruno Leubner (studio
   work)
Assistant camera: Robert Dahlmeier
Art direction: Leopold Blonder
Editing: Arnold Fanck
Sound: Hans Bittmann, Emil Specht
Sound editing: Fritz Seeger
Composer: Paul Dessau, Fritz
   Goldschmidt (assistant)
Production company: Sokal-Film,
   Berlin, on behalf of Aafa-Film, Berlin
Producers: Heinrich (in the US: Henry)
   Sokal, Harry R. Sokal

Cast
Leni Riefenstahl: Leni
Hannes Schneider: Hannes
Rudi Matt: Rudi Matt
Guzzi Lantschner, Walter Riml:
   Hamburg carpenters
Lothar Ebersberg: young Lothar

Premiere: December 10, 1931, UFA
Palast am Zoo, Berlin

Arnold Fanck
Born March 6, 1889, Frankenthal,
German Empire; died September 28,
1974, Freiburg im Breisgau, West
Germany. No exile

Selected Weimar films: *Das Wunder
des Schneeschuhs* (documentary,
1920), *Der heilige Berg* (1926),
Stürme über dem Montblanc (1930);
as codirector: *Die weisse Hölle von Piz
Palü* (with G. W. Pabst, 1929), *SOS
Eisberg* (with Tay Garnett, 1933)

Thrilled by the daring descents of experienced skiers, Leni, a naive tourist from Berlin, wants to try them herself. Although she does not know how to ski or jump, she finds herself in an advanced course taught by Rudi Matt. Completely overwhelmed, she arranges for private instruction with Hannes. She seems hopelessly untalented at first, but in a race the following winter, Leni proves that she has turned into a pro.

"After a hearty breakfast, the column of fifty top skiers in the new Fanck film *Der weisse Rausch* marches in serpentine curves up the fairy-tale ski slopes above St. Christoph. We cameramen wheeze and groan. Cameras, tripods, lenses, batteries, motors, light shades, film—everything that would better have belonged in an equipment van we had to carry on our own shoulders. Finally the director cries: 'Stop—a great shot—we'll stay here!' Neubert and I set up our equipment—one a normal camera, the other a slow-motion one. . . . ¶Sweating despite the cold, we attempt to 'anchor' the forty-kilogram cameras in the powdery snow. Three skis are quickly placed under the legs of the tripod and Dr. Fanck calls, 'Action!' ¶Like hunters with rifles at the ready, we wait at the foot of snow-covered slopes in the Arlberg for this daredevil bunch of skiers. The cameras roll, and above us the tiny dots begin to move—it is the 'pack,' which now comes racing down the slope. ¶The plucky Leni Riefenstahl keeps pace with Hannes Schneider. . . . [They race] toward our cameras at the speed of an express train. We carefully track the scene through the viewfinder—until we are blinded by the snow flung in our faces."

Richard Angst, "Mit Kameras im Skigelände," in the January 1932 program for *Der weisse Rausch* at Lichtburg Cinema, Berlin. Schriftgutarchiv, Stiftung Deutsche Kinemathek, Berlin.

Das Blaue vom Himmel 1932
The Blue from the Sky

Germany
Director: Victor Janson
Artistic supervision: Rudolf Walther-Fein
Screenplay: Billie (in the US: Billy) Wilder, Max Kolpe (born Max Kolpenitzky)
Cinematography: Heinrich Gärtner
Art direction: Jack (born Jacek) Rotmil
Costume design: Karl Gillmore
Sound: Fritz Seeger
Sound editing: Else Baum
Composer: Paul Abraham
Lyrics: Fritz Rotter, Max Kolpe
Songs: "Was kümmert mich die ganze Welt?" "Ich könnte jetzt zu Ihnen sagen," "Einen Tag möcht' ich bei dir sein"
Production company: Aafa-Film, Berlin
Producer: Gabriel Levy

Cast
Marta Eggerth: Anni Müller
Hermann Thimig: Hans Mayer, mail pilot
Fritz Kampers: Tobias
Margarete Schlegel: Cigarette Cilly
Ernö Verebes: Swift Hugo, train dispatcher
Jakob Tiedtke: stationmaster
Margarete Kupfer: Mrs. Breitsprecher
Hans Richter: Tommy
Walter Steinbeck: Director General Pieper
Mathilde Sussin: Miss Fischer
Erich Kestin: Mrs. Pieper's chauffeur
Gerhard Dammann: taxi driver

Premiere: December 20, 1932, Berlin
First US screening: September 7, 1934, Yorkville Theatre, New York

Victor Janson
Born September 25, 1884, Riga, Russia (now Latvia); died June 29, 1960, Berlin. No exile

(continued)

Anni, a ticket seller in a Berlin subway station, who is courted by countless men, and the mail pilot Hans have fallen in love. Their trysts are hindered by their irreconcilable working hours: she works days; he works nights. Moreover, Hans has a number of competitors, since Anni is also being courted by both the stationmaster and the director of a cigarette factory. She manages to get her lover a job as a skywriter for the cigarette company, but instead of an advertising slogan, he writes against the blue of the sky, "Anni, I love you!"

"Wilder has followed the recipe of *Ein blonder Traum* [Paul Martin, 1932]. But for his subway dream he has mixed even more sky-blue and rose-red shades. On top of that, a setting that has considerable charm simply because of its banality. . . . ¶For the station, here called Wallenstein-Platz, the director Victor Janson and his architect have created a triumph. Truly, no one notices that it was all constructed in the studio. This world of make-believe and cardboard is the only genuine thing in the film! The characters, the subway officials, are not of this world! Whether on a Sunday outing together in white trousers or at work, they are all bewitched princes and princesses. They always have sunlight in their hearts and a song on their lips, most notably the carefree conductor (Verebes) and the very elegant young woman at the ticket counter (Marta Eggerth). The only somewhat believable figure is Jakob Tiedtke's stationmaster."

-ap-, *Vossische Zeitung*, December 21, 1932, evening edition.

"The acting of the principals, all of whom are prominent in the Teutonic theater and film world, is excellent. Despite occasional flaws in the sound reproduction, Miss Eggerth's singing is well worth hearing, and some of the airs are likely to stick in the listener's memory for a while."

H. T. S. [Harry T. Smith], *New York Times*, September 8, 1934.

Das Blaue vom Himmel

Selected Weimar films: *Das Skelett des
Herrn Markutius* (1920), *Der dumme
August des Zirkus Romanelli* (1926),
Der schwarze Domino (1930), *Die
Frau, von der man spricht* (1931), *Es
war einmal ein Walzer* (1932)

Ein blonder Traum 1932

A Blonde Dream

Germany
Director: Paul Martin
Screenplay: Walter Reisch, Billie (in
    the US: Billy) Wilder
Cinematography: Günther Rittau, Otto
    Baecker, Konstantin Irmen-Tschet
Art direction: Erich Kettelhut
Sound: Fritz Thiery
Editing: Willy Zeyn, Jr.
Choreography: Franz Roth
Composer: Werner Richard Heymann
Lyrics: Walter Reisch
Songs: "Irgendwo auf der Welt gibt's
    ein kleines bisschen Glück" ("In
    a Year, in a Day," lyrics: Robert
    Gilbert), "Einmal schafft's jeder,"
    "Wir zahlen keine Miete mehr,"
    "Alles verstehen heisst alles
    verzeihen"
Production company: Universum Film
    AG (UFA), Berlin
Producer: Erich Pommer

Cast
Lilian Harvey: Jou-Jou
Willy Fritsch: Willy I
Willi Forst: Willy II
Paul Hörbiger: Scarecrow Man,
    vagrant
Trude Hesterberg: Bookstall Ilse, news-
    paper seller
C. Hooper Trask: Charles J. Merryman,
    American manager
Hans Deppe: his secretary
Wolfgang Heinz: doorman

Premiere: September 23, 1932,
Gloria Palast, Berlin
British premiere: (as *Happy Ever
After*, codirected by Robert Stevenson)
October 1932, London

Paul Martin
Born February 8, 1899, Kolozsvár
(Klausenburg), Austria-Hungary (now
Cluj-Napoca, Romania); died January
23, 1967, Berlin. Exile: 1933:
worked with companion Lilian Harvey
(continued)

Two window washers, Willy I and Willy II, have spied a ravishing blonde in the American embassy and have immediately fallen in love with her. The blonde, Jou-Jou works as a live target for a knife thrower in a traveling circus, but she feels she was meant to be a Hollywood star, so she pays Merrymaker, who claims to be a manager, a large fee to make her dream come true. She moves into an abandoned train car with her two admirers and their vagabond friend Scarecrow but leaves again on Scarecrow's advice, since Willy I and Willy II are competing for her and jealous of each other. At the American embassy Jou-Jou learns that she has been deceived by a confidence man. When she suddenly comes across the true Mr. Merrymaker, he gives her a film contract, in spite of her minimal gifts, to keep her from getting on his nerves. Willy II picks a fight with Merryman, accusing him of promoting the hated American cult of stardom. Impressed by this impassioned speech, Merryman promptly engages Willy II for a delicate job: protecting him from the tiresome people who think they are destined for a fairy-tale career in Hollywood. Thrilled at this unexpected promotion in the land of unlimited opportunity, Willy II lets Willy I have Jou-Jou.

"Lilian Harvey, the woman determined to get to Hollywood, virtually parodies her America trip in this film. It is particularly charming to note that this small, blond creature, with her obsession with dance and her determination, has hit the jackpot that is denied her in this film. . . . Paul Martin has allowed her to dance around her own life."

Georg Herzberg, *Film-Kurier*, no. 226
(September 24, 1932).

Lilian Harvey Willy Fritsch 3695

in the US on *Orient Express*, was
unable to find further work on planned
projects; 1935: returned to Berlin from
Los Angeles and subsequently worked
for the National Socialist film industry

In Weimar-era Germany Martin
directed only one other film: *Der Sieger*
(1932, codirected by Hans Hinrich).

F.P. 1 antwortet nicht 1932
F.P. 1

Germany and Great Britain
Director: Karl Hartl
Assistant director: Ernst Rechenmacher
Screenplay: Walter Reisch, Kurt
  Siodmak, from the novel by
  Siodmak (1931)
English screenplay: Donovan Parsons
English dialogue: Robert Stevenson,
  Peter McFarlane
Cinematography: Günther Rittau,
  Konstantin Irmen-Tschet, Otto Baecker
Art direction: Erich Kettelhut, with
  technical assistance from Albert
  Berthold Henninger
Editing: Willy Zeyn, Jr.
Sound editing: Rudolf Schaad
Sound: Fritz Thiery
Composer: Allan Gray (born Josef
  Zmigrod)
Music: UFA Jazz Orchestra, conducted
  by Hans-Otto Borgmann
Lyrics for German version: Walter
  Reisch
Lyrics for English version: Rowland
  Leigh, Donovan Parsons.
Songs: "Flieger, grüss mir die Sonne,"
  "Ganz dahinten, wo der Leuchtturm
  steht," "Hoch oben im Äther"
Production companies: Universum Film
  AG (UFA), Berlin, and Gaumont-
  British, London
Producer: Erich Pommer

Cast
Conrad Veidt: Major Ellissen
Jill Esmond: Claire Lennartz
Leslie Fenton: Captain E. B. Droste
George Merritt: Lubin
Donald Calthrop: Sunshine,
  photographer
Nicholas Hannen: Matthias Lennartz
William Freshman: Conrad Lennartz
Hermann Speelmans: Damsky, chief
  engineer
Warwick Ward: first officer
Alexander Field, Francis L. Sullivan:
  sailors
Philipp Manning: ship's doctor

(continued)

F.P. 1 is the abbreviation for Flugplattform (flight platform) 1, a fictional landing strip in the middle of the ocean, where planes flying between America and Europe would be able to land. It was conceived and planned by Droste, a former naval officer. His friend Ellissen, an aggressive pilot, supports the plan and convinces the Lennartz Shipyard to build it. Ellissen decides to accept an attractive offer from an aircraft factory: he will be the first man to fly non-stop around the world, starting from Berlin, an adventure that means more to him than committing to his lover, Claire Lennartz. He leaves, and while he is away, Droste and Claire become close. Droste is directing the construction of F.P. 1, which takes two years because of repeated acts of sabotage, and shortly before it is completed, all radio contact is suddenly interrupted. Claire convinces Ellissen to go with her to clear up the situation. When they land on F.P. 1 they discover that Damsky, the chief engineer, is destroying the platform under orders from another country. Damsky escapes in the ensuing shoot-out. Claire attends to the wounded Droste; Ellissen is enraged about her concern but finally recognizes that the lives of his friend, of Claire, and of the rest of the F.P. 1 crew depend on him alone.

"Our task was to create the illusion of a technological miracle. The script of the UFA sound film, the Erich Pommer production F.P. 1 antwortet nicht, called for the construction of an artificial island floating in the sea, which, outfitted with marvelous machinery, was to serve as a stopover for future international air traffic. In the script this huge floating pontoon was 500 meters long and 150 meters wide. It was stabilized by thirty-two bearing pillars, whose cavities were constructed so that they could be filled with water in emergencies to either raise or lower the island depending on weather conditions. . . . [The] difficulties began with our search for the ideal spot for the creation of the Atlantic station F.P. 1. . . . After much back and forth we decided on the Greifswalder Oie—the small island 17 kilometers off the southwest point of Rügen [in the North Sea]. It is a strip of land some 11½ kilometers long and 500 meters wide that has a lighthouse and a normal population of seventeen people. . . . Before we could begin with the construction, the pitted surface had to be laboriously leveled and the postal cable network leading to the lighthouse had to be removed. ¶The film's action, the illusion, and safety concerns required that the structure be completely stable. The wooden platform had to be covered with real iron plates of standard thickness. A special iron structure held the giant fuel tanks, submersible in case of danger. The command tower, the radio room, and the diesel motor room were outfitted with the actual machines and equipment that experts assured us were appropriate to the imaginary island. The fact that we needed thirteen rail cars for the iron plates covering the platform alone provides some idea of the fantastic quantities of building materials we were required to assemble! . . . Construction of the platform took roughly ten weeks."

Erich Kettelhut, "F.P. 1 wird gebaut," *Film-Kurier*, no. 297 (December 17, 1932).

Film Notes:
The English-language version was rereleased in England in 1938 under the title *The Secrets of F.P. 1.*

Premiere: December 22, 1932, Berlin
British premiere: April 3, 1933,
London
US premiere: September 15, 1933,
Roxy, New York

Karl (born Karl Anton) Hartl
Born May 10, 1899, Vienna; died
August 29, 1978, Vienna. No exile

Weimar films: *Ein Burschenlied aus
Heidelberg* (1930), *Die Gräfin von
Monte Christo* (1932), *Der Prinz von
Arkadien* (1932); as codirector: *Berge
in Flammen* (with Luis Trenker, 1931)

Ich bei Tag und Du bei Nacht 1932
Early to Bed

Germany
Director: Ludwig Berger
Screenplay: Hans Székely, Robert
Liebmann
Cinematography: Friedl Behn-Grund,
Bernhard Wentzel
Assistant camera: Kurt Hiller, Franz von
Klepacki, Gerhard Brieger
Art direction: Otto Hunte
Costume design: Joe Strassner
Editing: Viktor Gertler, Heinz G. Janson
Sound: Gerhard Goldbaum
Composer: Werner Richard Heymann
Lyrics: Robert Gilbert
Music: UFA Jazz Orchestra, conducted
by Gérard Jacobson
Singers: Comedian Harmonists, Leo
Monosson
Songs: "Uns kann keiner," "Wenn Du
nicht kommst, haben die Rosen
umsonst geblüht," "Wenn ich
Sonntags in mein Kino geh"
Production company: Universum Film
AG (UFA), Berlin
Producer: Erich Pommer

Cast
Käthe von Nagy: Grete, manicurist
Willy Fritsch: Hans, night waiter
Amanda Lindner: Cornelia Seidelbast,
landlady
Julius Falkenstein: Herr Krüger
Elisabeth Lennartz: Trude, his daughter
Anton Pointner: Meyer, banker
Comedian Harmonists
Leo Monosson: singer at Casanova

Premiere: November 18, 1932,
Hamburg

Ludwig Berger (born Ludwig Gottfried
Heinrich Bamberger)
Born January 6, 1892, Mainz,
German Empire; died May 18, 1969,
Schlangenbad, West Germany. Exile:
1928–30: directed five films in the
US; 1930: returned to Germany;
1936: went into exile in Amsterdam
(continued)

Grete and Hans share a room and sleep in the same bed but do not know each other: she works days as a manicurist; he works nights as a waiter. Frau Seidelbast, the landlady, makes sure that her two roomers never run into each other. They happen to meet away from their shared room and fall in love. Each feels the other to be special, anything but an unknown roommate. To Grete, Hans appears to be a well-to-do bon vivant. Hans, in turn, believes that Grete is the daughter of the wealthy Herr Krüger, who in reality is one of her impoverished patrons. The confusion escalates when Krüger tries to match up his daughter, Trude, with Hans, in the false assumption that Hans is the banker Meyer. In the end Hans may have lost his job, but he has won Grete.

"The two poor but decent people are juxtaposed with a Kintopp film with a heroic tenor, with a blaring Gitta Alpar, with countless pages. . . . The Kintopp appears to be more or less the typical social narcotic. And when the plot situation comes all too close to what you'd expect of Kintopp, the delightful Käthe von Nagy says: 'Just like in the Kintopp!' . . . ¶The film has been directed and edited by Berger with an agile, very experienced hand. It flows easily and pleasantly and with the delicate sparkle of a good wine flowing from the bottle into the glass."
  W. H-s [Willy Haas], *Film-Kurier*, no. 282 (November 29, 1932).

and France; 1939: codirected *The Thief of Bagdad* (with Michael Powell) for producer Alexander Korda; survived World War II in the Netherlands thanks to falsified papers

Selected Weimar films: *Der Richter von Zalamea* (1920), *Ein Glas Wasser* (1922), *Der verlorene Schuh* (1923), *Ein Walzertraum* (1925), *Der Meister von Nürnberg* (1928)

Kuhle Wampe oder Wem gehört die Welt? 1932
Whither Germany?

Germany

Director: Slatan Dudow

Screenplay: Bertolt Brecht, Ernst Ottwalt

Cinematography: Günther Krampf

Art direction: Robert Scharfenberg, Carl Haacker

Sound: Carl-Erich Kroschke, Fritz Michelis

Editing: Peter Meyrowitz

Composer: Hanns Eisler

Music: Lewis Ruth Band, choirs of the Berlin Workers' Athletics and the Berlin State Opera, directed by Josef Schmid

Lyrics: Bertolt Brecht

Ballad singers: Helene Weigel, Ernst Busch

Songs: "Lied von der Solidarität: Vorwärts und nicht vergessen," "Das Spiel der Geschlechter," "Wir sprechen aus, was Euch berührt," "Schöner Gigolo, armer Gigolo" (music: Leonello Casucci, lyrics: Julius Brammer), "Deutsche Kaiserklänge"

Production companies: Prometheus-Film, Berlin, finished by Praesens-Film, Berlin

Producers: Willi Münzenberg, Lazar Wechsler

Cast

Hertha Thiele: Anni Bönicke

Ernst Busch: Fritz, her friend

Lili Schönborn: Anni's mother

Max Sablotzki: Anni's father

Adolf Fischer: Kurt

Martha Wolter: Gerda

Alfred Schäfer: Anni's brother, unemployed worker

Gerhard Bienert: newspaper reader on the train

Berlin Workers' Athletics Choir, Greater Berlin Workers' Choir, Uthmann Choir, North Choral Society, Das rote Sprachrohr

During Germany's massive unemployment at the beginning of the 1930s, with countless workers competing for too few jobs, the father of the working-class Bönicke family in Berlin blames his son for being unable to find employment. The humiliated son throws himself from a window of the family's tenement and dies. His sister, Anni, is the only one bringing in money. She works in a factory, and her salary is small. Since the family can no longer pay the rent, the owner of the building evicts them. They move in with Anni's lover, Fritz, in Kuhle Wampe, a tent city on Berlin's outskirts. Anni is carrying Fritz's child, but he only agrees to marry her under pressure from her parents and his friend Kurt. At the engagement party the guests drink and eat far too much. Anni and Fritz have a quarrel and separate. Anni goes to live with her friend Gerda, and both of them take part in athletic events and political-theory classes organized by the communist workers' movement. Anni and Fritz meet again and become reconciled. On their train ride back into the city after a sports festival, Anni and her comrades discuss the contradictions of capitalism with some petit bourgeois passengers. When one of them objects that everything will remain as it always was and asks who would want to change the world, Gerda responds, "Those who don't like it as it is!"

"In the tiresome series of operetta and honky-tonk films only interrupted by blood-curdling tales, one has to welcome the work of Brecht and Ottwalt. This film is a rallying cry. It presents a harsh vision of the world. It forgoes an epic plot, contents itself with simple suggestions. . . . The dialogue is crisp. Brecht was sparing with words. He sticks to clear, sober, indisputable facts. This is what makes the film worthwhile. When the actors speak they accuse, they expose a new environment, they point to the future."

Kurt London, *Der Film*, no. 23 (June 4, 1932).

Film Notes:

When the Berlin censorship board banned the film on March 31, 1932, Prometheus, the production company, appealed. On review, the superior censorship board upheld the ban on April 9, 1932. After protests, a shortened version appeared briefly in theaters. On March 26, 1933, the National Socialists banned any further screenings.

(The Red Megaphone, a workers' theater troupe, directed by Maxim Vallentin), choir of the Berlin State Opera

First Russian screening: May 14, 1932, Moscow
First German screening: May 30, 1932, Berlin
First US screening: week of April 21, 1933, Cameo, New York

Slatan Dudow

Born January 30, 1903, Caribrod (now Dimitrovgrad), Bulgaria; died July 12, 1963, Fürstenwalde, East Germany. Exile: 1933: went into exile in Paris; 1939: left France, moved to Switzerland; 1946: returned to Germany

In Weimar-era Germany, Dudow directed only one other film, the short documentary *Zeitprobleme. Wie der Arbeiter wohnt* (1930).

Razzia in St. Pauli 1932

Germany
Director: Werner Hochbaum
Screenplay: Werner Hochbaum
Cinematography: Alfred Otto
  Weitzenberg
Art direction: Willy Schiller
Sound: Franz Schröder
Editing: Carl Behr
Composer: Kurt Levaal
Lyrics: Carl Behr, Hedy Knorr
Musical direction: Giuseppe Becce
Song: "Song vom Heer der
  Hafenarbeiter"
Production company: Orbis-Film, Berlin
Producer: Justin Rosenfeld

Cast
Gina Falckenberg: Dance-Hall Else
Friedrich Gnass: Karl Burmeister, called
  Sailor Karl
Wolfgang Zilzer (in the US: Paul
  Andor): Leo, musician
Charly Wittong: Charly, folksinger
Max Zilzer: barkeep
Also featuring: Kurt Appel, Käthe
  Hüter, Friedrich Rittmeyer, Hamburg
  policemen, members of the St. Pauli
  underworld

Premiere: May 20, 1932, Berlin

Werner (born Werner Paul Adolf)
Hochbaum
Born March 7, 1899, Kiel, German
Empire; died April 15, 1946,
Potsdam, East Germany. No exile

Weimar films: *Vorwärts* (documentary,
1928), *Brüder* (1929), *Wille und
Werk* (documentary, 1929), *Zwei
Welten* (documentary, 1930), *Besserer
Herr gesucht zwecks . . .* (short film,
1932)

"Dance-Hall Else, one of the many street-walkers in St. Pauli, near Hamburg, finds life unbearable with the musician Leo, a boozy wimp. And when she meets a man who appears to understand her secret desires in Sailor Karl, a notorious burglar, she falls in love with him. The two decide to leave Hamburg and head for the Kongo Bar, a meeting place of crooks and prostitutes, to tell Leo that Else is leaving him forever. ¶Karl is sought by the police for a break-in. In the Kongo Bar there is a terrible fight between the underworld and the police, in the course of which Karl is finally overpowered and led away. 'I'll be back,' he calls to Else. The girl returns, desperate, without hope, to her little room with Leo, just as always."

Mein Film (Vienna), no. 353 (1932).

"Nothing else happens there in twenty-four hours, but only rarely is as much included in a film: the whole milieu, St. Pauli with its port facilities, alleys, amusement parks; the hardworking, pleasure-loving men who never really find it; and nature with its cycle of days and nights. In numerous highly impressive montages, overlappings, and lyrical shots, the camera of A. O. Weitzenberg ties the fates of the three characters into the life of the underworld."

Hermann Gressieker, *Berliner Börsen-Courier*, May 21, 1932,
evening edition.

Film Notes:
"Song vom Heer der Hafenarbeiter" is sung by Ernst Busch.

National Socialist censors banned the film on December 7, 1933.

Max Zilzer was the father of Wolfgang Zilzer.

Ein toller Einfall 1932
A Crazy Idea

Germany
Director: Kurt Gerron
Screenplay: Philipp Lothar Mayring, Friedrich Zeckendorf, from the play by Karl Laufs (1891)
Cinematography: Konstantin Irmen-Tschet, Werner Bohne
Art direction: Julius von Borsody
Costume design: Hermann Hoffmann
Editing: Konstantin Mick
Sound: Gerhard Goldbaum
Musical direction: Hans-Otto Borgmann
Composers: Walter Jurmann, Bronislaw Kaper
Lyrics: Fritz Rotter
Songs: "Du bist der Mann, der den Frauen gefällt!" "Heut' bin ich gut aufgelegt!" "Ich suche Eine, die mir allein gehört"
Choreography: Franz Rott
Production company: Universum Film AG (UFA), Berlin
Producer: Bruno Duday

Cast
Willy Fritsch: Paul Lüders, painter
Jakob Tiedtke: Michael Lüders, his uncle
Max Adalbert: Birnstiel, art dealer
Heinz Salfner: Mr. Miller, wealthy Englishman
Dorothea Wieck: Mabel, his daughter
Harry Halm: Bob, Mabel's friend
Leo Slezak: Theo Müller, manager of the Miller Girls
Ellen Schwanneke: Evelyn, his daughter
Wilhelm Bendow: Wendolin, chairman of a study committee on combating urban noise
Fritz Odemar: Werner Schubart, composer
Genia Nikolajewa: Marga, his wife
Rosy Barsony: Anita, dancer
Paul Hörbiger: Emil, servant
Theo Lingen: headwaiter
Adele Sandrock: landlady
Oskar Sima: man from the finance office

Paul Lüders, a painter, is supposed to be taking care of a castle belonging to his uncle, the impoverished German art dealer Michael Lüders, who is in London arranging the sale of the castle to the wealthy Englishman Mr. Miller. For Paul, also impoverished, this is a splendid opportunity to live for free in extreme comfort for a few days. His uncle, aware of Paul's notorious weakness, has forbidden him all contact with women. Moreover, Paul has been commissioned by the art dealer Birnstiel, a relative of his uncle, to design a poster for a winter sports hotel. Theo Müller, the manager of the famous dancers the Miller Girls, searching for decent accommodations for his performers, sees the poster and mistakes Paul for a hotel owner and the castle for a luxury hotel. Believing he is acting in Paul's best interests, Birnstiel rents rooms to Müller, his daughter, Evelyn, his Miller Girls, and additional illustrious guests. Evelyn and the dancers all fall in love with Paul, as does Mabel Miller, just arrived from London and the daughter of the man interested in buying the castle. In addition, Paul's former girlfriend, the lively dancer Anita, visits him, hoping to revive their love affair. After some hemming and hawing, Paul finally ends up with Evelyn, the woman he truly loves, and Bob and Anita are a happy new couple as well. Mabel, however, prefers to remain single.

"This film is somewhat topical in that no one in it has any money. . . . Kurt Gerron continues his series of directorial successes. His films bubble with life. . . . Barsony is delightful, whether murdering the language, making faces, or swinging her legs in unlikely curves."

Georg Herzberg, *Film-Kurier*, no. 113 (May 14, 1932).

Film Notes:
At Theresienstadt, Gerron was forced by the SS to direct, from August 16 through September 11, 1944, *Theresienstadt. Ein Dokumentarfilm aus dem jüdischen Siedlungsleben* (later retitled *Der Führer schenkt den Juden eine Stadt*), a propaganda film meant to demonstrate to representatives of the International Red Cross and the Vatican, as well as the public in the neutral states such as Switzerland and Sweden, that the Jews in Theresienstadt were treated well.

„Ein toller Einfall"

Premiere: May 13, 1932, Berlin
First US screening: May 20, 1934,
79th Street Theatre, New York

Kurt Gerron (born Kurt Gerson)
Born May 11, 1897, Berlin; died
October 28, 1944, Auschwitz
concentration camp, Poland. Exile:
1933: went to France, Austria, Italy,
and the Netherlands; mid-1943:
captured by the Germans in the
Netherlands and sent to Westerbork,
a concentration camp; 1944: on
February 25 interned at Theresienstadt,
(Terezín, Czechoslovakia, now Czech
Republic). On October 28, 1944,
Gerron and most of the crew were
deported to Auschwitz and gassed.

In Weimar-era Germany Gerron was
mainly active as an actor in films and
variety theaters. Other films as director:
Der Liebe Lust und Leid. Kellerkavaliere
(1926), *Meine Frau, die Hochstaplerin*
(1931), *Der Stumme von Portici* (short
film, 1931), *Der weisse Dämon* (1932),
Heut' kommt's drauf an (1933)

Vampyr 1932

Vampire

Germany and France

Director: Carl Theodor Dreyer

Screenplay: Christen Jul, Carl Theodor Dreyer, from the short story collection *In a Glass Darkly* (1872) by Joseph Sheridan Le Fanu

Dialogue director: Paul Falkenberg

Cinematography: Rudolf Maté

Art direction: Hermann Warm, Cesare Silvagni

Editing: Carl Theodor Dreyer, Tonka Taldy

Sound: Hans Bittmann

Sound editing: Paul Falkenberg

Composer: Wolfgang Zeller

Artistic advisor: Hermann Warm

Production companies: Carl Theodor Dreyer-Filmproduktion, Paris, and Tobis-Melofilm, Berlin (Tonherstellung)

Producers: Baron Nicolas de Gunzburg, Carl Theodor Dreyer

Cast

Julian West (aka Baron Nicolas de Gunzburg): David (also: Allan) Gray

Maurice Schutz: lord of the manor

Rena Mandel: Gisèle, his elder daughter

Sybille Schmitz: Léone, his younger daughter

Jan Hieronimko: Dr. Marc, village doctor

Henriette Gérard: Marguerite Chopin, old woman from the cemetery

Albert Bras: old servant at the manor

N. Babanini: his wife, maid at the manor

Jane Mora: nurse

Premiere: May 6, 1932, Berlin

Carl Theodor Dreyer

Born February 3, 1889, Copenhagen; died March 20, 1968, Copenhagen. Exile: 1943: went into exile in Sweden

(continued)

Gray, a sportfisherman, spends the night at an inn. Strange figures appear outside and inside the house, and from his window he sees a man with a scythe at the river. In his room an old man gives him a package with the inscription "To be opened after my death." In a castle near the inn Gray meets the old man again and discovers that he is the father of two daughters, one of whom, Léone, is cared for by a nurse. Suddenly a figure visible only as a shadow shoots the old man, and he dies with his elder daughter, Gisèle, kneeling beside him. A servant woman begs Gray to stay with them. He opens the package entrusted to him, which contains the *Book of Vampires*, written in Gothic script. Léone leaves her bed and runs into the surrounding park, and Gisèle and Gray follow her. They find her lying motionless on a rock in the garden, with an old female vampire bent over her, sucking her blood. The vampire turns away and disappears. Léone is carried back to her room, conscious and making gestures of both deep sorrow and great joy. A doctor examines her and determines that she urgently needs fresh blood, which is drawn from Gray. During the procedure he has a nightmare that the doctor tries to poison Léone, and he wakes to find it taking place in reality. Gray prevents the murder and destroys the monster, which he knows how to do thanks to the *Book of Vampires*: they open the coffin in which the vampire sleeps, and with a hammer the old servant drives a metal rod through her heart. The face of the vampire is transformed into a skull, and Léone awakens. Smiling, she says, "My soul is free," and then dies.

"But what a spook! It was not pulled from the chest of scary stories à la [Edgar] Wallace. For Dreyer composes . . . with artistic means. With the most filmic ones ever been applied. . . . A Renaissance of silent-film writing. . . . Dreyer brings to the very real world of film description the time- and space-dissolving sense of the supernatural. He beats all the French Surrealists. ¶Shadows of things that do not happen, contours of creatures that are not identified. Events and people who senselessly and yet with a secret mission operate between heaven and earth, [in a manner] heretofore undreamed of by film-school wisdom.

-g, *Film-Kurier*, no. 107 (May 7, 1932).

Film Notes:

The film was shot in 1930 in France. "Although *Vampyr* was filmed without sound, the actors performed dialogue scenes in French, German, and English, and the film was subsequently synchronized in these three languages in Berlin." (David Rudkin, *Vampyr* [London: British Film Institute (BFI) Film Classics, 2005] p. 79.

The French subtitle is *L'Étrange Aventure de David Gray*. The English version in the BFI collection is subtitled *The Strange Adventure of David Gray*, and the version distributed by Jorgen S. Jorgensen, Gloria Film, is subtitled *The Dream of Allan Gray*.

shortly after directing *Vredens Dag*,
when the German army occupied
Denmark

Weimar films: *Die Gezeichneten* 1922),
Michael (1924)

Morgenrot 1933

Dawn

Germany
Director: Gustav Ucicky
Screenplay: Gerhard Menzel, from a story idea by E. Freiherr von Spiegel
Cinematography: Carl Hoffmann
Assistant camera: Günther Anders
Art direction: Robert Herlth, Walter Röhrig
Costume design: Fritz Schilling
Editing: Eduard von Borsody
Sound: Hermann Fritzsching, Reimar Kuntze
Composer: Herbert Windt
Production company: Universum Film AG (UFA), Berlin
Producer: Günther Stapenhorst

Cast
Rudolf Forster: Captain Liers, U-boat commander
Adele Sandrock: his mother
Fritz Genschow: First Lieutenant Fredericks, called Fips
Paul Westermeier: Jaul, radio operator
Camilla Spira: Grete Jaul, his daughter
Gerhard Bienert: Böhm, helmsman
Friedrich Gnass: Juraczik, torpedo seaman
Frank Nicklisch: Petermann, seaman
Hans Leibelt: mayor of Meerskirchen
Else Knott: Helga, his daughter
Eduard von Winterstein: Captain Kolch
Charles Bush, Frank Ferfitt, William Cavanagh, G. W. Stroud, A. A. F. Trebes: English sailors

Premiere: January 31, 1933, Essen
First US screening: May 15, 1933, Little Carnegie Playhouse, New York

Gustav Ucicky
Born July 6, 1899, Vienna; died April 26, 1961, Hamburg. No exile

Selected Weimar films: *Ein besserer Herr* (1928), *Hokuspokus* (1930), *Das Flötenkonzert von Sanssouci* (1930), *Im Geheimdienst* (1931), *Mensch ohne Namen* (1932)

The crew of a World War I U-boat takes leave of their families at the train station in the small town of Meerskirchen; they are about to make another attack on the British fleet. In a speech the mayor praises the U-boat commander Liers and his crew, calling them heroes. Liers's mother wishes he would stay and work in the family business; she is the widow of a major and has already lost two sons in the war. First Lieutenant Fredericks is rebuffed by the mayor's daughter, Helga, whom he has courted for a long time. She is more interested in Liers, although he is unaware of it. At sea the U-boat is on a secret mission to prevent a cruiser carrying high-ranking British military experts from reaching Russia, where they plan to support their ally in the struggle against the German Empire. Liers and his crew sink the British warship, while barely avoiding depth charges from enemy boats. On the return trip they locate a suspicious ship. The U-boat surfaces. In response to a warning shot, the ship, presumably serving a civilian function, hoists the Danish flag. Suddenly the German U-boat comes under fire. Liers realizes too late he has fallen into a British ambush. When the British commander of the badly damaged ship orders his crew to board the lifeboats, Liers tells his men to cease fire and rescue the enemy in distress. Then to the Germans' surprise they sight a British destroyer. It rams the diving U-boat as swiftly as possible. Badly damaged, it sinks to the bottom of the sea. Of the ten surviving seamen only eight have a chance to escape, so the commander and Fredericks choose to stay on board. But their comrades decide to die with them. Only after Fredericks and Petermann have committed suicide do the survivors leave the U-boat. After a brief shore leave they once again set out to hunt the British.

"With sure instinct Gustav Ucicky . . . once again finds the difference between national and nationalistic. He does not allow any patriotic hurrahs; in some episodes he even chides those who fail to recognize the frightful earnestness of war. At the news of the sinking of the British ship the captain's mother, wonderfully played by Adele Sandrock, laments the deaths of many hundreds of men. No pontificating for bloodthirsty chauvinists."

Georg Herzberg, *Film-Kurier*, no. 30 (February 3, 1933).

"Considerable interest revolves around this film because it was the last big picture made by UFA before the Hitler thing broke. England, Holland, Poland, and several other countries have barred it on its German nationalism and it probably won't get much of a welcome in the US. Rather too bad, because the picture is intrinsically well made and an outstanding production. Under normal conditions it could be booked without trouble into regular American houses despite its German dialogue. But conditions are not normal for a German picture."

Kauf., *Variety*, May 23, 1933.

Viktor und Viktoria 1933

Germany
Director: Reinhold Schünzel
Screenplay: Reinhold Schünzel
Cinematography: Konstantin
Irmen-Tschet
Art direction: Benno von Arent, Artur
Günther
Editing: Arnfried Heyne
Sound: Fritz Thiery, Walter Tjaden
Composer: Franz Doelle
Lyrics: Bruno Balz
Songs: "An einem Tag im Frühling
klopft das Glück an deine Tür,"
"Komm' doch ein bisschen mit
nach Madrid," "Man sagt bei einer
Dame nicht beim ersten Mal: Komm
mit!" "Rosen und Liebe sollst du mir
schenken," "Wir müssen's auf jeden
Fall erreichen"
Choreography: Sabine Ress
Production company: Universum Film
AG (UFA), Berlin

Cast
Renate Müller: Susanne Lohr
Hermann Thimig: Viktor Hempel, actor
Adolf Wohlbrück (in the US: Anton
Walbrook): Robert
Hilde Hildebrand: Ellinor
Friedel Pisetta: Lilian, showgirl
Fritz Odemar: Douglas
Aribert Wäscher: F. A. Punkertin, theat-
rical agent

Premiere: December 23, 1933, Berlin
First US screening: January 1935,
55th Street Playhouse, New York

Reinhold Schünzel
Born November 7, 1888, Hamburg;
died September 11, 1954, Munich.
Exile: 1937: left Germany when his
film *Land der Liebe* (with the provisional
working title *Hofloge*) was banned
and traveled by way of Vienna to
Budapest; in early September went into
(continued)

The revue artist and female impersonator Viktor Hempel considers himself an unrecognized genius. After another flop, he turns to fostering the career of Susanne Lohr, an ambitious, beautiful blonde singer. In return, she offers to help him out of his difficulty: he has been struck hoarse and cannot make his usual appearance as Viktoria. Susanne takes over the job and receives thunderous applause for her perfect imitation. Impressed by the talent of this unusually feminine-looking man, Punkertin, an internationally known manager, arranges a permanent engagement for Viktoria. Viktor accompanies her as an assistant on her first world tour. While Viktor courts Lilian, a chorus girl, Viktoria and Robert, an enthusiastic fan, feel drawn to each other. Robert soon confirms his suspicion that Viktoria is playing a man pretending to be a woman, and when her female identity is revealed, the lovers can enjoy their happy ending.

"The director Schünzel . . . has accomplished an astonishing feat. With Franz Doelle, the composer of [the very successful song] 'Weisser Flieder,' and cameraman Konstantin Irmen-Tschet, he has formed a triumvirate that functions as an . . . ensemble in the best sense. Light, sound, and acting are here combined the way we often wish they were. . . . Schünzel's earlier discovery was Renate Müller. Here he discovers her a second time [after *Wie sag' ich's meinem Mann?*, 1932]. Not swept up in spiritual flights, but also no longer trapped in a petit bourgeois existence. . . . An innocuous, lighthearted, and amusing film that takes on importance thanks to the musical element; one almost listens more than one watches."

Dr. loh, *Film-Kurier*, no. 302
(December 27, 1933).

"Renate Müller storms the hearts of the audience. Her laughing, singing, crying, dancing, and leaping are utterly delightful. Looks stunning both as a woman and—as a man. Perhaps her finest achievement since *Die Privatsekretärin* [Wilhelm Thiele, 1931]—and once again it is confirmed that a director with a good eye and firm hand can always guide a gifted actor to success."

Der Film, no. 53 (December 30, 1933).

exile in the US with Wilhelm Dieterle;
1949 onward: returned periodically to
Germany for extended periods of work

Selected Weimar films: *Maria
Magdalene* (1920); *Alles für Geld*
(1923); *Peter, der Matrose* (1929);
Ronny (1931); *Wie sag' ich's meinem
Mann?* (1932)

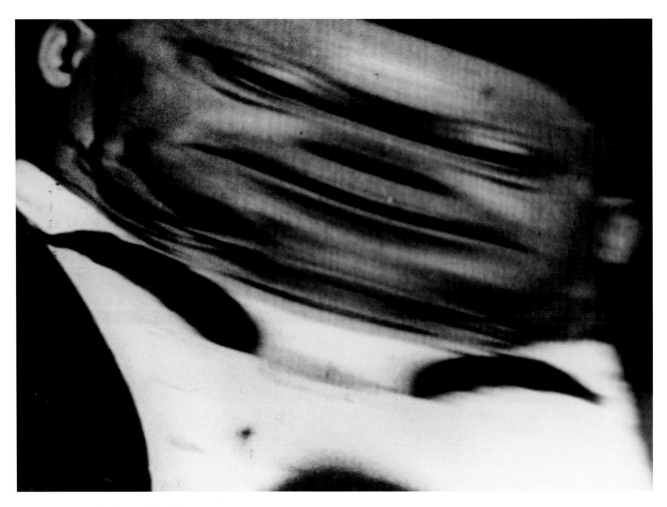

Ernö Metzner. *Polizeibericht Überfall.* 1928

Short Films

Die Mysterien eines Frisiersalons   The Mysteries of a Hairdresser's Shop, 1923

Germany
Directors: Erich Engel, Bertolt Brecht
Screenplay: Erich Engel, Bertolt Brecht,
  Karl Vallentin
Production company:
  Kunstproduktionsgesellschaft (Kupro),
  Munich
Producer: Dr. Koch

Cast
Karl Vallentin: apprentice hairdresser
Blandine Ebinger: hairdresser
Erwin Faber: Professor Moras
Annemarie Hase: his lover
Hans Leibelt: owner of the shop

Erich Engel
Born February 14, 1891, Hamburg;
died May 10, 1966, Berlin. No exile

Bertolt Brecht
Born February 10, 1898, Augsburg,
German Empire; died August 3, 1956,
East Berlin. Exile: 1933: went into exile
in Switzerland and Demnark; 1939–41;
sought asylum in the US; 1948: returned
to Germany

Strange goings-on in a hairdresser's shop.

Film Notes:
Engel, a theater director and playwright,
became acquainted with Brecht in Munich
in 1922 and directed several of his plays.

On July 14, 1923, the censors approved
a shorter version of the original. There is no
documention of the film's premiere or distribution, nor have any contemporary reviews
been discovered.

Short Films

Polizeibericht Überfall   Accident, 1928

Germany
Director: Ernö Metzner
Screenplay: Ernö Metzner, Grace Chiang
Cinematography: Eduard von Borsody
Art direction: Ernö Metzner
Production company: Deutscher
   Werkfilm, Berlin

Cast
Heinrich Gotho: main character
Also featuring: Eva Schmid-Kayser,
Alfred Loretto, Sybille Schmitz, Hans
Ruys, Kurt Gerron, Gustav Püttjer

Ernö Metzner
Born February 25, 1892, Szabadka,
Austria-Hungary (now Subotica,
Serbia); died September 25, 1953,
Hollywood. Exile: 1933: went into
exile in England by way of France;
1937: moved to the US

A man finds a coin on the street, and as a result is involved in a nasty series of situations.

"The film . . . is a criminal film. . . . The events represent outrages, shown with impressive lucidity to the spectators, so that they might induce persons who incline to the commitment of crime to the execution thereof. The culmination of brutalities is reached in the scene where the hidden aggressor strikes the man, already lying on the ground, on his head with a truncheon. . . . The film, which does not reveal an equal artistic equivalent to induce milder interpretation, could not be released because of its brutal and demoralizing effect."
   Censor's letter to *Deutscher Werkfilm*,
   quoted in "German Censor's
   Incomprehensible Ban,"
   Close up 4, no. 5 (May 1929): 14.

Film Notes:
On April 3, 1929, the Berlin censors banned public screening of this film, and on April 13, 1929, on review by the highest censorship agency in Berlin, the ban was upheld.

Markt in Berlin   Market in Berlin, 1929

Germany
Director, screenplay, cinematography,
   editing: Wilfried Basse
Production company: Basse-Film, Berlin
Premiere: November 10, 1929, Berlin

Wilfried Basse
Born August 17, 1899, Hanover; died
June 6, 1946, Berlin. No exile

"A short film of day-to-day life, and precisely for that reason greeted with extraordinary approval."
   Lichtbild-Bühne, no. 269
   (November 11, 1929).

Film Notes:
This was the first short version of *Wochenmarkt auf dem Wittenbergplatz* approved by the censors, on November 7, 1929; a second, slightly longer version was passed by the censors on December 20, 1929.

In der Nacht, 1931

Germany
Director: Walther Ruttmann
Screenplay: Walther Ruttmann
Camera: Reimar Kuntze
Composer: Robert Schumann
Production company: Tobis-Melofilm,
    Berlin
Premiere: October 12, 1931, Tatania-
    Palast, Berlin

Walther Ruttmann
See page 118

An abstract work with images suggested
by the music of Schumann.

Ins Blaue hinein   Into the Blue, 1931

Germany
Director: Eugen Schüfftan
Camera: László Schäffer
Screenplay: Herbert Rona
Composer: Harry Ralton
Sound: Franz Schröder

Cast
Carl Ballhaus, Alice Iverson, Theo
Lingen, Aribert Mog, Helene Robert,
Werner Scharf, Wolfgang Staudte,
Franz Stein, Tony van Eyck

Eugen (in the US: Eugene) Schüfftan
Born July 21, 1893 Breslau, German
Empire (now Wroclaw, Poland); died
September 6, 1977, New York. Exile:
1929–33: shot Robert Siodmak's
Menschen am Sonntag and *Abschied*,
among other films; 1933: traveled
through Austria to France; 1940: came
to the US; 1947: became US citizen

Three fellows, suddenly unemployed, take
a girl for a spin in the countryside around
Berlin.

Film Notes:
This film is a recent discovery with little existing
documentation. A Swiss film collector gave a
copy of this film to the Archives Françaises
du Film, Bois-d'Arcy, where it was preserved
and restored. It has been given conflicting
production dates—both 1929 and 1930—
but its first public screening appears to have
been in 1931, although where it was shown
is not certain. *Ins Blaue hinein* appears to be
the only film Schüfftan directed himself.

Index to the Catalogue of Weimar Films

Friedrich-Wilhelm-Murnau-Stiftung

Eva Orbanz

Friedrich-Wilhelm-Murnau-Stiftung
Wiesbaden

Founded: April 26, 1966

Responsibilities:
Salvaging and restoring films and making them accessible to the public, and awarding the annual short-film prize for young filmmakers in Germany

Rights holdings:
2,000 silent films, 1,000 sound films, and 3,000 short, advertising, and documentary films

Selected production companies represented in the foundation's holdings:
UFA, Universum Film, Bavaria, Terra-Film, Tobis, Berlin-Film

1

The Friedrich-Wilhelm-Murnau-Stiftung, Wiesbaden, is a foundation dedicated to preserving and maintaining a large part of the German film legacy, whose golden age is frequently considered to have been the Weimar years. Its stock of films encompasses six decades of production, extending from the Wilhelmine period (before 1918) through the Weimar Republic (1918–33), the Third Reich (1933–45), and the occupation (1945–49) to the postwar period in the Federal Republic (1949–early 1960s). This unique inventory includes copies and materials (along with the attendant rights) from the production firms of the time.

The Friedrich-Wilhelm-Murnau-Stiftung is thus one of the most important organizations devoted to the preservation of Germany's audiovisual legacy. It is an active collaborator in a growing international network of film archives, museums, cultural institutions, and initiatives. Its expertise in film restoration is of great importance for all film archives.

By lending copies of films to cinemas and festivals, licensing television screenings, and issuing the films in new formats, it makes its holdings accessible to a broad public on a nonprofit basis.

2

The foundation's history is closely linked to developments in Germany after World War II. At the end of the war, the Allied High Command sequestered all of the state-owned film assets, including the film holdings of numerous firms that for propaganda purposes had been integrated, between 1937 and 1942, into UFA-Film GmbH (UFI), a single concern directly controlled by the state.

After the establishment of the Federal Republic, UFI's holdings were returned to German hands and sold, in 1956, to a consortium of firms. Bertelsmann acquired these assets in 1962 and two years later began negotiations to sell the film rights to an American company. Out of concern for the preservation and treatment of the nation's film legacy, the rights were instead acquired by Spitzenorganisation der Filmwirtschaft (SPIO), Germany's top film-industry organization, for 13.8 million marks, and given to the Friedrich-Wilhelm-Murnau-Stiftung, established for that purpose, in 1966.

3

The foundation, without funds or personnel, began the job of sorting through the acquired film material, which was stored in a former air-raid shelter. Ulrich Pöschke, the foundation's director at the time, recalled, "When we opened the doors, we were met with a stinking cloud. The stored cellulose nitrate material had not been rereeled for years and was partly disintegrated." The first chore was to inventory the holdings and analyze their condition, so they could be adequately stored and copied.

In the following decades the foundation's activities were limited, with most of its funds going to repay a government loan for the purchase of the rights and materials. It was only when the government freed the foundation from its debt in the 1980s that it was placed on a solid financial footing, able to generate income through Transit Film's utilization of its film rights.

Since the 1980s the foundation has salvaged, restored, or digitally processed two hundred films, many of them available on DVD and some in a special edition developed with Transit Film.

4

The Friedrich-Wilhelm-Murnau-Stiftung began a new phase of expansion in 2009, with the opening of the Deutsches Filmhaus, Wiesbaden, its own cinema. Recently the foundation has brought about two of its most important restorations: Fritz Lang's classic *Metropolis*, which has been almost completely restored thanks to the sensational discovery of yet another copy in 2008, and both parts of Lang's *Die Nibelungen*, with a running time of nearly five hours. These have been the foundation's most ambitious projects.

Transit Film

Eva Orbanz

Transit Film
Munich

Founded: January 18, 1966

Responsibilities:
Utilizing the holdings of the Friedrich-
Wilhelm-Murnau-Stiftung and the
Bundesarchiv-Filmarchiv

Rights holdings:
2,000 silent films, 1,000 sound films,
and 3,000 short, advertising, and
documentary films

Selected production companies
represented by Transit Film's holdings:
UFA, Universum Film, Bavaria, Terra-
Film, Tobis, Berlin-Film

Film-rental agency:
Roughly 600 titles in 35mm format and
many more DVDs

1

On January 18, 1966, Transit Film was founded by the German government to utilize the holdings of the Friedrich-Wilhelm-Murnau-Stiftung.

2

Transit Film markets the films salvaged and restored by the Friedrich-Wilhelm-Murnau-Stiftung and the Bundesarchiv-Filmarchiv to television, film distributors, and cinemas on a for-profit basis. Its chief business lies in the international licensing of feature films, pictorial documents, and film clips.

Transit Film has its own rental agency with roughly six hundred feature films in 35mm format and even more DVDs, both of which are rented at home and abroad.

Transit Film organizes film presentations with branches of the Goethe-Institut around the world; screenings in which silent films are shown with live music are especially popular.

3

Transit Film also offers salvaged films from the holdings of the Bundesarchiv-Filmarchiv, such as German newsreels and documentaries.

4

Transit Film produces the DVD edition Transit Classics, films processed with the most up-to-date technology and supplemented by bonus features of interest to film scholars.

In its production of DVDs, Transit Film works with German film archives and the Goethe-Institut as well as with the Friedrich-Wilhelm-Murnau-Stiftung.

5

Transit Film has been engaged in the production and coproduction of films since 1998, issuing an average of two films a year on subjects relating to the history of film. In addition, it has made digital copies of interviews with film personalities, among them the UFA stars Carola Höhn, Liane Haid, and Lída Baarová.

6

The income from Transit Film's activities supports the culture of film, funding the preservation of the German film legacy through the Friedrich-Wilhelm-Murnau-Stiftung and the Bundesarchiv-Filmarchiv and supporting the film industry.